COACH 2

the bottom line

ISBN 1552122840

9 781552 122846

COACH2 THE BOTTOM LINE:

An executive guide to coaching performance, change and transformation in organizations

VERSION 1.0
Visit the website
www.coach2-the-bottom-line.com

Library of Congress Catalog Card Number 99-0035

Cover design by Bonnie Mitchell

Canadian Cataloguing in Publication Data

Jay, Mike R. (Mike Robert), 1952-
  Coach2 the bottom line

  ISBN 1-55212-284-0

  1. Employees--Training of. 2. Employee motivation. 3. Teams in the
workplace. I. Title. II. Title: Coach to the bottom line.
HF5549.5.T7J39 1999   658.3'12404 C99-911051-9

TRAFFORD

This book was published *on-demand* in cooperation with Trafford Publishing.
On-demand publishing is a unique process and service of making a book available for retail sale to the public taking advantage of on-demand manufacturing and Internet marketing.
On-demand publishing includes promotions, retail sales, manufacturing, order fulfilment, accounting and collecting royalties on behalf of the author.

Suite 2, 3050 Nanaimo St., Victoria, B.C. V8T 4Z1, CANADA

Phone	250-383-6864	Toll-free	1-888-232-4444 (Canada & US)
Fax	250-383-6804	E-mail	sales@trafford.com
Web site	www.trafford.com	TRAFFORD PUBLISHING IS A DIVISION OF TRAFFORD HOLDINGS LTD.
Trafford Catalogue #99-0035		www.trafford.com/robots/99-0035.html	

10   9   8   7   6   5   4   3

Acknowledgements

I could not have accomplished the tasks of writing this book, or been as motivated to learn *what I had to learn* without the expressed and continued support of two of my dearest friends; Steve Baisch, MD--forever my friend, Sheila Jordan, CPA, who steadfastly held the mirror—what better coach could one have and last but never least my confidante, my partner in discovery and support, Connie Davis.

Without the regular drinks from the examples set by my mother, whose long and debilitating illness has never gotten her down and my father who stands beside her and cares for her in a loving spirit of long-time marriage the epitome of *"for better or worse—I salute you!"*

To grandparents who are gone now, children of immigrants who toiled quietly and dutifully, I am you and you are me—together we are better in our children—you would be proud of them.

To my children, Ali, Katy and Ryan who constantly provide me with reasons why I need to continue growing and learning around reasons to keep my priorities straight, may your days be filled with choices around challenge and opportunity.

To the many teachers, coaches and friends who have made an indelible image on my life--and to those of you who thought I was too small—THANK YOU! In life, the master truly does appear when the student is ready, however we don't always realize until later that they were there.

Undying gratitude and respect to all of you,

mike

TABLE OF CONTENTS

Introduction: Why we're here!

Thank you for picking up this book! And I mean it!

Please feel free to own it! [See our special offer!]

> *The primary aim or purpose of this book is to provide a methodology for creating a CoachSystem™ in an organization.*

I wrote this book to put into print a <u>methodology of coaching,</u> devised in my 25 odd years of working in and being worked in teams, groups and organizations. I have had many *successful failures* and have learned more from failing than succeeding. I am also glad to know that it is now considered "normal" to fail and in some cases, even championed. To have the right to fail is leveraging; to learn from it, is an organizational dream.

The book you are about to read is a composite of my learning from those failures woven into the various successes I have been fortunate enough to enjoy, the greatest of which are two wonderful daughters who constantly find ways to challenge and delight me. (Hi, Ali & Katy!)

This book is not THE BOOK on COACHING. I would ask you not to misunderstand my intentions in that regard. In it, I offer many of my own pet theories, some of which are not indicative of thoroughly researched materials but they work! Nowadays, things are changing so rapidly that *what works* is changing as rapidly.

With the proliferation of the world wide web, we now see things changing before our own eyes without having to wait a month, a year or a decade for a new iteration. Iterations occur literally overnight and in recognition of that, I chose an electronic online publisher to record the metamorphosis of my own thinking on how I practice and write about the methodology of coaching. You are, therefore, the beneficiary of these times.

Once you purchase either the print or online version, the changes made will be available to you in real time. You will be able to adapt your learning as the evolution of coaching is recorded. This WILL be an adaptive—emergent—constantly changing process!

I have tried to answer your questions ahead of time by bringing together the process of relating to you "how" as much as "what" to think about during your own journey towards *generati*--a term coined to reflect the type of person and circumstances surrounding those people who effortlessly facilitate generative conditions around them. In my view, *people who coach* stand the best chance of being those people.

Business is challenging these days. There is no question about it. In your roles as managers and leaders, you will need to find and use every possible leverage point to make things add up. **Your people, structure and technology, they all have to be integrated into a cohesive system in order to compete with global challenges. This book is about those needs.**

In *MANAGING IN A TIME OF GREAT CHANGE*, Peter Drucker reveals that managers are being obsoleted for executives. I think what he means by that is that the role of the manager stems from our long past of scientific management. That paradigm was and is still important to the organization to get the work done.

We have, however, entered a new age where the organization is proliferated by knowledge workers, and the systems that surround and amplify knowledge work will require, as Drucker states, an *executive mentality* rather than a management one. The person in charge will need to be an amalgam of leader, manager, coach, facilitator, teacher, mentor, consultant, counselor, alchemist and perhaps—even guru. Those of you who are executives know what I mean. To those of you who do not yet consider yourselves "executives" I would challenge to adapt your thinking.

This book lays out for you a coaching methodology you can *teach* to your line managers or use in your customer service department—even with your kids! It helps you build a CoachSystem™, integrating coaching into every level in your organization.

> *The book is about creating outcomes for the individual and the organization that lead to well-being, purpose, competence and awareness. It is based on proven methods of improving performance, creating generative rather than destructive change and facilitating individual and organizational transformation towards effectiveness.*

No, it will not be easy but throughout your journey recognize that you alone can make a difference in those around you by using the coaching knowledge, skill and abilities outlined in this *manual*.

I wish you the best of luck and hope you will forward your thoughts, comments and suggestions to me at coach2@leadwise.com, visit the book's website at www.coach2-the-bottom-line.com or give our office a call at 800-823-1251.

SPECIAL OFFER

Please be sure to send in the feedback and registration form at the end of the book (after reading the book, of course) to receive access to the book's online version and knowledgebase, including the entire dialog from reviewers, readers and pundits that will appear with the book—online—over time.

I look forward to any opportunity to meet with you to discuss coaching and success in your organization.

If you still have not decided to own this book of coaching, here is one last enticement.

Anyone purchasing the book will gain access to a special membership on the web and access to our *coach-wise knowledgebase*—only available to members. This value alone is worth more than the price of the book. We would be happy to help you find answers to your coaching and leadership dilemmas through membership.

Again, thanks for picking up this book and GOOD LUCK!

Mike R. Jay, 1999
www.leadwise.com/leader

For information on Membership:
www.i-cbc.com

Executive Brief

The COACH2 CoachSystem™

> *"Any company that aspires to succeed in the tougher business climate of the 1990's must first resolve a basic dilemma: success in the marketplace increasingly depends on learning, yet most people don't know how to learn...*
>
> *First, most people define learning too narrowly as mere "problem solving," so they focus on identifying and correcting errors in the external environment. Solving problems is important. But if learning is to persist, managers and employees must also look inward. They need to reflect critically on their own behavior, identify the ways they often inadvertently contribute to the organization's problems, and then change how they act."*
>
> Chris Argyris, Teaching Smart People to Learn,
> HBR, May-June 1991

Every leader of any team or organization dreams of creating a purposeful, highly competent organization of self-directed team members who on a regular basis, achieves extraordinary results.

Yet, how many managers, leaders and professional coaches possess a clear—adaptive—proven roadmap for designing and integrating leadership, management and coaching systems into their lives and organizations?

Unfortunately, most people in leadership roles believe that setting ambitious goals and providing regular corrective feedback will create the results they need in a competitive marketspace. In general, research and experience prove that this is NOT enough.

The COACH2 CoachSystem ™ creates openings, possibilities, plans, outcomes and action steps that connect people, clarify expectations and foster high commitment, while supporting personal and organizational learning and development.

How do people and your organization benefit?

- Increased levels of personal and professional well-being
- Clarity and alignment of individual and organizational purpose
- Improved levels of personal and organizational competence
- Higher levels of awareness resulting in adaptive responses to change
- Organizational effectiveness

What does this book provide?

- A *foundational* Theory of coaching methodologies
- Coaching practices that lead to measurable results
- How to design a coaching system in your workgroup or organization
- How to use the COACH2 Model to improve other coaching methods
- The barriers and pitfalls to the successful use of coaching systems in organizations

- A model for improving performance and learning at the unit or line level
- A methodology for facilitating generative individual and organizational change
- A proven framework for transforming people and organizations

What specific skills will readers gain an understanding of?

- How to use *process* to coach performance, change and transformation
- How to *facilitate* an effective coaching system in your organization
- How to use: feedback, questions, statements, challenges and ideas in coaching delivery
- Basic coaching skills: observing, listening, discerning, modeling, delivering
- Creating a methodology that *values* a person's theory of action

How the book is laid out

- Prologue: The Reasons to Coach
- Part I: Coaching as a Theory of Action
- Part II: Coaching as a System of Change
- Part III: Coaching: Where it's Headed
- Epilogue: Coaching Insights so far

For more information or a personal consultation contact us by email: execoach2@leadwise.com or phone 1.800.823.1251
Visit us on the web www.coach2-the-bottom-line.com

Prologue

In the Beginning...Right Action

> *When people ask me what the responsibilities of leadership, management and coaching are in an organization, I offer the following statement: "The right people doing the right things at the right time in the right way for the right reasons."*
>
> Mike Jay

It is imperative that we discuss why the above statement has a place in the back of every person's mind who may employ coaching as a strategy for improving and developing people and organizations—*right action.*

We often view the ability to create wealth and keep a customer as the most important role of leadership. Yet, it really isn't *enough* of a noble cause to accomplish the real big things, is it?

In this book the organization is considered to be a *framework for the exchange of value.* It helps us to keep organizational life in perspective--the structure that surrounds us including all those functional but impersonal issues—and the people, the personal side of an organization. I admit I still struggle with the definition of an organization, and while I don't think it is necessarily a bad thing, it is not about struggle.

You will hear the term *effortless* used throughout the book with many different nouns, as work in today's world with all of our modern attributes should not be about effort and work, but about contribution and flow. Never before have we had the opportunities that abound today. We literally are at the dawn of a new age, hardly capable of being known, yet fully emerging as we live and breathe.

This book is about this "new age," living and prospering in it and finding an uncommon happiness through effortless contribution. My goal is to help you help others find their own place in organization, their own best way of contributing, and that inner sense of well being that burns deep within all of us—everyday. Work and organization need not be about struggle and strife--scarcity and greed. Work is probably the most significant human bond, lying ready to afford us the abundance and satisfaction that is common to the least of us.

Organizational Effectiveness

The short sidetrack above should not distract you from the central issue of *right action*—for it is merely the underlying foundation for it. Right action depends on the individual and on the collective action taken as a matter of choice each and every moment we process our thoughts—and behave. Right action is a matter of deep inner being that is often prevented from surfacing by personal and organizational barriers. However, in each and every moment, we have the opportunity, and some would say the obligation, to surface right action.

> *"Understanding how we diagnose and construct our experience, take action, and monitor our behavior while simultaneously achieving our goals is crucial to understanding and enhancing effectiveness."*

Argyris & Schon, <u>Theory in Practice</u>, 1974

This is, of course, easier said than done. While this book contains the *where with all or theory and practices* to help facilitate that for individuals and organizations, it is beyond the scope of our time here together to fully explore right action for you in all of your roles and their dimensions. Perhaps someday I will finish the work in progress that addresses those personal leadership issues, but for now allow me to offer to you my experience and synthesis of how to coach right action in organizations—*to create organizational effectiveness.*

Separating Right Action?

Please, do not think for a moment that I intend anything other than a synthesis of personal and organizational effectiveness--simultaneously. However, I have to focus the light of our attention and consciousness on the task at hand, that is, of helping us to understand how to create a system in an organization or workgroup that allows the opportunities for *right action* to surface and persist.

You will notice that we make reference to the *surfacing* of right action as opposed to having to create it? This is done on purpose. If we view the process of surfacing as something that already exists rather than constructing it from scratch, I think we can see that our *system of approach* will be much different. The methods, along with the knowledge, skills and abilities (KSAs) that are required for competence in surfacing right action as opposed to constructing it, are not always similar.

While this book is about developing and improving the competencies we will need to master in order to remove the barriers to *right action,* it is also about people. These competencies are made up of the KSAs that people will learn and master. In later chapters we will discuss fully the integration of theory and practice.

Components of Right Action

Let's for a moment go back to the concept of right action. We said that *right action* was "the **right people** doing the **right things** at the **right time** in the **right way** for the **right reasons**."

If we look at each component in the right action system, we will discover the reason for including it in the equation.

Right People

> *"It is a lot easier to hire the right people to begin with than to fix them later."*

Bradford D. Smart, Ph.D.

The above quote from Bradford Smart's latest book, *TOPGRADING: How leading companies win by hiring, coaching and keeping the right people,* sums up the importance of the right people in my view. So much of our time as change agents is spent working with the wrong people—people we are stuck with? It is clear that in order to be a great company or great workgroup you need to have great people. Yet, so much of the time, we find ourselves working with people who are not ready, willing and able to do the job they have been assigned.

While this book deals effectively with coaching in this situation, that is preventing a mismatch; recruiting, hiring and training the best person for the job cannot be overlooked. Fix your problems before they start! Coaching a person who is ready, willing and able is a whole lot different than interacting with someone who is not. Surfacing right action in the former is truly effortless, while the latter can be a challenge for even the most masterful of coaches at *best*, impossible in the least. Many coaching programs discuss the person who is not "coachable." A person who is not *ready, willing, or able* populates that subset.

I would recommend *TOPGRADING* for no other reason than to see how Smart helps us understand how different people fit into A, B and C possibilities. He fully demonstrates the effectiveness of how leading companies prosper because they spend 80% of their time with the people falling into the A class. He indicates that an effective strategy is to hire the *best possible candidate* available for the job based on an extensive interviewing process that is delineated in his book.

> *The old adage "People are your most important asset" is wrong. The right people are your most important asset.*
>
> Jim Collins, <u>Turning Goals Into Results</u>, HBR, July-Aug, 1999, p.77

Right Things

The first part of the equation is fairly simple, *start well—end well.* However from here on things get pretty complex. What is the *right thing*? This question in itself is probably responsible for more books, papers, articles and conversation than most other topics except the *right reasons.*

The right thing has a way of being highly elusive especially when the right thing today is not the right thing tomorrow in an ambiguous environment! However, the right thing can also be surfaced with the proper methodology. In fact, the **quality** of the right thing will improve with the use of the coaching methodology we describe in this book.

The focus throughout the book often centers on the question *what is the right thing--for the person coaching, the person being coached, the system or the organization?* Simply put, the right thing is whatever content, delivery, product or service meets the needs—that have value--to the person/organization and situation you are dealing with at the time. Many of these values will be in conflict, hence the turbulence and ambiguity of business today and tomorrow.

In the case of the *person coaching*, the right thing may be something we say or refrain from saying. It might appear as a question, a form of feedback, an idea or perhaps even silence. For a *customer service person*, the solution might appear in what the customer wants and the company can afford. For a *leader*, the right thing might be that *vision* thing, the correct selection of CFO, a new product idea or even a smooth, quiet ride through the countryside.

Each moment in time defines rightness or fit. The ability to do the right thing is within each of us. It may not be the right thing for everyone but at that precise moment it might be the right thing for us—a chance to work for another company, an opportunity to pursue a lifelong interest or the action taken to help someone in need.

To do the right thing requires an awareness and understanding of one's self, the situation and the desired outcomes, either shared or held individually. It must meet a host of moral and legal criteria, all so complex that at times we find ourselves pulled in two directions at once, yet underneath it all, we *know* the right thing.

An effective coaching interaction surfaces the right thing at the right time, even under the most ambiguous of circumstances.

Right Time

Timing is essential. Almost everything can be fixed except time. Time passes and often you get just one chance to do it right. Accountants talk of efficiency. In systems, we measure efficiency, the time and resources it takes to do it right the first *time*. As an individual or organization, we need to focus on doing the right thing at the right time because of the costs involved in doing it over and the speed in which the business environment is changing shape. Regis McKenna's book called *REAL TIME: Preparing for the Age of the Never Satisfied Customer* brings into view how critical *timing* is to both individuals and organizations.

> *"Companies best equipped for the twenty-first century will consider investment in real time systems as essential to maintaining their competitive edge and keeping their customers. By this I mean that they will use information and telecommunications technology to respond to changing circumstances and even more important, customer expectations within the smallest lapse of time."*

> Regis McKenna

Clearly, we have no choice but to take into consideration how time affects everything in our personal and organizational lives. From being on time to seeing your child perform in a play, to having the right thing ready for a customer precisely—on time. People and organizations have NO CHOICE but to seriously consider the impact of time on everything—including the right time to relax!

Coaching is about timing!

Without a doubt, the most exciting thing about coaching is that it brings about the consideration and importance of timing—through interaction. When we take the time or the opportunity to connect with people, to clarify meaning and to make commitments that are healthy, wealthy and wise—our time is well spent.

Right Way

This book is about *a* right way because the right way is the way that it needs to be or what works! On the surface, however, we don't always know the right way and many times will unconsciously do things in a way that is not representative of this *knowing* we all have access to deep inside us.

> *"The environment in which we operate is significantly more complex than what the human mind can process at a given moment. In order for the human mind to deal with reality, we must abstract from the buzzing confusion of everyday life by using abstract concepts."*

> Chris Argyris, <u>Org Dynamics</u>, Autumn 1982

Quite often, the right way becomes something that has worked in the past or something that is familiar. Due to complexity we tend to use these previously successful *right ways* to handle more and more challenges—to the point that they are no longer the right way. One of my favorite quotes from Abraham Maslow demonstrates this modus operandi, *"he who is good with a hammer thinks everything is a nail."*

The *right way syndrome* can be tested and often determined from using coaching methods. This is why coaching has become so popular among the *fad of the month* practicioners. As a way, coaching is participative and not directive as other *ways* and by rule, much more appreciative of people. It allows for the surfacing and development—not just the substitution—of the right way in each circumstance. At the very minimum, an awareness that we often fall into using the same abstract concepts-- for making meaning and decisions stated by Argyris--to solve a variety of solutions. In organization, it is easy to sub-optimize the system by using less than ideal solutions.

Ask anyone who has been in a coaching relationship for any period of time and regardless of whether they like their coach or not, they will *feel* more *aware* of themself and the organizational patterns. The mere fact that two people relate to one another and discuss things that are not normally discussed has the power of unleashing forces within us that are seldom seem. No wonder everybody is a coach!

> *[If we were on the internet I would have put a <g> (stands for an emotion of smiling or grinning) but since we are not I will just say the statement was meant facetiously<g>].*

One mistake that is often made—addressed clearly throughout the book—is that not everyone can or should be a coach, however, everyone should learn to use coaching KSAs (knowledge, skills and abilities).

The right way is therefore, determined mostly by the actor acting in accordance with the situational needs with unbending principles. If we understand that paradox, then using coaching KSAs can *surface or test the right way*, whether we are a coach or not. Most times, the right way is a perception and not a truth. This confuses most people because so many people have been taught to believe that there is a one right way to everything (remember Maslow?).

> *In a complex and ambiguous world such as we live and work in, very few things are universally true. We perceive them to be, but such is just not the case. We do not see the world as it is, but how we are.*

If I asked you—for just one moment—to suspend all your *truths* and ask you to find the *right way* to do something, you would probably use coaching KSAs automatically. Not knowing—that is, starting with a beginner's mind—you would have to probably connect with someone, clarify some issues—testing alternatives—and then commit to the *right way* for that situation.

Of course, we always consider the *right reasons* while we are discovering the right way, but that goes without saying.

Right Reasons

I saved the best for last! For the *right reasons* **is** the most written and talked about subject of mankind. Whole nations have been annihilated for not having the right reason on their side! Our entire democracy exists for the *right reasons.* Each and everyday we think we are doing things for the right reasons. We are individually and collectively guided by the right reasons, yet why don't we all have the **same** reasons?

> *Because the right reasons are highly personal and often very subjective—often hidden deep within our cognitive and emotional conditioning—being*

*interpreted from rising complexity, arising out of
abstract concepts.*

As we discussed in *right way*, there are universal truths but
not as many as we subscribe to and believe. In business, the
right reasons have to be motivating, empowering, energizing,
on solid legal ground, compassionate. Compassionate? Yes,
that too! It is no longer acceptable to hide behind a stoic
truth about how the organization is all-powerful and dictates
the lives of its constituents, its market and its buyers! A new
world has dawned and we now live in a buyer's market,
driven by overcapacity, global competition, ambiguous and
turbulent circumstances, a deteriorating environment and a
deep need to connect and belong to each other.

The Right Reasons?

The right reasons today are different from the right reasons
of yesterday. Yes, we need to have the same moral compass,
yet the moral points have become more graduated. We
cannot live and work any longer at the benefit of our
environment. No longer are there people lined up at our
doors willing to work for anything we chose to declare as fit.

> *The time has passed that we are able to command the
> world's markets and our employee's time, life and
> existence. A fragile, yet dynamic balance is coming
> into vogue where we must—for the right reasons—
> conduct ourselves individually and collectively in
> harmony with one another and our environment.*

Coaching is one of the few *ways* to approach and dialog
about the right reasons at the individual level.

- Leaders describe for us the right reasons in their
  noble visions.

- Managers decide our course of actions for the right reasons.
- Trainers teach us what to do for the right reasons and
- *actors* perform their roles for the right reasons.

Yet, in coaching, we <u>explore</u> the right reasons; we test the *assumptions* those right reasons are based upon. Through discovery, appreciative inquiry as well as dialogue and conversation with another person, we generate the right reasons through interaction.

Throughout this book, we will discover why coaching is not just another *program du jour*. We will come to understand how coaching fits in the modern day organizational structure. We will learn how to conduct coaching interactions to develop well being, purpose, competence and awareness in an individual and in an organization.

> *"I recommend that we account for behavior by understanding it as what follows from the way the world is showing up for someone. In other words, it is not events, communication, or stimuli that lead to behavior, it is the interpretation [my emphasis] an individual gives to the phenomenon that leads to actions taken."*
>
> James Flaherty from *COACHING: Evoking Excellence in Others.*

Clearly, right action is determined *through interpretation* of the interaction of a variety of factors. This is not always defined in terms of standards but often emergent according to interpretation or one's governing variables as Argyris might conclude. The role of coaching in an organization and for the individual can facilitate interpretations that are more generative for all concerned.

Generati

In a sense, people who practice this methodology as a lifestyle rather than in a part of their lives evoke for me the term *generati*. I coined this term a number of years ago to describe this very condition—*people who continuously create generative outcomes for others.*

The term is derived from the forms of literati and digerati describing conditions surrounding the literary and digital worlds. I offer this coaching methodology to a new world. This new world is about right action…is about creating generative conditions for all involved and…is about a practice of understanding and acting in harmony with our goals, our work, our communities and ourselves.

Please join me in the following chapters on a journey towards *generati*. Coaching is a path you will find generative for you and your organization.

Part 1

Coaching as a Theory of Action

The following excerpt is paraphrased from a speech given by David Whyte, speaking to a group of coaches in Boston, MA at a Linkage, Inc. Coaching Conference in 1999. It frames the basis for coaching, the coaching model as an intervention process and highlights a theory of action that can be used to create organizational effectiveness.

David Whyte speaking…

> *Business in a way is always at some kind of frontier or another. And the people who have founded the business or run the business also have to put their own identities at a certain kind of frontier. I'm interested in this frontier conversation, this conversation with the great unknown, which is forming around us at any one moment in time. To which, we have not only to bring our empirical and our strategic inheritance, but also, the inheritance of the imagination and what it means to be a full human being.*
>
> *…I see a commonality of exploration, which has to do with a new kind of dispensation, which is broad…and a new understanding…and the understanding is really one of not knowing really…an understanding that there is a new territory that we are gazing over but have not yet entered.*
>
> *There is a new direction that our grandparents and parents could only have imagined but which we are now about to experience. It has to do with a pilgrimage of identity that we are all going through.*

In which many of the old names we gave to things no longer are fluid enough or changeable enough to actually be useful in the new oceanic world in a way.

...so the word manager actually comes from the root of this idea that you would get on the back of this beast, you would dig your knees in, you would pull the reins and you would head it in a certain direction.   I think we've all come to the place now where we understand that the words "giddy-up there" only go so far in creating participation...a sense of commitment.

Of all the qualities that most individuals and companies are looking for right now we identify those of adaptability, vitality, meaning and the willingness to go the extra mile. And these qualities really, they all belong to the eternal sense of what it means to be fully human.

So, we are at an astonishing crossroads now. We are at a place where the very things that organizations are looking for, that is, the qualities of adaptability, vitality, passion and the willingness to go the extra mile are the very things human beings have wanted for themselves since the beginning of time.

Both sides are equally frightened of embracing these qualities. These are not qualities you can coerce or legislate, nor can you invite people into your office and say: I would like an increase in the creativity quotient of 8.9%. The request is absurd because there is no lever you can pull inside that person that will turn on their qualities of creativity. If there was a lever, they would have pulled it themselves, years ago.

Their own creativity is just as much a mystery to them as it is to someone outside, trying to engage it. What I do believe is that you can create a conversation in which people will find themselves emboldened and excited as well as part of a much larger story in which they actually surprise themselves into giving gifts that quite often they did not even know they had themselves. It is this conversation that we are all entering together…

Chapter 1

Only a few achieve the colossal task of holding together, without being split asunder, the clarity of their vision alongside an ability to take their place in a materialistic world. They are the modern heroes...Artists at least have a form within which they can hold their own conflicting opposites together. But there are some who have no recognized artistic form to serve this purpose, they are artists of the living. To my mind these last are the supreme heroes in our soulless society.

Irene Claremont de Castillejo

A Theory of Coaching

Welcome to COACH 2 THE BOTTOM LINE. Over the next few pages I want to introduce you to personal and organizational coaching. Coaching is a fairly young professional discipline—appearing formally in business organizations during the 1970s if not before. As we approach the beginning of a new millennium, coaching as a practice, is being introduced into modern organizations at all levels.

Defining Coaching

The COACH2 Model is designed to help you experience coaching and how it fits into fast, *organic,* flexible and adaptive organizations. Throughout this book, we refer to the *coach* as the *person coaching (pc).* This is purposefully done to remove the confusion around who is a coach and what is coaching. In the simplest terms, **a coach is someone who uses coaching knowledge, skills and abilities (KSAs) without responsibility, accountability or authority over the outcomes of the *person being coached (pbc)* while seeking to co-generate well-being, purpose, competence and awareness as a result of a coaching interaction.**

A person using coaching KSAs is not necessarily a coach and should not be considered a coach unless he/she meets the specific criteria above. A modern day illusion is that everyone is a coach, as many pundits have indicated. Often an organization failing to recognize the following distinctions sets up people—they call coaches—to fail.

A more correct term to describe the current phenomena around coaching would be to state that everyone should be coaching—using the coaching KSAs to promote personal and organizational effectiveness. While this may seem like a minor distinction, I can tell you from first hand experience that you cannot be someone's coach and maintain responsibility, accountability and authority (RAA) over their outcomes. What was to be *their agenda*, quickly becomes influenced by your agenda and that, effectively disqualifies an essential property of the coach designation.

Coaching Distinctions

1. A *coach* normally has many years of specialized training and experience; a person coaching is often not formally trained as a coach, only in coaching KSAs.
2. Coaching is practiced through openings; management coaching through gaps.
3. Leaders, managers, mentors, counselors and teachers all practice coaching but are not coaches.

4. The significant issue differentiating coaches and people coaching is agenda; *a coach does not have one.* In addition, the coach lacks the RAA to see that the person performs or achieves a specified outcome.

5. A coach, as stated previously, has no RAA over the performance of the pbc, while a pc often has at least one and often all three.

6. A *true coach* practices in a strictly voluntary environment.

7. Almost anyone can, should develop and must use coaching KSAs, however it often takes many years of practice to become masterful at coaching.

8. The difference between personal coaching and organizational coaching is that in personal coaching, the pbc is figuratively the center of the universe in terms of focus. In organizational coaching, there are at a minimum of two universes of intention and attention, the individual and the organization. There may indeed be others as role complexity increases dramatically in personal and organizational life, but in organizational coaching there are **two sets** of governing values or variables.

Coaching Outcomes

In short, here is the remainder of the theory surrounding the COACH2 Coaching Methodology. Any kind of coaching has in common at least one, and more often than not, all **four critical coaching outcomes**—personal and organizational—in all cases.

- An improvement in well-being
- Purposeful behavior
- Higher levels of competence
- Increased awareness

These crucial outcomes of effective coaching are often judged by the pbc and not the pc. Many times personal and organizational outcomes are directly and inextricably linked. There are many ways to reach these essential outcomes in an interactive process between pc and pbc and frequently, those processes will emerge or be unique to the relationship.

However, there are **three *core competencies*** that under gird **any** coaching process, methodology or system. Any other system of coaching can be mapped onto the COACH2 Model creating enormous personal and organizational leverage, but all must attain competence in a minimum of these three key areas:

- Connection
- Clarification
- Commitment

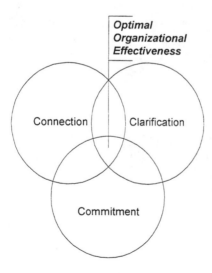

Without all three of these competencies evident in the coaching methodology or technology, it will be difficult to achieve the stated and desired outcomes of well-being, purpose, competence and awareness—leading to personal and organizational effectiveness.

With regard to outcomes and core competencies, there is a host of other KSAs that contribute toward fulfillment of these significant virtues. Many processes are involved, triggered and co-created during coaching interactions but all have five important sub-processes in common. They are:

- Openings
- Possibilities
- Plans
- Outcomes
- Action

There are key abilities that must be continuously developed and improved. Those abilities are:

- Observing
- Listening
- Discerning
- Modeling
- Delivering

These five abilities in concert with the five key subject areas of openings, possibilities, plans, outcomes and action create the realization of the three core competencies and resultant desired outcomes listed previously. What is also interesting is that the key abilities are directly represented by our five senses in one-way or another: Sight, Sound, Feeling, Action and Speech.

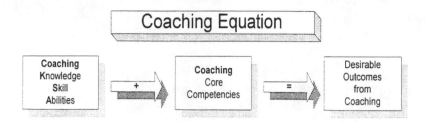

This equation assumes that a coaching interaction includes an appreciative interaction with a person or system and is based on these basic values:

- **RIGHT ACTION**
- **RESPECT**
- **CONFIDENTIALITY**
- **DEVELOPMENT**
- **MASTERY**

There are literally hundreds of KSAs available to coaches. They all have their place and their time, however, they must all flow-through these essential components of the equation in full view of governing values or variables.

To complete the abridged version of the COACH2 Methodology, there are two remaining factors to consider as central to the model. A coaching conversation, approach or interaction basically, consists of two things: content and process (delivery). Delivery is only one aspect of communication, but it is central to coaching. You will notice that all five key abilities: observing, listening, discerning, modeling and delivery are required components of communication.

We know that at times, coaching occurs in every discipline and in every possible situation. Content is often created about and through those unique circumstances. However, the *delivery methods* used by a person coaching can be categorized as feedback, ideas, questions and challenges. Every one of these methods can be charged positive or negative and can be perceived as such to the pbc.

Effective coaching actualizes the agenda of the pbc, or when the agenda and desired outcomes are not the same-- whichever the desired state of the pbc--each method can be masterfully used. A continuum from past to future helps to dimensionalize the delivery.

Effective use of timing, placement, force and focus of delivery provide the appropriate impact on the interaction or relationship. To evoke excellence in others requires the effective use of coaching KSAs and practice. The co-generation of well-being, purpose, competence and awareness requires that our coaching be value-based and compassionate, clear and courageous, empathetic and masterful.

Coaching Guidelines

To close this overview of COACH2, here are some simple, yet elegant guidelines:

1. People are different. Seek understanding of those differences with a beginner's mind.
2. Spend the *appropriate* amount of time connecting with the pbc.
3. When in doubt, listen deeply and ask a clarifying question: "Say more about that?"

4. Coach through openings. Use coaching KSAs to create openings out of gaps.
5. Coach the pbc where he/she is and with an eye on his/her desired future.
6. Challenge the pbc's status quo when they are stuck.
7. Use the C.A.R.E.S. Model to guide the coach approach:

8. Control-Assurance-Reliability-Empathy-Safety

    Provide the pbc with all of these in the interaction!

9. Ask for commitment to action
10. Embrace the concepts of *blameless error* and successful failure.
11. Smile a lot and enjoy the interaction with the pbc.

Summary

If you can change just 20% of your organization or your beliefs through coaching, you will create a structural change in your company and in yourself toward more desirable outcomes. The coaching interaction is the medium to produce sustainable cultures, adaptable organizations and generative futures.

Finally, remember that people are different and what we intend does not always produce a similar effect. It takes skill to relate to the differences we all share because *the only thing common to all of us is that we are all different.* Valuing another human being is the essential nature of coaching. Learning to approach coaching from an appreciative standpoint helps us to focus on solutions rather than being oriented towards problem solving.

CHAPTER 2

"In this chapter, I describe the coaching model, its constituent parts and how it fits into the organizational climate. We also discuss what coaching is and what it is not and why it is necessary to differentiate the coach from a manager, a leader, a therapist or consultant. I offer the reasoning behind why managers cannot be coaches and how an executive must understand this distinction in order to create a successful coaching system that contributes to high personal function."

An Overview of Coaching in Organizations

In this chapter, we need to proceed around some assumptions. These assumptions concern the model of coaching called COACH2 (C2), how it was developed and how coaching in general fits into personal and organizational life. Without some basic articulated beliefs, the discussion throughout the book has no foundation or guiding theory of action (mental model). In effect, this book is about a mental model of coaching and how coaching permeates organizational life towards effectiveness.

Coaching is...

MORE	LESS
• listening	• talking
• observing	• doing
• about connection	• about hierarchy
• clarifying	• knowing
• commitment	• democracy
• modeling	• teaching

- practice
- about development
- EQ
- about adapting
- about transformation
- results
- discovery
- about goal design

- performing
- about perfection
- IQ
- about being best
- about maximizing
- activity
- prediction
- goal directed

The C2 coaching model is formed by an essential need for well-being, purpose, competence and awareness in people and organizations. It is founded on the premise that improving performance, creating generative change and effecting transformation is possible without the degeneration of self, our environment and our need to be fully human in pursuit of happiness.

Coach & Coaching Defined

To have direct control is to manage, not to coach. It is the coach's lack of direct control or authority that makes the coaching task difficult and challenging. A coach, however, can have considerable power depending on reputation, track record, access to other parts of the organization, and so forth. Absence of authority also makes possible major change, because the person being coached must be motivated internally. True, a coach can be instrumental in encouraging or motivating the executive to learn and to change, but ultimately the changes must be embraced by the executive if they are to be effective.

Four Essential Ways that Coaching can help
Executives, R. Whiterspoon and R. White

Coaching: an interaction that occurs between people that produces desired performance, change or transformation in consideration of personal and organizational awareness, purpose, competence and well-being.

Coach: a person participating in a voluntary interaction with neither responsibility, accountability or authority over the outcomes of the person being coached towards a result of mutually desirable performance, generative change and development of the whole person.

Person coaching (pc): a person who engages in a coaching interaction towards performance, change and transformation.

Person being coached (pbc): a person who is coached in an interaction towards a result of increasing performance, exploring change and transformation.

Corporate Coaching: A Definition from ICF

Another viewpoint is listed below from working documents of the International Coaches Federation (ICF), a committee of volunteer coaches seeking to define and represent the case for corporate coaching in an organization. This is a work in progress but the information below is valuable towards our understanding of the difference between coaching individuals and coaching in organizations of individuals.

[My future goal is to demonstrate yet another category of a business or systems coach, where the "coachee or object" is the business or organizational system as a whole.]

What follows is the initial definition agreed to by the Committee for use in determining a category of corporate coach:

In corporate coaching, an **organization** has hired a coach to work with **people**, whether individuals or teams, to facilitate shifts within the **context of the organization's culture** to achieve extraordinary results.

Emphasis is placed on the three key elements around which the definition was built and which are most important in distinguishing corporate coaching from other types of coaching. This definition was intended to include ideas of:

- ◆ coaches who are internal and external to the hiring organization
- ◆ for profit and not for profit organizations
- ◆ professional, executive, leadership and team coaching
- ◆ personal development coaching
- ◆ shifts in the area of organizational development
- ◆ situational coaching or on-going relationship coaching

This definition does not include some of the concepts that the term "coaching" has meant in some corporate settings. Not included in the ICF definition are the following concepts:

- ◆ managers who change their title to "coach" with no change in role or approach
- ◆ mentors who change their title to "coach" and exclude the evoking element of coaching
- ◆ consultants who change their title to "coach" and are hired to address specific performance concerns where the consultant is responsible for prescribing the solution

In the future, more and more organizations will define coaching for their organization. Those parameters of coaching will require the coaching system to be reflective of personal and organizational needs for performance, change and transformation towards awareness, competence, purpose and well-being--personal and organizational.

Performance, Change and Transformation

For the sake of discussion throughout the book, let us define the constructs of performance, change and transformation. The four outcomes (well-being, purpose, competence and awareness) of effective coaching are discussed later. It is important at this point to explore why we're here before proceeding with ideas about a theory of action.

- **Performance**: improving the current need—doing current things better
- **Change**: satisfying or creating the need to do things differently
- **Transformation**: recognizing and satisfying the need to do *different things differently*

These three levels of *learning* mirror the model created in systems learning that led to the concept of learning organizations. The third loop is added by Robert Hargrove in Masterful Coaching.

Level 1 learning—**performance**—is single loop learning, which requires us to practice getting better at what we are currently doing. It is a goal-oriented activity usually surrounding skill development or process improvement.

Level 2 learning—**change**—asks us to reframe our context in terms of modifying what we are currently doing by using different methods or techniques and certainly how we think about what we are doing. It is oriented around innovation. Should we be doing something different?

Peter Drucker's concept of systemized abandonment asks that we examine what we are doing and if we had to do it all over again, would we be doing this now? It also concerns a personal and organizational dispensation to change what they are currently doing in response to changes in the environment, and to create a *system of change* that requires multiple responses to change concurrently.

Level 3 learning—**transformation**—asks a completely different question. Do we have the capability and the ability to learn at learning, improve while improving—to ask those questions of ourselves, of our organization, about who we are? It is about development and not only doing different things differently, but doing ***better*** things.

Transformation not only requires changes in frame or context but changes in development. We can borrow some adult development theory and look at what we know we know, what we know we don't know and what we don't know we don't know, all three mirroring consequent levels in development and learning loops. While seemingly complex and ambiguous, I hope you will feel differently about "what you don't know you don't know" after reading this book on coaching.

Where Transformation Lives

To fully integrate the self with all three of these levels of learning forces fundamental change in the way we approach everything on our path. Argyris and Schon spent a great deal of time and research talking about theories in action. Their research presented in *THEORIES OF PRACTICE: Increasing Professional Effectiveness, 1974,* lays the groundwork for a good deal of developmental coaching theory (Basically an under-researched area of interest.) and an amalgam of adult development theory and the theories of action needed to create an organization that is fluid, flexible and adaptive in real time.

To summarize a rather complex theory in a few lines does injustice to the elegance presented by Argyris and Schon, after which I encourage you to fully explore their treatise in their book. Basically, we have two theories of operation—personally and organizationally. A theory we use called "theory in use" and a theory we say we use—"espoused theory." In a nutshell, coaching provides a methodology—the methodology—in my view, to surface the discrepancies and incongruencies between these theories—appreciatively, rather than by decree or gap analysis.

Argyris has given significantly to the process of coaching with his Model I and II theories because as a person coaching (pc) we can engage the person being coached (pbc) in a dialog to surface the discrepancies between what they say they believe and how they act—a most difficult journey for us all.

 In recognizing these principles we can then begin to reformulate our beliefs and approach the more effective functioning of the Model II set of governing variables that release us individually and collectively from the personal and organizational defensive patterns that block high performance. More is spoken about Model I and Model II in Part II and a summary of these theories from Argyris is contained in the appendicies.

Yes, we can't ignore that the realities of the current organizational climate coerce us to embrace all of these forms of learning, including goal achievement in level 1. It would be ludicrous to think that we can bypass performance and head straight to transformation as both are a part of the other.

In some organizations, performance will provide us with a platform to launch higher levels of coaching and that is the key...to find a way to introduce the coaching methodology into a personal and organizational system. The following model provides a conduit into organization by enabling the least common denominator in the organization with a model of how to approach personal and organizational performance, change and transformation--systematically.

The COACH2 Model

The COACH2 (C2) model is a prime or source model.

In other words, it is not reducible any further and other
coaching methodologies can be mapped onto it to create
additional sophistication and efficacy. The prime actionable
components of the C2 model are connect, clarify and commit.
This is the model in its simplest form. It is a hologram of
coaching and in its purest sense any coaching methodology
will contain all three elements. We start with a solid
foundation and add layers of sophistication to meet
complexity in our personal and organizational lives.

The C2 model is targeted to the bottom-line in personal and
organizational systems. The bottom-line has a connotation of
money, however many factors contribute to financial
performance, not just money. The bottom-line for a person
can be their family, friends, and success at work and
relationships. The bottom line recognizes that people are
different, and we need an appreciative not a punitive
methodology that promotes and meets those concerns,
whatever they may be. The one overriding assumption that
must always be at the forefront of your thinking is that while
people have many things in common—the thing most in
common—is that we are all different!

This bottom line orientation is meant to draw your attention **to
what is most important** to you, personally, towards a higher
level of adaptability, vitality, passion and the willingness to go
the extra mile. Since it is impossible to separate our lives
from our daily bread—and our organizations, whether they're
profit, non-profit, community or group—we must create
systems that recognize this point of leverage.

The C2 Model is designed to provide a simple framework with which to address more and more complex interactions. From the counter person at McDonald's Restaurant to an interaction between heads of state, the C2 model can be utilized to successfully address performance, change and transformation among two people or two world powers.

Within that continuum lies a simple fact, that people need to connect with each other, clarify meaning and commit to some action—presumably an action that becomes a winning proposition for all concerned. I refer to this condition as the "third win." Pundits have discussed win-win philosophies for decades, yet few have taken the time to explain the third win.

The third win is generative and represents the capability created when *win-win* is achieved in full recognition of producing a *system win* or capacity to generate additional leverage. Here is a quick example. The sales manager of a department store exchanges the tires of an unhappy customer even though the tires belong to some other brand. The customer is happy and goes on to become a continuous customer and an *advocate* of the brand. (True story!)

Another example: a manager coaching a subordinate towards performance realizes that the subordinate is underemployed and desires more responsibility. The manager sends the employee to night school and pays the tuition while the employee performs at a higher level in his/her current position in anticipation of the promotion likely to occur at the completion of his/her education. The third win generating leverage for all concerned. Clearly, the C2 model provides the methodology for that *simple* success.

C2 is also scalable and adaptable in real time: two critical factors to people and organizations. It also provides a methodology to address rising complexity in our lives—

effectively. C2 is NOT a reductionistic model where complexity is addressed by fractionalizing the whole and dealing with those separate parts. In the simplicity of the model lie the tools to address any situation in terms of scale, adaptability and complexity.

C2 can be taught to someone who has never been exposed to coaching methods in a matter of minutes with benefits to the organization and to the individual over time. Those small initial benefits will amplify in time as the model provides the *beginning* of a developmental journey for both the person and the organization—a spiral of effectiveness. While remaining skeptical of the efficacy of such a benefit from three simple words, allow yourself as the reader/skeptic, to remain cautiously open and considerate of your own journey through this book.

A couple of essential things will happen along this journey with C2. First, you will easily remember the model. When situations arise with others, you will find yourself becoming aware either in the moment or afterwards, of the power and ease of the model during interactions. The other factor will be that the model allows you to adapt any methodology you are currently using or will learn in the future towards a greater level of mastery in dealing with performance, change and transformation.

> *What is key about the simplicity in the C2 Model is while in a coaching interaction you can become a witness to the process rather than focusing on judgments about your agenda!*

Any current and future methodology, skill and ability can be *mapped onto* the C2 model. It is precisely why your journey will be rich and full of success, as you understand connection, clarification and commitment—all at the core of the COACH2

Model. These three fundamental ways of being form the *"core competence"* for coaching. There will be knowledge, skill and abilities that have to be learned and developed but all of them flow essentially into and through these three core competencies. These competencies discussed in Part II flow towards values of TRUST, COMPASSION and "RIGHT-ACTION." Within these core beliefs lay the keys to high performance, generative change and effective personal and organizational transformation.

COACH2 & Fit

How does coaching and the C2 model fit into our lives to effect *performance, change and transformation*?

Levels of Complexity	Graduated layers of Attention	Levels of Intention
5	————————————	Practice
4	————————————	Ksa's
3	————————————	Methdology
2	————————————	Business System
1	————————————	MarketSpace
0	- - - - - - - - - - - - - - -	Environment

1. An **environment** encapsulates *everything.*
   - *a simple, yet complex array of choices and opportunity*

2. We define a **marketspace** or focus of *attention using strategic intention.* (Space used to denote inclusion of cyberspace into marketplace.)
   - *consciously or unconsciously*

3. An organizing **system** arises from intention—personal/organizational.
   - *using people-structure-technology*
   - seeks and responds to **needs** in the environment
   - *towards well being, purpose, competence, awareness*

4. **A methodology** is used to manage complexity.
   - *connect, clarify, and commit*

5. **Knowledge, skills and abilities are directed to**
   - *openings-possibilities (ideas)-plans-outcomes (scenarios)-action*
   - leveraging a continuum of ***direct to indirect* methodologies**:
   - *used by teaching-management-consulting-leadership-counseling-facilitating-mentoring-coaching, etc.*
   - with a combination of interconnected **resources**:
   - *content/products/services-capital-connectivity-clients*

6. **Practice and learning towards development**

You can see all these essential components in this hierarchy of complexity that we have in our personal lives as well as in our organizational systems. You will notice these interrelated parts are woven inextricably and cannot be separated without affecting the identity of the whole. The interesting assumptions of this unending cycle are:

- all parts of the cycle are necessary and cannot be reduced any further
- performance, change and transformation are effected by the combination of the parts and also affect those parts in return (as in a quantum field)
- coaching is not **the** preferred methodology but **one** of many
- the situation will dictate the most effective methodology rather than the method dictating the situation
- to reach high levels of performance, all methods will be used
- there is no beginning and no end—a journey, *"dance where you like, but dance you must"*
- *any* action will be in respect to the whole
- the ability of C2 to scale and adapt to complexity is limitless

Coaching has a Place

It is important to establish the place of coaching and C2 in the scheme of things. It is now clear that coaching **is** a separate discipline, however young and fragile at this time. Some say that coaching is a part of an overriding discipline, however my research has shown that coaching is in fact a *separate discipline when it meets certain criteria*. Those criteria will be demonstrated throughout the book and the definition that is reflected by those criteria at the beginning of this chapter.

The following model shows how easily the aspects of the C2 model provide a cyclical spiral of development that can be used in our personal lives and our organizational lives *to improve performance, create generative change,* and *transform our lives*.

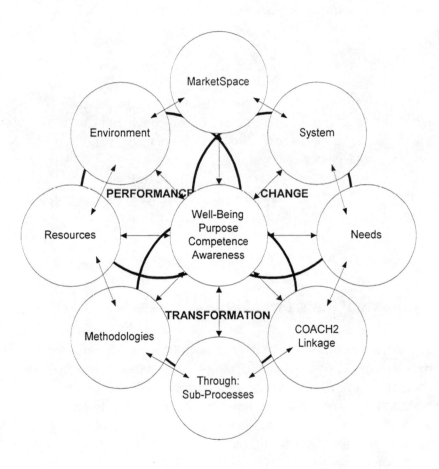

The Paradox of Coaching

In order to frame the context of the model we must frame the general context of coaching. Coaching knowledge, skills and abilities (KSAs) lay separate from and are at the same time a part of being a coach. In other words, you can coach someone, use coaching KSAs and not be a coach—you are a (leader, manager, teacher, facilitator, etc.,--a person coaching (pc). This is an important conceptual demarcation that **must** be understood as the coaching discipline stands today in 1999.

Too many people are labeling themselves coaches because they practice coaching KSAs. This is confusing the industry and the environment. The matrix that follows *helps* put into perspective what I mean in terms of being a coach and practicing coaching—a critical distinction we must make. *Everyone* should practice coaching KSAs as those KSAs overlay on any discipline and on any person's life and organization. However, very few people will need to become a coach or want to become a coach to achieve those means.

A Contextual Matrix of Methodologies

This matrix was arrived at over time from trying to discern the particular aspects of each methodology that separated it from another method of focusing content. It appears that there are basically two prime considerations, one of content and one of process (delivery). Each methodology has a set of KSAs as well as responsibility, accountability and authority that differentiate it and make it similar with others. Many **share** commonalities with as few as one differentiating aspect of their content and delivery, however, that **one** difference may be crucial.

The **Methodology Matrix**: [explanation follows]

Methodology*	For Business Processes that involve the person being coached										
	1 To 1	1 to Many	Respons-ability	Account ability	Has Authority	Owns Process	Owns Outcome	Owns Problem	Transfer Tacit Knowledge	Transfer Explicit Knowledge	Develop Future Ability
Teacher	X	X	X	X	X	X	X	X		X	X
Manager	X	X	X	X	X	X	X	X	X	X	X
Consultant	X	X	X	X		X		X		X	
Facilitator		X		X	X[1]	X					X
Leader	X	X	X	X	X[2]		X	X[3]	X	X	X
Counselor[a]	X			X		X	X		X	X	X
Mentor	X		X			X	X		X[4]		X
Coach	X					X			X	X[5]	X
Mediate		X				X					X

* Some related disciplines that practice coaching KSAs—does not include all

[a] Therapist is grouped with counselor for the purposes of the criteria in the table

[1] Facilitators are often given authority

[2] Leaders can have authority as well as not, i.e. volunteer

[3] Leaders may not own the problem

[4] Mentoring maybe the most effective method of tacit knowledge transfer

[5] Three kinds of coaching: process, content and combination

coach2-the-bottom-line.com

You can see from the matrix that many assumptions are made and there are some with which you will probably not agree. However, the major factors I would like to draw your attention to are the differences between **coach** and the rest of the major disciplines. The coach has no responsibility, accountability, and authority and does not own the outcome. These are crucial demarcations and while any of the disciplines listed may claim total *coverage of all others*, it is not practical to do so.

If anyone discipline could function—if it were possible—to resemble all the various attributes of all disciplines, then we could picture mediocrity rather than mastery, or perhaps enlightenment, you pick. The person and our organizations are too complex to master all the requirements of every discipline, every situation and every need.

The fact remains that being a coach is NOT the same as being one of the other disciplines and practicing coaching KSAs.

The matrix is clearly delineated to strike a particular chord that will not be in harmony to many people at the present. Organizations have began to adopt more consultative approaches as we move from mechanical, hierarchical, inflexible organizations to those that resemble organisms that are highly flexible, adaptable and living forms of doing work. This rush to participative forms of management has precipitated many consequences, the least of which is labeling everyone in the organization as a coach.

If you review the matrix, you can seen the direct conflict between a coach and a manager regarding responsibility, accountability and authority, none of which are held by the coach for either problems or outcomes. **Again, I state that this is a bifurcation in the current coaching landscape for**

both personal and organizational coaches and a clear statement of definition.

A coach does not have responsibility, accountability or authority for problems or outcomes concerning the client's actions. If they do, they may be coaching and using coaching KSAs but they are not a coach as the definition requires such of a coach.

These critical distinctions **must be understood** in order for executives and leaders to properly implement a **CoachSystem™** in their organization. Should you adopt coaching KSAs —**YES**! Should everyone be coaches—**NO**!

It is impossible. Someone must take responsibility, accountability and authority for personal and organizational outcomes. In a personal sense (and in a new organizational sense), it is the individual who is required to take those factors into account. In an organizational sense, it will be leadership and management that direct and assign these critical issues.

This may throw many of you for a loop and it should. Coaching is at a precipice as people scramble to credential, build brands and create coach training programs. However, without this clear set of distinctions, organizations will create havoc among people and structure in the organization and in the coaching environment as well—we can literally have anyone state or claim they are a coach (and many are) confusing even more the ability of leaders and managers to establish credible systems and outcomes.

Such confusion and mediocrity created by ineffective coaching systems and unclear responsibility, accountability and authority will diffuse and cripple performance, change and transformation among people and organizations. Please understand this, if you are bound and determined to create coaches throughout your organization internally, do not make these people responsible, accountable or give them authority over those they coach. IF YOU DO, you will be destroying the essential nature of the coach/client relationship—TRUST!

Take all other elements from the coaching relationship except trust and you can still create effective performance, change and transformation in people and in organizations—it will emerge—with trust! However, if you break the bond of trust between coach and client, you have severed the *heart* of the coaching relationship between coach and client.

Trust is the fountain of all *free and informed* choice. Without the clear, safe elixir of trust, anything we do with a person being coached--by a coach--becomes less.

- First, you cannot have trust if the person you are coaching—as a coach—believes you have anything to gain from his/her actions in the organization.
- Secondly, it is impossible to coach someone without *participating* in the outcome. No more than it is possible to measure a particle in a quantum field without influencing its measurement as an observer in that field.

  If you have responsibility, accountability or authority as a *coach*, you cannot be impartial, neutral and without agenda—the essential prerequisites of a professional coach. Therefore, you participate in the success or failure of the client's actions—*with benefit*—either positive or negative.

Can you coach in organization and have responsibility, accountability and authority (RAA) for business processes of those you coach? Of course! However, coaching and being a coach are two different aspects of the same set of KSAs. When you add RAA to the situation, you can be coaching, however you are not a coach. You CANNOT be a coach (in the sense of a new coaching discipline being defined—of course we all have grown up with athletic coaches, singing coaches, etc.) if you have responsibility, accountability and authority for those processes that are a part of the individuals you coach!

A simple way to view this distinction is that you may practice leadership KSAs in an organization without being the leader. You may practice management KSAs without being a manager, therefore, it goes without saying that you may practice coaching KSAs without being a coach.

Once we see this distinction clearly, then we may institute a coaching system that is designed for success rather than for failure. In Part II, I provide the necessary explanations on how to design a CoachSystem™ in view of these distinctions that is designed for success leading to improvement in performance, generative change and effective transformation of people and organizations.

Chapter 3

Using Coaching to Match Capability

Based on the largest study of its kind ever undertaken, more than 80,000 managers in 400 companies reveal revolutionary insights about successful managerial behavior.

Great managers do not help people overcome their weaknesses. They do not believe that each person has unlimited potential. They play favorites and they break the "Golden Rule" every day. This amazing book explains why great managers break all the rules of conventional wisdom.

In today's tight labor markets, companies compete to find and keep the best employees, using pay, benefits, promotions, and training. But these well-intentioned efforts miss the mark. The front-line manager is the key to attracting and retaining talented employees. No matter how generous its pay or renowned its training, the company that lacks great, front-line managers will bleed talent. Talented employees know that managers trump companies.

Great managers are the heroes of this book. Vivid examples draw readers into the world of real-life managers and show how -- as they select, focus, motivate, and develop their people -- great managers turn talent into performance, and build a great company, one employee at a time.

First, Break All the Rules: What the World's Greatest Managers Do Differently
Marcus Buckingham and Curt Coffman, Simon & Schuster, May 1999

In all areas of life we search for a level of consistency. This consistency is usually derived from how we explain reality. So we develop models that help us to understand and "categorize" reality into manageable constructs—retaining a strong hold on constancy. In organization we use models as a system of standardizing behavior both in and outside the organization—creating cultural norms.

Our task is to create a model of coaching that builds capability and can be utilized throughout the organization to match capability, whether it is personally or with others in the organization. Creating a coaching model for an organization is no easy task in view of the discrepancies in deciding what coaching actually is in the first place.

As a person considering the implementation, administration and maintenance of a coaching program–personally or organizationally, it becomes imperative to understand the issues involved. Organizationally, it is becoming more difficult to decide on coaching because we are faced with deciding "who" gets coaching. Personally, we can always opt for coaching if we feel that coaching is the best choice for our personal requirements outside of work. However in organization, it is becoming more critical to relate the coaching requirements across the board and NOT as an executive perk in order to establish cultural norms that leverage the organization.

The question becomes, how do we create a coach program for executives who have demonstrated need in terms of development and leading the organization and those rank and file members who have a right to development and success methodologies by virtue of their membership in organization? This may seem like a far-fetched question to ask while developing a coaching model, but it is in fact a question that somehow must be answered at some point during the design process.

Our task then, is to create a model that can be used by and for executives, and at the same time be available to the line manager who seeks improvement and development of subordinates—towards improving performance and building future capability. Our human resources are becoming too capital intensive to merely play a game of substitution. We must recruit, train and develop those resources over time, efficiently and effectively, in order to remain competitive under the umbrella of global competitiveness.

Obviously, this is not a question easily answered. Executives and line managers have differing needs and responsibilities to the organization. In discovering and exploring these issues as well as many other questions that are often asked about coaching programs, we found some interesting research.

> A few years ago, The Gallup Organization decided to initiate a multi-year research project to try and define a great workplace. Our first task was to define what "great" was. We decided that while a great workplace should be one where employees are satisfied with their jobs, it could not be considered "great" if it was not producing positive business outcomes. So we studied workplaces with an eye on four key outcome variables: employee retention, customer satisfaction, productivity and profitability.

> *First, Break All the Rules*, Buckingham and Coffman,

What Gallup discovered was that, contrary to conventional wisdom, there was no such thing as a great company but merely a great workgroup. While actually true or not, their research uncovered "12 critical issues" common to these great workgroups. These issues were later developed into questions that we can ask about these workgroups and are tied directly to the four key outcome variables: employee retention, customer satisfaction, productivity and profitability.

[By the way, these variables match very closely the *Balanced Scorecard* issues that were popularized by Kaplan & Norton. Articles about the Balanced Scorecard are available on Harvard Business School Publishing website.]

[http://www.hbsp.harvard.edu/hbsp/prod_detail.asp?92105]

A Great Workplace by Gallup?

What is germane to our discussion of coaching models is two-fold. On one-hand we want to achieve personal and organizational goals concurrently. Secondly, we need to design the appropriate interventional strategy with a coaching program. It does not do us any good to talk about coaching in terms of second and third order consequences, as is the case with most soft-skill development. We must connect the relevance of coaching to key desired outcomes that are *bottom-line focused*.

[The following is from: What is a Great Workplace?
http://www.gallup.com/poll/managing/managing.asp]

The following list of questions are distilled from the meta-survey conducted by The Gallup Organization as a result of studying and interviewing over 1 million employees. The following 12 areas have been demonstrated by research to relate to Business Unit Productivity, Profitability and Customer Loyalty. The essential components of the 12 areas have been reframed as "audit questions" and are listed by and ©copyrighted by the Gallup organization as the following:

1. I know what is expected of me at work.
2. I have the materials and equipment I need to do my work right.
3. At work, I have the opportunity to do what I do best every day.
4. In the last seven days, I have received recognition or praise for good work.
5. My supervisor or the person I report seems to care about me as a person.
6. There is someone at work who encourages my development.
7. In the last six months, someone at work has talked with me about my progress.
8. At work, my opinions seem to count.
9. The mission/purpose of my company makes me feel my job is important.
10. My associates (fellow employees) are committed to doing quality work.
11. I have a best friend at work.
12. The last year, I have had opportunities at work to learn and grow.

```
[Further discussion of these twelve elements is
located at on the www.gallup.com,
or
http://www.gallup.com/poll/managing/managing.asp]
```

We could dissect those twelve questions and show how each one is related to direct coaching outcomes but I believe it is sufficient to demonstrate by their listing that a *coaching program is central to key personal and organizational outcomes!*

I need to add a disclaimer at this point and remove from your mind the thought that coaching is an answer to everything—it is NOT! Coaching happens to be a key to certain personal and organizational issues but it is not a panacea for every situation. In the questions above we can see the need for a *systems* approach to reaching generative outcomes personally and in organizations. A CoachSystem™ approach is discussed in Part II as a systemized approach producing the best short and long-term business results.

OUTCOMES of Coaching

Gallup identified four key variables that are supported by our reference to the Balanced Scorecard Research by Kaplan and Norton. With those in mind as key business outcomes, we need to synthesize a clear set of outcomes that pertain to both personal and organizational environments. We know that "high function" in people working in organizations whether they are family, community or workscape oriented occurs at a junction between the goals of the person and the goals of the organization. At that juncture we create opportunities for highly cohesive effort and resultant strong intrinsic motivational drive to move the personal and organizational agenda forward jointly.

We are also aware that when personal and organizational goals are in conflict we have a much lower motivation to accomplish what appear to be disparate goals. It goes without saying that in order for us to succeed personally and in organization we need alignment between goals. With that in mind, the following four constructs—as capabilities--were synthesized to depict the desired outcomes of the COACH2 Model.

Desirable Outcomes of a Coaching System

- <u>Well-being</u>: defined individually and organizationally
- <u>Purpose</u>: action taken according to intention
- <u>Competence</u>: the quality of action and the development and mastery of skills
- <u>Awareness</u>: the ability to self-discover, self-correct and self-generate

We might say that if an individual or organization has these four states or capabilities, most of what they want and need is within their reach. It is important to understand that each of us relates to these four *capabilities* **differently** and that is the elegance of the COACH2 model. A theory or model, to be successful, must be adaptable and flexible as well as applicable and predictable in almost any situation or practice.

People will identify differently with each of the four constructs and will be able to induce or mold their own individual performance, change and transformation in alignment with their own ways of making meaning about reality for *them or the organization*. At the same time, they will be able to identify with others on a similar journey and appreciate through awareness that each of us marches to the sound of a different drum. And that is ok.

WELL-BEING

In searching for critical capability, we know that a person or organization seeks one form or another of well-being. Well-being can be articulated by any one of a thousand different adjectives: happiness, success, sustainability, wellness, compassion, money, security, comfort, health, family, richness of experience and so on. What is *key* is that well-being as related by the person being coached (pbc) is at issue, not a predetermined mark established by another entity.

However, with this realization comes the paradox always associated with most any so-called *universal truthes*; and that is when we *agree* to pursue a course of action inside an organization, we automatically become bound or aligned (your choice) with the well-being of the organization. Therefore we may feel or the organization may insist that our own personal well-being—whatever well-being as defined by us means—be subjugated to the good of the many.

In the case of family, it may be child, parents or even a spouse. The construct of well-being always rides on the horns of a dilemma, existing often fully in paradox between person and organizing form. Any coaching program must understand the existence of this dilemma and be prepared to exercise it in full view among others towards the benefit of the pbc as well as the organization.

[Complexity in life often increases with the number of ambiguous forms our life encounters, and the four capabilities as outcomes listed above are always affected by one's clear choice.]

As you might imagine, almost everything we do is done within the context of how it affects us personally and how it affects the organization. When you introduce multiple organizations as most of us are interfaced with daily, e.g. family, friends, work, community, it is easy to see how complex our interrelationships become and how difficult it is to remain apart from the effects of any one of them.

Prior to the industrial age, many of the modern ambiguities were absent: multiple family units (divorce), organizational life in terms of work (people working together in groups to produce outcomes not related to their personal life requirements) and the enormous number of connections afforded by personal mobility, connectivity and leisure.

When we coach, we coach to all of these issues often concurrently. In the past, we attempted to deconstruct reality and deal with each part individually—separating people from work and vice versa—but this was just too inefficient and ineffective. When someone has a performance problem, we bring in a performance specialist. When someone encountered domestic issues, we sent them to EAP (employee assistance programs) for *help*. We fractionalized reality and created separate solutions to each challenge.

Well-being concerns the *whole* person, not just one portion of our reality at work, or at home. Well-being consists of a state that affects how we function. It is a complex, ambiguous interconnected reality that flows through all of our function. To create well-being must be the intentioned outcome of an effective coaching program. A person capable of well-being stands able to perform, change and transform with least effort in higher states of function and in longer periods of flow. This is not to say that we can **prescribe** well-being, for when we attempt to do so, it often fails, and it will be and is the reason why so many *programs* fail.

Well-being is a complex issue and requires intention. As a desired outcome, it should be approached with respect for its power to affect people and organization at work or at play. Yet, because of the overriding complexity, it is often pushed back for *easier*, more concrete objectives that are not as messy or ambiguous. However, the greatest store of desire to perform, change and transform lies with each individual's concept of well-being.

PURPOSE

Many of the same arguments discussed in well-being hold true for each of the four key outcomes of a successful coaching program. Purpose can be as simple or as complex as a project purpose to *put a man on the moon*. Clear as mud, right? Yet simple, easily understood, of course, and a very powerful, compelling purpose that guided a nation to do exactly that as a result of John F. Kennedy's goal for the nation after being elected president.

Yet, how many of us are on purpose?

What is purpose? How does holding a purpose clearly in mind promote well-being or any of the other key outcomes we have discussed? Purpose is <u>essential</u> in focusing our thoughts, beliefs, intention and consequent actions. Purpose is about choice. And about the capability to choose among competing variables and resources to make a decision that will lead us to accomplish what matters most. Tony Schwarz wrote an entire book on *WHAT REALLY MATTERS*, and after more than two years of research and hundreds of pages of dialog the conclusion resulted in a discovery of one's purpose. Purpose is what matters most.

Purpose in organization can guide the collective action of the group to make choices that matter. Well-defined purpose can be the difference between success and failure. Individual purpose, or mission as Stephen Covey wrote in his book *7 Habits for Effective People* is the driving force behind individual and organizational success.

> Creating a Personal Mission Statement™ will be, without question, one of the most powerful and significant things you will ever do to take leadership of

your life. In it you will identify the first, most important roles, relationships, and things in your life—who you want to be, what you want to do, to whom and what you want to give your life, the principles you want to anchor your life to, the legacy you want to leave. All the goals and decisions you will make in the future will be based upon it. It's like deciding first which wall you want to lean your ladder of life against, and then beginning to climb. It will be a compass—a strong source of guidance amid the stormy seas and pressing, pulling currents of your life.

Dr. Stephen R. Covey

[Franklin-Covey's Mission Builder Exercise is drafted from Covey's book and is available for free at http://www.franklincovey.com/customer/missionform.html]

There are many correlations to Covey's mission statement, hence we use the term purpose rather than mission because of the connotation of mission--something which has defined boundaries. In some respects, purpose as well as mission *will* change over your lifetime.

Some of us will struggle with purpose as each new level of cognitive, emotional and physical development will lead to insights into ourselves and into the organizations we associate or align with, yet purpose in organization—or primary aim as W.Edwards Deming proposed—is key to alignment with one's inner and outer forces.

"A system must create something of value, in other
words, results. The intended results, along with
consideration of recipients and cost, mould* the
aim of the system. It is thus management's task
to determine those aims, to manage the whole
organization toward the accomplishment of those
aims."

W. Edwards Deming **The New Economics** (p.51-2)

* "mould" *is* his spelling and not a typo

Maslow's reference to self-actualization concerned purpose
and moving along one's inner-directed course. Purpose means
many different things but the construct of pursuing a course of
action dictated by a predetermined path—individually and
organizationally, is a key capability of an effective coaching
program.

Recognizing that purpose is highly individual, effective
coaching helps create the awareness needed to align
purposeful individual action with purposeful organizational
action. It does not matter whether it is creating high
performance at the customer interface in a fast food restaurant
or sending a man to the moon.

COMPETENCE

Simply, competence means capability. Again, we must be
reminded that capability comes in a number of forms and
flavors, and it is the individual and the organization that create
the value of that form. An important aspect of competence in
terms of how we are referring to it in this discussion is that it
must be competence with purpose. The link between what is
needed and what is done is, therefore, solidified.

If I am a manager and I supervise a team of customer service teleworkers, competence will have meaning to the extent that it relates to the purpose of our workgroup in context with ourselves and our organization. I could have a wonderful competence in painting, however, it may not be related to the competence required in customer service to the extent that my competence in painting would automatically transfer to the customer service requirements. However, in some cases it might. Being able to demonstrate capability in painting may lead directly to my capability to demonstrate capability in customer service-yet our reference to competence combines both in organizational coaching systems.

We must always link competence with requirements otherwise the capability resident in ourselves will not amplify our intrinsic value in our lives or in our organization. This is a critical distinction for someone coaching to remember. Does the pbc demonstrate capability in the requirements or purpose important to them and, are they aware of the gaps? Clarifying these distinctions have high value for the person and the organization as capability is a much-needed resource in organizations and constitutes high value.

[An article on building capability towards organizational competence is located at http://www.leadwise.com/articles/fifthelement.htm. This article references the four elements of the Balanced Scorecard and adds a fifth to organizational competence.]

[An extraordinarily interesting treatise of competence (possibly first used as a linguistic term) is delivered by David S. Taylor, School of Education, University of Leeds at http://www.cbl.leeds.ac.uk/~edu/inted/icu/compete1.htm. It is good background, however, it does not necessarily promote the manner in which competence is used in this model.]

AWARENESS

Awareness is the ability or capability to stand apart from or to perceive an event such as a thought, feeling or action separate from the actual process--my definition. In creating the ability to become aware, we have to ask ourselves in inner dialog or outer dialog what is actually happening versus our awareness of the causes and effects of what is or has occurred. The attempt to define this construct of reality brings about its own ambiguous nature. It is normally referred to as becoming a witness, as opposed to being a part of in terms of the process.

Obviously, we are all aware. Does this mean we have achieved this capability? I wish that were true. In my own discovery of awareness I realize how far that is from the actual need I have to become more aware. More aware of my inborn preferences, my strengths, weaknesses, opportunities and threats, my unconscious nature to behave in accordance with my conditioned reflexes, and to allow myself the freedom of expression I *seem* to be aware of at times—is often fleeting.

Yet this ability for personal awareness often stands in the way of relating to others, approaching needed change and moving to more empowering levels of development through transformation.

Awareness of who we are, how we see ourselves and our own reality, can be as simple as seeing an upset customer--being compassionate and sensing his/her needs--or as complex as knowing we need to understand our relationship to our unconscious motives in order to lead a project team more effectively. Awareness in our personal lives and in our organizations will create the adaptive response to challenges that will occur on a steady basis—often, in real time.

Improved performance, generative change and welcome transformation depend on this capability.

SUMMARY

Each of the factors: well-being, purpose, competence depend upon each other and on the awareness of the interconnected nature of each. The area of high function and flow will always be where these factors are aligned with one another, and between individual and organization. This may seem like a utopian dream, however it is possible in both theory and practice—*creating personal and organizational effectiveness.*

Chapter 4

The COACH2 (C2) Model

In coming to grips with a methodology that can be used to facilitate personal and organizational success, we have identified three *prime* core competencies. Any coaching program must master, at a minimum, these competencies—often using many others—in order to provide the efficacy required for organizational effectiveness.

This is not to say that these are the only competencies, but importantly, the essential building blocks needed by the program to meet key personal and business developmental outcomes. The three competencies are: <u>connection</u>, <u>clarification</u> and <u>commitment</u>.

C2 Core Competencies

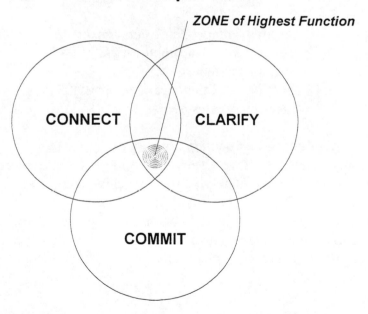

Each one of these competencies deserves in depth treatment but for the purposes of our journey a summary version follows:

CONNECTION

In the C2 Model, we use the active tense "to connect" in order to identify the actions taken by the person coaching (pc).

[We need to be careful and bear in mind through this treatise that much of coaching is done by someone other than a coach. To confuse coaching with coach is going to be detrimental to both the system and the intended outcomes in many cases.]

One thing that must always be at the forefront of our intention with others is to *connect*. Why? Several important things happen as a result of connecting with others in either a coaching relationship or any kind of relationship.

1. Connecting with people fosters **trust**.
2. Connection creates **opportunities.**
3. Connecting facilitates **openings.**
4. Connecting amplifies **"want to, or will."**
5. **Connecting creates ownership**

The by-products of connection are very desirable and necessary outcomes. If we would do nothing else but connect to people, the chances of helping them reaching their most desirable states is enhanced. Part of the problem we have today is that we are in large part unable to feel connected to people in business and organizations—our environments have become rootless and less structured and we lack belonging.

The tremendous advances made in technology have propelled our society both forward and backward in terms of relating to one another. We have, today, many forms of communications that to a large extent *depersonalize* the need for connections. Voicemail, email and paging all are asynchronous methods of communication that rely only slightly on the KSAs of connection—many preferring to do business completely "out of touch."

If the McDonald's Restaurant Clerk does nothing more than engage you with eye contact and a warm smile indicating a willingness to be of service, the entire transaction becomes *easier*. Even if the clerk is incompetent, inexperienced and the system supporting him/her inferior, that slight connection changes your attribution of blame and fault. Because "that clerk" connected with you, you are willing to forgive almost anything and will do whatever you can to make that person's job smoother in light of that connection—if only just out of empathy.

When we are connected, there is something in our psyche that trips a switch. Personally, I feel it has to do with attribution and the method we assign to cause and effect. If we are connected, we look for somewhere or someone else to assign the cause and effect to—so as to not damage the connection.

If we are connected, the person we are connected with becomes a part of our own psychic protection and we attribute failure, incompetence and incongruence to an *outside* force. In fact, in many cases we hold the concept of *blameless error*—a truly exciting concept in a management world replete with blame finders!

When someone is using coaching KSAs in either a *coaching moment, conversation* or coaching interaction, they need to remember to fully connect as much as the situation allows with the *other person. This connection* increases dramatically the chances of creating desirable coaching outcomes. You do not need to be a coach to use this model, however as a person coaching or someone setting up a coach approach, you should not minimize this step.

Talking about connecting is pretty straightforward and in this short discussion, I think you will agree me in the merits of using this step. However, doing it is something altogether more difficult. The first aspect of connecting that is most challenging is the realization that *connecting* means different things to different people. We will revisit this issue in a later chapter when we discuss the chapter on differences. This will provide you with some insights on individual differences from which to probe more fully the manners of connecting and building rapport with someone.

The second major issue concerning connecting is time. How much time do you really have to set up the relationship and reach *right action?* Obviously, there is a difference between setting up a coaching relationship with many sessions versus touring the factory floor or customer interface and having an opening to coach. In the latter, your time to connect is very narrow, yet *still* as important as the former to reach positive outcomes. A connection can start with eye contact, a firm handshake, a respectful bow or an embrace. Yet, connection is what we most lack and need in order to reach the openings, opportunities and levels of trust and motivation to learn, grow and develop as people in organizations.

CLARIFICATION

At the center of the C2 Model and between connection and commitment is <u>clarification</u>. Without clarity around meaning-making, developmental level, structure of interpretation, condition of mind, situational demands and personal needs, performance change and transformation are sub-optimized.

In a coaching relationship, unlike any other, we find ourselves uncovering, exploring, discovering, questioning, surfacing and removing barriers to right action. This is done through a process of clarification. One listening technique goes like this: *receive, reflect and re-state*. This simple process is indicative of the process of clarification. It usually involves a highly developed degree of skill on behalf of the person coaching to refrain (before stepping into the gap to be clarify the opening), another "r" I would like to add to the above formula.

Refrain means withholding your own needs, agenda, judgment and content before fully understanding what is best for the person being coached (pbc) in terms of developmental processes. Many people will come to coaching being open to help with performance of some kind, or wanting to change certain aspects of their life and find themselves being transformed as a result. This, of course, is highly desirable for both the person coaching (pc) and the pbc.

Do you recall Chapter 1 where we discussed adult development? You remember, the stuff like what we know we know, what we know we don't know and what we don't know that we don't know? Clarification is where an *appreciative dialogue* takes place to help the person coaching and the pbc discover some developmental issues.

The person coaching as well as the person being coached is interested in exploring several issues either by choice or by need (perhaps unconscious in the pbc at this time). Maybe the reason the pbc came to the opening for coaching was precisely that they could not see how to get from where they are to where they want to be. It is possible that through the clarification process, the person coaching (pc) can be the *catalyst* for this quantum leap in performance, change or transformation

Research by Argyris and others has shown that we carry a theory in our heads and often practice incongruently to that theory. This discrepancy is *unknown* to us—we don't know we don't know. Effective coaching helps us uncover this *espoused theory* and its assumptions, and compare it with our *theory in use.* Often, this is why we get stuck and cannot seem to crawl out of the rut we have found ourselves in…it was working, but now it's not, so what happened?

As the environment changes, we must modify our espoused theory to be more congruent with the needs in the environment. Continuous changes in complex and ambiguous business systems demand flexibility. How does this demand for adaptation fit with our own personal need for constancy? Really, not very well.

Most of us change because we have to not because we want to—so we are constantly lagging behind change in the environment, constantly feeling more ambiguous about our own assumptions and those of others. Coaching helps to clarify and surface these discrepancies and move out from under the rock we find ourselves trapped under.

I should mention a few aspects of looking at clarification in terms that do not become *interrogation.* There are many ways to clarify the issues between the pc and the pbc. Depending on the *connection* and the differences between pc/pbc, clarification as inquiry can be seen as an invasion or interrogation. It is important for the pc to identify and respect the differences between pc/pbc in order for clarification to proceed through openings and NOT through gaps.

Later on, when we demonstrate a critical sub-process of the COACH2 Model, we will understand the difference between *opening* and *gap*. In my view, **this is the single most important transformational concept** contained in this model. The difference between an opening and a gap is that an opening is *known by the pc* as "what they don't know" and know they want and are willing to be objective about getting it. On the other hand, someone, externally, perceives a *gap* about the pbc. The pbc is unaware of the difference between what is expected and what is being delivered by the pbc.

This is the **MOST** important difference to a pc. If you coach in the gap, you will meet more resistance and the coaching interaction for both pc and pbc will be filled with effort and often failure. Coaching occurs in the opening and not in the gap. *Management occurs in gaps!*

COMMITMENT

Without commitment, coaching is anemic.

Commitment comes from a number of convergent factors. Mostly, as a result of integration in the pbc of motivation, ability and the will to do the right thing. This third leg of the C2 stool is imperative in order for the foundation of performance, change and transformation to occur as benefit to the personal and organizational systems involved.

When the pc considers the desired outcomes of well-being, purpose, competence and awareness—commitment is then an essential component of the model. Most people can " talk" the talk, however, walking the walk is critical to meeting key personal and business outcomes.

How does the pc create commitment?

Through the integration of the connecting and clarifying processes. Commitment comes from holding a *personally relevant* position. In terms of the organization, we see we have organizational goals as well. In order to gain commitment, we need to integrate the personal and organizational goals.

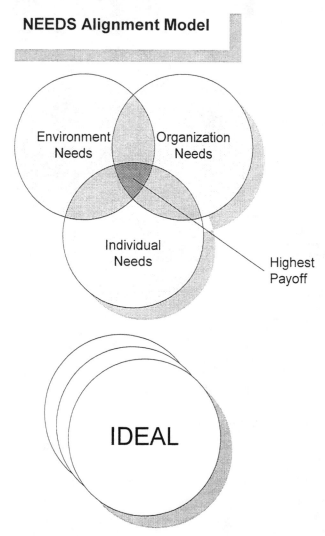

NEEDS Alignment Model

Environment Needs

Organization Needs

Individual Needs

Highest Payoff

IDEAL

The diagram provides a visual view of the competing factors for commitment. In the drawing labeled as <u>ideal</u> we see how commitment is created through the alignment of individual, environmental and organizational needs. The process of commitment is a <u>derived</u> process—from connection and clarification—but it must also be confirmed through appropriate strategies.

When right action fails to occur, commitment to action may be the limiting factor. However, for right action to occur, commitment must be integrated with personal, organizational and environmental demands. This sounds quite simple and straightforward but in practice, it is extraordinarily difficult to accomplish.

Because of the competing and conflicting demands and *value sets* between the big three, it is often fairly easy to gain commitment in one area or another, however, a challenge results when right action must be fully representative of all constituent factors. In fact, what we actually create a hologram where fractally, all of the parts contain a representation of the whole. It becomes impossible to fracture reality and separate personal, organizational and environmental needs!

Personal commitment is usually fairly easy to understand and acquire, however, when people are mismatched with job opportunities, we find the *tension* between personal and organizational goals beyond the capacity of the individual to overcome. Therefore, we virtually create a can of worms when we fail to understand the integration of all three paradigms. In an organizational sense, the environment plays a huge role in regards to marketspace. If the organization fails to gain sufficient commitment to environmental demands, then the organization itself will be obsolete in terms of providing a sufficient *value framework* for individuals.

Revisiting our definition of organization as a framework for the exchange of value, the organization must provide sufficient leverage and efficiency to remain as a viable means of attracting value in terms of the environment and effective individuals. These critical reinforcing loops are what differentiates right action in terms of integrated wholeness. Without a commitment to right action that stimulates and develops ALL three areas—personal—organizational—environmental demands, all parts of the whole suffer and will become obsolete in a short time.

A fairly broad but excellent example of this outcome is the fact that only one company listed in the Fortune 10 at the beginning of the century, is still on the list. GE is representative of a successful commitment and integration of the constituent parts. By contrast, the companies missing are excellent examples of a failure to integrate those parts. Commitment is a simple outcome of integration through the pc/pbc interaction at the basal level in an organization. Yet, this interaction MUST represent and produce an integrated solution to right action based on a holistic approach.

Here is an interesting quote from Harvard Management Update, September 1999 article on *How to keep your 50-Somethings.*

> *This is the age of human capital—and of tight labor markets. Companies have finally realized that competitive advantage resides mostly in people, and finding and keeping good managers and employees is a strategic necessity. But how do you attract and retain the best and brightest when the competition for people is so brutal?*

...[on fifty-somethings] while they're on the job, surveys show, baby boomers [almost anyone?] want autonomy, a sense of meaning, and a chance to learn new things. That, say several experts, means redesigning the way tasks get done. Let people work on their own. Teach the basics of business; help people understand how their job contributes to company performance. Give them a chance to take on new challenges and pick up new skills—but don't assume everyone will get up to speed without help.

"You have to make a conscious investment in training for a more mature workforce," says Mark Francis, a vice president at Age Wave. "particularly in the technology area." But it is money well spent.

Clearly what comes out of most research today is to make investments in people pay off in the long run. Coaching is a longitudinal, *helping, appreciative* intervention that can integrate leadership, management, training and results to a personal and organizational level. In the next chapter we discuss the process where interaction can produce personal and organizational awareness, competence, purpose and well-being.

Chapter 5

"No one has to change but everyone has to have the conversation—change will come out of that."

David Whyte

The Coaching Interaction Model (CIM)

One of the main reasons that the CIM was developed was to take coaching to the lowest common denominator of business—the customer interface, or *zero time* as some call the space where the business and customers interact. This means that performance, change and transformation and their outcomes, well-being, purpose, competence and awareness need to occur at the prime organizational levels—where work is done at the customer interface.

It seems there is a great movement to coach at the Executive Level because that is where the money and power reside, but in my view, the organization of the future will create a CoachSystem™ that permeats the organization from top to bottom! The CIM is a model that consists of an interface between conversation and action--***interaction***, between theory and process linking the goals of the individual with the goals of the organization at time zero.

> *When people at every level in the organization learn—fundamentally—that they can use coaching skills to increase well-being, work on purpose—competently—becoming increasingly aware of themselves and others in view of environmental demands, then the organization truly becomes capable.*

In my view, this latent ability residing in every organization from the smallest to the largest is the key to unleashing the magnificence of people. We, as leaders, must understand that coaching is not just for executives but a skill-set for improving and linking the organization's capability at every level in the organization.

Coaching cannot be so complex that individuals at line levels in the organization cannot begin to use it. It must be straightforward enough that people can see *into* it and use it easily—if not completely. We all are in different places regarding our mastery of coaching KSAs. We all started somewhere. A Chinese philosopher once said that *a journey of a thousand miles begins with but a single step*. In that same vein, we have to begin to integrate coaching KSAs into the organization at the work levels, in order to create the leverage that the individual and the organization--as a fundamental provider of value--deserve.

In this model, the issues surround Five *Actionable* Factors:

- Identify openings
- Generate possibilities
- Develop plans
- Preview outcomes
- Commit to ACT

The CIM is designed to create a *fluid structure* for the interaction between the pc (person coaching) and pbc (person being coached). This structure allows the interaction to *find* a focus and commitment to action through the process.

Coaching Interaction Model (CIM)

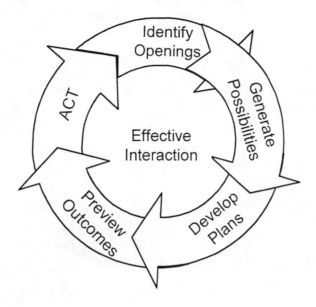

At any point in the structure, the process steps can be combined or skipped depending on the appropriateness of doing so and the framework of the interaction. However, strong commitment is achieved through a clear understanding and development of the action steps leading to desired outcomes. In its most succinct form, this structure provides a guide to author beginnings and endings that achieve desirable business results.

This process is vital to move from abstractions such as perceived openings into clearly labeled steps of action that are measurable in terms of *what is expected and what is to be delivered.* This process launches the coaching interaction into what can be a coaching relationship--longitudinal over time, but provides the necessary accountability for the action steps to be taken at each step in the process.

When we examine the most abstract development in the pbc, it still requires some measure of understanding and commitment to action, whether that action is merely *reflection* or a specific project plan. These five factors are critical to effective coaching.

- Identify openings -- into the consistency or coherence of theories of action

- Generate possibilities -- at this point we know that we have options and choices

- Develop plans -- formulate a plan of *right action* that is integrated as a whole

- Previewing outcomes or scenarios -- asking the question, what if?

- Commitment to take defined actionable steps to learn, grow, develop and perform

Conversation or Interaction?

Conversation: Informally talking together

Interaction: Mutually influence

There was a quote by Albert Bandura in a piece about how we learn and how TV Violence affects learning in young people [http://www.afirstlook.com/docs/Bandura.html] where "Stanford psychologist Albert Bandura agrees that conversation is not an effective way of altering human behavior." In the treatise involving how we learn, several interesting factors come to light regarding how we learn.

The comment made by Bandura, even when taken from context, suggests that conversation is NOT enough in coaching. I realize that it is probably *splitting hairs* but it helps us to understand that just talking with people does not qualify the conversation as coaching. I am reminded of a story told by the poet-philosopher-consultant-speaker David Whyte that brings to light some interesting aspects of conversation.

In the story, Whyte speaks of living in the Pacific Northwest and being more of a mountaineer and less of a kayaker, and one day being invited to a kayak trip. Upon arriving on the scene of embarkment, he noticed in contrast to his own very well-organized and light backpack, that the others had brought along dutch ovens, ice chests and so forth. It dawned on him at that point that HE was not going to carry the weight but that the *water* was going to carry the weight of him and his portage. The metaphor is a great one for us in coaching as the *medium--conversation* carries the weight of the performance, change and transformation.

His quote "no one has to change but everyone has to have the conversation" depicts the relationship between allowing change to emerge from conversation. The *weight of performance, change and transformation* is carried by the medium—the conversation that creates the interaction.

Here is the difference between a conversation and an interaction—perhaps the difference between managing and coaching?

...*"in a real conversation, you don't actually know where you are going to arrive!"* David Whyte

Again, it may seem like splitting hairs, but in coaching we may start with conversation but we often must embrace the *interaction*. This subtle distinction may help us understand the model and coaching even more. While we need to understand that the conversation during the interaction—mutual influence, not unlike a particle in a quantum field--become one and become one with the other. In this dance, coaching occurs.

Coaching is MORE than conversation; coaching is interaction. Effective coaching concerns itself with the subtle, yet distinctive openings that are discovered and explored during the interaction. Through the dance of interaction, the pc and pbc try not to step on each other's toes (make-wrongs), are respectful of the differences in interpretation of the *music* and seek harmony in movement—adjusting pace, force, distance, dependence and need according to the subtleties and variations in the dance.

The needs of the pbc emerge out of the subtle cues in the interaction that are discerned by the pc. Influence is mutual. Mastery in coaching comes from interaction not conversation. Conversation becomes the medium, the weight of change is carried through conversation, but interaction—the dance—is where effective coaching occurs. *Real conversation* has no defined point of arrival. A coaching interaction is directed by the pbc and guided by the pc—it has a definite point of arrival—a destiny of sorts that is co-created by the mutual influence—the dance of interaction. Anyone can have a conversation but effective coaching occurs in an interaction.

I think of an interesting set of comparisons:

- Managing has a focus; Coaching occurs through openings

- Managers begin with the end of mind; Coaching has the means in mind
- Managing is concerned with product; Coaching is concerned with people
- Managing has objectives; Coaching has interactions

In all of the cases, the nuances between management and coaching are clear. The agenda *shifts* from pc as a manager to you as a person being coached. We are both concerned with outcome, yet what outcomes, first order, second order, third order, or all combined? Management is focused usually on performance—coaching is focused on development. If we go into the interaction thinking the way we always have, we will get what we have always gotten.

The Organizational Coaching Dilemma

The Coaching Interaction Model is designed to be a dance. Yes, it has a predetermined step, but if the music changes…so can the dance. We, as coaches, listen for the music within the pbc. We seek to orchestrate and guide the medium in such ways that development emerges. When we hear the sound of music in the pbc, we can draw upon our experience and our view of reality to help guide the dance. There must always be some kind of action as a result of effective coaching. As we keep in mind the possible ways we can mutually influence committed action to be taken through the dance, we are guided by the CIM model.

We seek openings through interaction, we evoke possibilities and plans, and we are careful to test the assumptions, the inferences made by the pbc before action is taken out of commitment. Through coaching we *invite the soul and language of the soul* into the interaction—we are not just concerned with doing, but with being.

[A Coaching Manifesto?]

...it is incumbent on each of us, to start telling our story in such a way that you can grant magnificence back to your work and back to what you do...if you can't grant magnificence to your work, you grant magnificence to yourself and have the courage to step out of it into something that is really commensurate to your gifts and is a place where you can really feel like you come alive again at the frontier of your destiny...

> *David Whyte speaking to coaches in 1999*

In this moment spoken about by Whyte, what comes clear to me as a coach is that not all organizations *really want personal magnificence.* The lip service that separates the organizational needs from the personal needs prevents *this very magnificence* from happening. In order for coaching to occur we must *invite the soul* into the interaction—the whole person, not just some facet of performance or organizational change!

Organizations are torn between keeping their best and brightest—the investment that those actions represent—and magnificence. In Whyte's admonition to us all, what is being said is the same thing that Robert Frost related in his poem of *Two Tramps in Mud Time*

[http://redfrog.norconnect.no/~poems/poems/02139.html]

> **But yield who will to their separation,**
> **My object in living is to unite**
> **My avocation and my vocation**
> **As my two eyes make one in sight**
> **Only where love and need are one,**
> **And the work is play for mortal stakes,**
> **Is the deed ever really done**
> **For Heaven and the future's sakes.**

The dilemma is expressed in clear terms, separating our avocation from our vocation. In coaching, the whole person is coached. We are NOT coaching just to *protect our investment in human resources*! We must give full rein to the interaction and allow it come in view of the whole person, and what we will find there…rides on the horns of a dilemma. People are caught between avocation and vocation. Especially the young, unclear about who they are and the frontier that lies ahead of them. Mediocrity, dissatisfaction, lack of adaptability, vitality, passion and the willingness to go the extra mile lie in the gap between avocation and vocation. If people are just putting in their time, they are not going to proactively respond to the environmental and competitive changes in the workscape.

What lies ahead for the organizational coach is discovery. A discovery of who people are, what they need and where their magnificence lies. As conversation turns to interaction, and credibility to trust, we will find ourselves at the frontier of their conversation. Will the organizational coach interact or merely try to close the deal through another organizational manipulative device? Will corporate coaching become another lever to pull or will the effective interaction consider the whole person?

A WARNING

The interaction—the dance of change—will create a conduit to magnificence without constraint. However, what organization will *invite the soul* into the dance? What organization will open the door to a person's story and allow that story to guide that person to magnificence—IF? IF the chances of losing that person to their own story are possible?

There is a saying out here on the Oregon Trail, "keep them dumb and keep them on the farm." The dilemma of allowing someone—a person coaching in an interaction—to invite the soul into the dance is not only provocative as I write this in 1999, but almost far-fetched in some cases.

For in those boardrooms lies the spirit of bureaucracy and determination. Determination to be the best, to win—at all costs—to *manage the bottom line!* We find ourselves facing the gap between margin and mission, between product and people, between personal and organizational, between performance and development, between well-being of the organization and well-being of the person.

What's best for the organization and what's best for the person.

If you are not prepared to let the chips fall where they may, bringing coaches—real coaches—into your organization may deter your attempt to KEEP your best and brightest, especially if they are mismatched in terms of their story and their jobs!

When you coach the whole person, when you create an interaction that invites someone to tell their story, to *come to their magnificence,* you are taking a chance that your system has flaws in terms of creating strong links between avocation and vocation. Not everyone wants to love their work, or do they?

This could be a rationalization as to why so many people are dissatisfied with their employment or merely satisfied and not delighted? Research has indicated that as many as 75% of satisfied customers will change brands for more value. Does this same principle hold true for people at work and in jobs that they are merely satisfied with…? Perhaps so?

So much of coaching that is currently being labeled as coaching is nothing more than <u>participative</u> <u>management by objectives</u>. The whole person is not sitting across from you as the pbc. It is the person doing the job that must achieve the organizational outcomes you have designed. We have not invited anything other than the task-master to the table. There is no story, no magnificence, only compliance.

Summary

A COACH2 coaching interaction of the kind we are talking about invites the whole person to the table. From management by objectives, we move to leadership and vision of mutually satisfying outcomes—to magnificence. But there are consequences, both good and bad. The freedom that people begin to feel, to exercise free and informed choice, to advocate their position without feeling they have to save face, and to feel commitment out of internal right action brings about magnificence…and change. Often, the change is individual and people become more fluid in terms of where they want to work and that flow often can be out of an organization that is *stuck* in the Model I mindset whose governing variables are:

- Design, manage, and plan unilaterally.
- Own and control the task.
- Unilaterally protect self and others.
- Evaluate others in ways that do not encourage testing the validity of the evaluation.

These factors are often present in the organization and through the coaching interaction we overlay the cultural norms onto the interaction. If the interaction is involved in double loop learning and the organizational norms do not permit double loop action strategies, then we are setting up the pbc with two differing sets of value systems.

In Part II we discuss how to transition people through interaction, and how you must begin to transition the organizational culture in order to create the fertile ground for the new seeds of double loop learning—Model II governing variables (Argyris)—to take root and grow.

Like *any other organizational interventions*, coaching in itself will begin to change the organization, however, whether or not people in the organization "unfreeze" at the same time the organization is frozen, it can be a difficult cold experience with detrimental effects on the coaching interaction. They can deteriorate to gripe sessions where what goes on in the culture is discussed and cussed without changes occurring in the organizational norms held stoic by the powers at be.

The coaching interaction creates a microcosm of change. These microcosms must be ***fully supported and integrated*** in order for the performance, change and transformation to occur effortlessly. This brings us to organizational design, structure and development and how do we integrate those needed elements into the coaching system. These issues are reviewed in Part II.

Chapter 6

"But do your thing and I shall know you."

Emerson

Differences

A Scorpion and a Frog.

It is told that there once lived a scorpion that wanted to cross a pond, but being a scorpion, he couldn't swim. So he scuttled up to a frog and asked: "Please, Mr. Frog, can you carry me across the pond on your back?"

"I would," replied the frog, "But, under the circumstances, I must refuse. You might sting me as I swim across." "But, why would I do that?" asked the scorpion, "It is not in my interest to sting you, because you will die and then I will drown."

Although the frog knew how lethal scorpions were, the logic proved quite persuasive. Perhaps, felt the frog, in this one instance the scorpion would keep his tail in check. And so the frog agreed. The scorpion climbed onto his back, and together they set off across the pond. Just as they reached the middle of the pond, the scorpion twitched his tail and stung the frog.

Mortally wounded, the frog cried out: "Why did you sting me? It is not in your interest to sting me, because now I will die and you will drown." "I know," replied the scorpion, as he sank into the pond. "But I am a scorpion. I have to sting you. It's in my nature."

[http://www.gallup.com/poll/managing/Insight.asp for reference]

Our Nature--Our Nurture

Both are critical to the way we make meaning in any situation. This chapter is perhaps my favorite. I will try to remember that you may not be as enthused as I am, and will try to remain lucid and to the point as I speak from my soapbox.

I have to tell you that I am still very much confused about differences. It seems that I have a tendency or preference to see things from my own point of view, often to my own detriment. A close friend of mine once asked during a conversation, why is it sometimes you seem more accepting than others? I think that question centers the dialog around differences for me.

Although once removed, the question reminds me that when I am conscious or aware, I can move out of the unconscious scripts that have been written into my mind and heart from nature and nurture—my conditioning. Yet, consciousness and awareness--for me! —are not always such an easy task. It often takes a blow of sorts to remind me to be aware of my thoughts and behaviors such that I might live…rather than be the result of my conditioning.

I am not going to go into a discourse about personality typology, naming my favorite *hammer*, as you might recall Maslow making reference to, in his quote that *"he who is good with a hammer thinks everything is a nail!"*

What I am determined to accomplish is to demonstrate how differences in people in specific areas can be observed and understood—utilized by the person coaching (pc) and person being coached (pbc) to become more purposeful, competent and aware of meaning-making—towards well-being without resorting to labeling.

People are different, but how?

Depending on the flavor of your favorite preference, value, trait, or *way of working*--a couple of hundred or so assessments can fix you right up. Being an assessor myself I can say without question that assessments are the most misused and abused instruments you have at your disposal. Need I refer you back to Maslow?

What each of us tries to accomplish through assessments is to categorize and then (innocently?) predict behavior based on...something. Now, there is a real good reason for this and while there are not a lot of credible (legal) ways to get away with using assessments to predict behavior, we all knowingly and unknowingly contribute to the problem. We crave simple answers to complex and abstract problems!

In attempting to move beyond stereotyping people, although it may be impossible, the next chapter attempts to discuss basic differences in people without placing a stereotypical label on someone as a result. I'm not against assessments, I am against the improper administration, use and simplistic labeling that occurs as a result. Some people argue that we have to start somewhere. Yet, why not talk about differences in terms of the effect they have on our ability to make meaning rather than trying to consistently predict one's future behavior?

Remember Emerson's quote?

> *"But do your thing and I shall know you."*

A recently developing field in forensic psychology helps create personality profiles to identify and predict behavior. The Subject-Object Assessment Interview developed by Kegan, et al creates an interview around discovering levels of consciousness and development. We are literally at the frontier of this conversation in terms of the types of tools becoming more available to everyone in our attempt to understand human and organizational complexity.

As leaders and managers (even coaches), prediction is something that provides a rationale for reducing complexity and uncertainty in our organizations and in our lives.

However, *simplicity reigns* and the minute someone gives us a 4-quadrant matrix to understand and reduce this ambiguity that we are all swimming in--we apply it to everything. I have done exactly that myself and even with more sophisticated tools, I find my mind categorizing, predicting and *judging* rather than connecting and clarifying—withholding judgment and prediction.

In coaching, we talk of coming to the interaction with a *beginner's mind*, full of curiosity, compassion and without prejudice. And yet, the first thing a lot of people coaching want to do is run an assessment. I think this may be limiting in some ways. It distorts reality from the start and creates prejudices in that beginner's mindset we strive to reach as people coaching.

Therefore, if we are cramped for time and resources (a leadership problem), what do we do? We often resort to the assembly line full of assessment tools and off we go to *design* the coach approach. Sounds like consulting or counseling to me, what about you?

The most difficult dilemma for leaders and managers in organizational systems is cost versus benefit.

There will be times when *satisficing* will create the need for the use of assessments as a short-cut to creating openings through which to coach. However, with everything being equal, the observation and discernment of openings through the coaching interaction is a preferred approach. It does require more experience and skill in the person coaching—a difficult issue for organizations under the gun and strapped for resources—and it limits the number of preconceptions delivered through assessment.

Over the past years I have truly struggled with personality typology. It seems they are all right…and all wrong —at times. I think we seek the unifying theory (for predictive reasons) and in that vein psychology today has come to in part, agreement on the *big five*.

For your information, they are: extroversion, openness, agreeableness, conscientiousness, and neurotism, with neurotism often replaced with <u>negative emotionality</u>—less pejorative for an *appreciative approach (intentional scoff<grin>) in the business community.*

I think it might be important for us to remember these centering traits throughout our discussion in order to ground us as we consider theory and practice. I want to say that I am not an expert. As I said before, my knowledge is cursory and not deep and wise, yet, like you, *"have to dance with the girl who brung me"—a former Texas University Coach Daryl Royal Euphemism* (gig 'em aggies!).

The Dance Begins

With that said, come and take a journey with me into the land of differences. More and more, what makes sense to me is that differences are more important than almost anything else in coaching. The way each individual makes meaning in and through a life of continuous development, is as unique as one's fingerprint, yet we all seem to have some *basic things in common.*

I will list some of them in the chapter that follows, and I am sure you can add others. The point is that we need to look at people in terms of how they are different and not what their type or trait makeup is. Clearly, people can be grouped by type and trait, and it is often meaningful to do so. However what is important for the person coaching (pc) is to understand what makes people different and how the "meaning" they make is unique to them—either blocking them or motivating them to right action. This one single factor makes coaching unique as long as we practice the coaching KSAs with mastery.

We are an amalgam or hologram of traits and preferences. Each of us possesses all of them, some in higher concentration and some with greater clarity in preference. Yet, each of us has all of them. The problem with "typing" is that people take type literally and fail to understand that we respond to circumstances as a whole person, not as some type or trait. This is the central mistake I see made by people who use type and trait psychology in coaching practice.

It is too easy to label and pigeon hole people because in our attempt to understand, we *fracture* reality. In every circumstance, we are a fractal of the complete hologram of our experience, type and traits. In every situation we respond to, we respond with our whole self.

Therefore, while we may prefer one action in one circumstance, we have the ability to bring to bear *other* preferences and traits when confronted with a different set of circumstances—especially in regards to role behavior--so much for <u>predictive ability</u>. We are, as Am de Lange--a very interesting teacher in South Africa--states, an *irreversible self-organizing system*.

If we have previously labeled someone—even unconsciously--
we have expectations about their behavior in ALL
circumstances (simplicity reigns!). This inference creates a
pre-judgment and a prejudice that *traps* the unsuspecting pc
into narrowing the aperture of their perspective, losing their
beginner's mind. This preconceived notion or inference
lessens the opportunity for beginner's mind to reveal the
essential truth of the person being coached.

When we succumb to the easy way and do not develop astute
interviewing and observation abilities, we too will then miss
the nuances present in the interaction and as a result, mis-time
or mis-direct our deliveries. If we come to the interaction with
prejudice we will be less than effective in helping the pbc
discover and explore those undiscovered or hidden parts of
himself/herself.

Awareness is an essential key to growth and development.
Growth and development is a key to uncovering and surfacing
our high potentials towards achieving personal and business
results of high value!.

It all filters back to mankind's conscious and unconscious
search for meaning—individual as well as collective. Victor
Frankl is reported to have said, "the problem with man's
search for happiness is man's search for happiness." Along
the way we seek well-being, whether that comes through free
expression of ideas, equality, security or having loving friends.
We are different in many ways. To discover and explore those
differences often leads to development over a lifetime towards
that potential we all carry inside of our souls—*a dance with an*
invisible partner.

And it is not just about *achievement*. David McClelland, a
Harvard Scientist spent years studying motivation and

articulated 3 additional major motive systems: *affiliation, power* and *avoidance*.

The interesting thing is that we all have some of each within us. In terms of the five traits spoken about earlier, we all have some of each within us. We all have the conscious ability to rise above our conditioning and our nature. Yet for the person coaching, where *effort-is-less* we find a match between our natural predispositions and environmental demands. We know that it is not always possible to do what we love— although I dare ask, **why not**?

Most of us are still discovering who we are and what we love to do because we have faced a life of *have-tos*—not always by choice, but in the end—mostly by choice.

In life we are many things and as we grow and experience our movements we dance with an invisible partner. We only feel and sense this partner but it often takes a whole life to fully realize their influence on our dance. It took me almost 30 years to fully grasp this concept and I am now offering that experience to you.

However, it will not be easy to discover this partner as it will take time to explore the nuances of the dance and the music, and many times you will be struck by the dance and not by the partner, but the partner remains and the music often changes.

*In this time and space, we have a unique opportunity to discover and surface that partner and to dance the dance of light and awareness with that partner. It is obvious we hold the key to every ability, save one, **to know ourselves**...let us find the key.*

Yet, what makes us so different?

Have you ever played the communication game? It is a game where one person tells another person a message and that person repeats it out of sound range to another and so on. With as few as three or four iterations, the message becomes so distorted that it hardly has any of the characteristics of the original message. Try it sometime with your workgroup, you will not be disappointed, but you will be enlightened!

Before we look at the basic differences among people, I want to draw your attention to <u>interpersonal communication</u>. Now, this may seem pretty simple to some of you, but if it is so simple why do we keep messing it up?

The following model was derived from a basic understanding that what we intend is often not related to the effect perceived by others. Take a look at this visual diagram.

A Person's Intention is usually private	becomes	A Person's Action	becomes	A perceived effect with meaning made by B
A's Intention		A's Action		Effect on B
A's Private Intention	A encodes	Observable by anyone	B decodes	B's Private Effect
Must be inferred by B				Must be inferred by A

Now, if A, and B are very different, you might imagine the effects on the inferences and consequences. Our system of 'meaning-making' is so critical to understanding and being understood. In one of Stephen Covey's 7 Habits, he states, *"seek to understand and then be understood."*

I think this has merit but also a hidden flaw. *We cannot take being understood for granted* just because we understand. As a pc, you will want to become aware of the differences between you and the pbc in order to fashion your communication in recognition of those differences and likely pitfalls.

There are many treatises on interpersonal communication in the literature and you will want to pursue your own learning and development beyond this orientation.

While it is not my role to recommend, if I did so, I would make required reading of *THAT'S NOT WHAT I MEANT!* By Deborah Tannen, Ph.D., Ballantine Books, 1986. Here is a short quote on *indirectness:*

"People prefer not to say exactly what they mean in so many words because they're not concerned only with the ideas they're expressing; they're also—even more—concerned with the effect their words will have on those they're talking to.

They want to make sure to maintain camaraderie, to avoid imposing, and to give (at least appear to give) the other person some choice in the matter being discussed. And different people have different ways of honoring these potentially conflicting goals."

Meaning-Making

How and what are you paying attention to? What matters and where is the focus of your intention—yourself, others? Who do you blame? How do you attribute the causes and effects in your life? What is your espoused theory? What is your theory in use?

These are only a few of the *assumptions* we use to create meaning from the phenomena occurring in our lives. In the coaching interaction, the pc and the pbc have occasion to explore these and other issues. As a result of this journey of exploration, discrepancy and incongruence can be questioned, tested and explained.

In the following chapter, we look at some of the opposing elements in behavioral continuums to gain clues into how we behave, think and assign meaning to the world and events around us; our world view so to speak. How do we arrive at our conclusions and what are the inferences we make along the way? How does all of this create a structure through which we interpret the phenomena in our personal and organizational lives?

A Baseball View

…three baseball umpires, who were debating when a ball, thrown by a pitcher, was in or out.

The first said: "I calls them as I sees them"

The second said: "I calls them as they are"

And the third added: "**they ain't nothing 'til I calls them**".

They ain't nothing 'til we calls them!

Be careful with your labels, they will often lead you astray in those circumstances that are most critical. Behavior in people is a phenomenon related to the environmental cues, the behavior itself and the person's most pressing need. They are often inconsistent and confusing.

Approach the coaching interaction with a beginner's mind, leave your ego and your assessments at the door, and discover fully the person being coached in all of their wit, charm and glory.

Chapter 7

I came to the conclusion that it is as difficult to get meaning out of an [assessment] as it is to get music out of a violin.

The violin is not about getting all the music into the four strings, but to get all the music out of those four strings. A violin is not an end but a source of music.

A master of violin learns to master his personality through mastering the violin. It is the opposite of a quick fix. Today you can buy for nearly anything "Courses in 30 Days."

Not so for a violin. Like "this personality stuff" it requires lifelong learning to grow in mastership. This is why Senge chose the word "discipline". I cannot put all the knowledge into my brain. My brain is not the end of knowledge but a source.

"Winfried Dressler" winfried.dressler@voith.de

What's the difference?

I have purposely avoided references to personality testing, typing, profiling and assessments without prejudice. What I am going to attempt to do is to briefly compare some dichotomies in terms of differences in order to illustrate summarily how our place on these paradoxical continuums creates confusion, misinterpretation and mistaken conclusions all the while climbing the ladder of inference given to us by Argyris.

Differences occur in many flavors. One of the best ways to use differences towards value in a coaching interaction is to understand how differences enable and disable performance, change and transformation. There is no scientific *proof* of my assumptions so I suggest you test them before you employ them. My point is to encourage you to explore the elements in the continuums and the paradoxes with the pbc during interaction and to generate a mutual understanding of differences, ways of being and meaning-making.

In my opinion, here is the real learning in studying differences: <u>attribution</u>. Can we attribute the interpretation, meaning-making and behavior a person displays to something other than his/her personal effect?

In other words, can we attribute the way someone is different towards a reason other than a personal dispensation or motivation to harm us, discredit us, show us up or become a threat to us? If we can mutually achieve this state where *attribution* is impersonal, then we can begin an open dialogue, free from defensive patterns that seek to shut down the interaction and growth available.

These defensive patterns become barriers to surfacing our assumptions and beliefs about our self and others that may block right action. Similarly, these personal and organizational patterns also lead to sub-optimal states of well-being, diluted focus on purpose, lower levels of competence and mastery as well as diminished awareness.

As we move through the following continuums, let us keep in mind how these theories of action foster defensive patterns from these differences. Visually, each continuum will have one constituent on one end and the other constituent part on the other. I do not think these are direct opposites in all cases, but in my view, they create a paradox of inference from the exact same data set.

Let us also keep in mind that these are mere summaries and are not intended to explore the full range of meaning in the paradox. You will, however, be able to use them to help connect, clarify and generate commitment to right action if you help the pbc understand how they are making-meaning out of the phenomena of life.

Some Continuums

Creativity -- Realization

The paradox noted through these two terms is often the position taken or avoided in terms of action or cognitive movement and motivation. Are we moving towards what we want—creativity, or are we moving to accept what occurs--realization?

Advocacy -- Inquiry

Are we so busy advocating our position that we forget to ask about another person's position--inquiry?

Deliberate -- Quick

Do we let things happen and evaluate them over time according to our plan and our experience; or are we fast to judge and form an opinion based on intuition?

Maturity -- Inexperience

Do we hold esteem for those that hold the history of the organization in their experience, or are we more concerned with how the present circumstances hold the keys to our actions and motivations?

Security -- Adventure

What is our risk tolerance? How likely are we to choose what is interesting over what is assured? What is our need for known versus the undiscovered, for safety in spite of everything?

Gratification -------------------------------------- Acceptance

Do we need to orchestrate the experience or are we willing to see things as they are? Are we constantly edged on towards a desired state or resting assured that whatever comes will be for a reason?

Stability --------------------------------------- Ambiguity

Do we have a high need for predictability and constancy or do we thrive at the edge of chaos? Do we spend most of our time stewarding steadiness or do we *provoke the environment* in need of experience? Are we more comfortable with routine or challenge?

Consistency -- Flexible

How important is it that we have closure, or is having options critical? Is it important for the experience to be planned, or spontaneous and just in time?

Action -- Resolve

When we are frightened and unsure, do we have to just DO something, or do we hunker down and lay in for the storm?

Experience -- Intuition

How important are things that have happened in our lives and what we are experiencing through our senses in forming our conclusions about things, or do answers just bubble-up from somewhere and we just sort of know things? How easy is the future to see versus feeling ok in the present with our experience? Is the big picture easy for us, or do we struggle with all the gaps in getting from here to there?

Thinking --- Feeling

Do we make sense according to what we think or what we feel? If something needs to be done, then it should be clear to everyone and what happens to people as a result is just a result of what had to be done? Is how people are affected really important, important enough to change what needs to be done?

Open -- Private

Do we feel comfortable with people we do not know, or do we need to trust someone before we offer anything other than superficial knowledge of ourselves? Are we willing to explore the issues among others, or do we prefer the company of trusted friends and people we know a lot about before discussing *important things*?

Internal --- External

Do we process our thinking inside our heads or through speech and conversation with others? Do we float trial balloons for effect, or only offer comments when we have come to an internal conclusion about the subject? Do we have to take things in and think about them for a while or are we comfortable brainstorming ideas and discussing difficult subjects with people with whom we have only a cursory or working relationship.

Innovative --Traditional

Do we need things to be suited to the situation at hand or are we willing to do things the way they have always been done? Is there a comfort in feeling or thinking that there is a reason to keep things

the same, or are we constantly looking for new and different ways
to do things.

Ideas -- Structure

Are we concerned with ideas and how they can make things better
no matter what, or do we place a great deal of faith in the powers
that be? Do we need expectations defined in advance or do we
make them up as we go? Are we comfortable with procedure and
rules or do we operate out of the box—feeling confined by
boundaries? Is ambiguity your friend or your enemy?

Tangible --Intangible

Where does our sense of security come from? From things in the
outside world that are manifestations of our diligence and
conscientious discipline to detail, or from knowing that we can do
anything if we want to bad enough—there isn't a challenge we
can't overcome with the appropriate effort or motivation?

Theoretical -------------------------------------- Practical

Do we love to learn new things, concepts and ways of being, or do
we decide on one particular path that works for us and stick to it,
thick and thin? Can we modify what we said yesterday because we
found some new information today, or find yesterday fine because
it is based on sound practices that have worked before and will
work again?

Solid -- Adaptive

Are we un-budging once we make up our mind, or do we waft
from flower to flower like a hummingbird searching for nectar?
Are we comfortable in a variety of changing environments or are
we most comfortable with the familiar—the tried and true.

Resistant -- Enthusiastic

Are we hesitant to change, willing to forego improvements for the bird in hand or, are we passionate about new ideas and the thought of what could be? Are we slow to move to new stances, weighing possible outcomes against probability or is it Katy bar the door, full speed ahead?

Direct --- Indirect

Do we say what we mean or do we leave room for the other person to have space to make a decision that might be better for them? Instead of asking, 'do you want to go with me?" do we ask, "what are you doing tomorrow evening?" Are you a bottom line person, need to skip to the part that asks the question, or are you comfortable in exploring the issues fully and moving to conclusions after you know what is at stake for you and others?

Task --- People

Are we oriented towards getting things done or how others feel about what is being done? Do we want to know what the goals are, or whom the people are going to be that we'll be working with?

Conscientious ------------------------------------ Laissez faire

Do things have to be done a certain way, on time and in a certain manner for them to be correct, or are we less concerned with the manner of things but whether things turn out all right? Are rules and structure our friend, or are they constraints?

Agreeable --- Oppositional

Are we willing to go along or are we always questioning things? Do we match or mismatch easily? Do we find ourselves constantly wondering about a better way or being comfortable trying to maintain things the way things they come?

Extra-punitive -------------------------------------Intra-punitive

Do we tend to blame others—look outside ourselves to external causes for failure or do we tend to blame ourselves or internal limitations and mistaken beliefs for failure? Jung indicated that there is a *tendency* for extraverts to blame others or outside causes for failure and for introverts to blame themselves or their internal limitations for failure.

There are many more nuances that create differences among us, but if we can get a handle on some of these basic dichotomies, we can begin to understand without labeling someone with *the burden of type*.

We must realize, however, that in some circumstances we will act contrary to our likes and dislikes due to super-ordinate goals or desires—with awareness, we will know why.

Something both easy and practical to do for any longitudinal relationship (long term coaching with multiple interactions over time) would be to ask the questions and explore the differences, even to mark the continuums in each case in order to explore the openings generated through the conversation about differences. (An assessment of sorts. <grin>)

This does two things for the people involved. It lets them get a feel for how they are different from each other and how they might be different from the people in their lives. These two factors can create the opportunities for impersonal attribution that we have discussed throughout this chapter.

Once we can move beyond self-protecting patterns and become open to exploring differences, the ease with which people work and play together becomes greater. Cognitive and emotional effort is translated into flow activities instead of resistant activities—lessening our ability to perform, change and transform our lives and organizations.

Level of Development and YOU

I would like to offer an untested theory that may or may not have already been proven but here is my intuition after working with people in coaching for the past 11 years. The level of a person's development affects how their preferences (inborn gifts) are muted, amplified, limited or leveraged. What I mean is that the higher level of consciousness and awareness a person attains, the greater their ability to transcend their unconscious scripts—not always but more often.

This is, in my view, another reason for coaching to be practiced in modern day organizations. Coaching directly affects development. Developmental level is a precursor to high function. High function is a key to innovation, motivation, performance and further transformation in people and organizations. If this one theory were true, then the impetus for using coaching as a methodology to optimize business systems would be imperative!

I personally have just begun a journey into the hallowed halls of adult development. A presentation at a coaching conference in Boston in 1999 spurred me to begin to research adult development theory and I have found that it contains a wealth of information along with the usual high-brow rhetoric of academics—some of it is just plain hard to understand and grasp--yet it truly holds the key for coaches.

An interviewing process developed out of research work by Kegan, et al called the <u>Subject-Object Interview</u> is truly interesting and while difficult to synthesize quickly, it serves as a *violin* representing a powerful body of knowledge for coaching. In my opinion, we will see coaching influenced heavily in years to come from this approach to differences.

SUMMARY

Developmental theory is the frontier of coaching. In order to become more effective as coaches we have to understand how people develop in terms of consciousness and higher order thinking. As more and more of what we do as a pc becomes centered around increasing returns—an ability to improve at improving—our ability to help people climb developmental ladders quickly in spite of their age or experience, can make drastic improvements in the business system and organizational effectiveness.

Understanding our role as part of the "business system" and what as the person coaching our role is in improving the organization, will help us enfold the various differences and potentialities of our human resources into an interconnected whole.

> *The criticality of our success as persons developing and maintaining an effective coaching system depends almost entirely on our ability to leverage and value differences among people.*

Chapter 8

"There's a problem with creating what I call the loving and caring workplace, and it is that no one person can love and care for all of the employees all the time. The daily act of caring is very hard work. So you have to choose other managers who have the willingness to care. You have to focus on nurturing your good, close managers, then teach them to pass it along. Spread the caring, spread the work."

James Autry, **The Art of Caring Leadership**

A Coaching Continuum

Process – Content

In this discussion, I have identified three fundamental forms of coaching. These are *generic* views and not intended to be inclusive of all the various types within the genres of coaching. There are three basic categories: <u>process</u>, <u>content</u> and <u>combined</u>—the latter a combination to some degree of both process and content; most coaching will fall here.

Why the need to establish these definitions?

As coaching grows, it is crucial both in importance and practice to define and distinguish categories of coaching. While newcomers will not find a great deal of use in these distinctions anyone attempting to design a coaching system will need to understand the nuances of these categories.

Coaching Combined—Process and Content

Coaching, as commonly thought of—athletic or performance coaching—consists of both content and process albeit heavy on the content side. The coach is thought to *know more* than the player. The coach commonly delivers feedback, ideas and challenges, both negative and positive, based on observation of the player/performer's actions. This method of coaching is designed to place equal emphasis on the coach and the player in a form of dynamic balance. *You will notice that it does not rely heavily on inquiry.*

Representing one category or another, most coaches will disagree in that anything other than their category is *true coaching.* It is important, however, not to throw the baby out with the bath water and provide a continuum of coaching from process to content with a measure of each in the middle. Visually, the continuum would appear as in the diagram that follows:

Continuum of Coaching

What makes this conceptually important is that in order to fully understand how and when to coach we must know <u>what</u> is needed. Here is an example of what I mean. Take a performance challenge with a customer service representative (csr). What kind of coaching is it going to be required in this situation?

Normally, what we find is that the csr will require a combined approach. In fact, almost all situations call for a <u>combined approach</u> with an emphasis on <u>process</u> whenever possible. It is important for the pc and the pbc to understand clearly that coaching is not a problem driven process but rather a <u>solution based process</u>.

Most employees have been taught to seek answers to problems rather than discover what solutions work best, and what is the difference between what is happening to create limitations in the system and what is happening that is working. Doing more of what works and less of what does not is a *solutions based* process. Yet, very few approaches in a traditional sense *take the time necessary* to involve the employee, in this specific case the csr, in the solutions process through inquiry. We are so addicted to problem solving that we do not even ask ourselves enough questions before we seek a remedy!

> *Coaching is an approach that can be taken to guide this process but it will be difficult to take full advantage of the coaching program if the system is dependent or has made employees dependent on a problem driven process, from where they go to the next higher echelon seeking answers rather than dialog.*

Back to our example.

In the case of a csr being coached rather than managed, we find that the pc will need to understand the situational environment (content knowledge) the csr faces. What dictates the approach on the part of the coach is whether or not we have *enough time and resources* to discover those content needs through dialog. If not, then the coaching interaction will be more content driven than process oriented.

If we have no content knowledge, then the pbc must drive that part of the agenda through process interaction with the coach. The coach can connect, clarify and strive to reach commitment, even if that is the introduction of more content-specific interaction through those *others* who do have content knowledge.

In a coaching interaction connected to or after training (which many programs are starting to implement) the pc has to have some clear understanding of the training program's objective in order to help guide the *refreezing* process—a process describing change as being unfreezing, the shift to the desired state and refreezing at the changed point—a classic OD change model derived by Kurt Lewin.

It is not *required* that a coach be content knowledgeable, as a masterful coaching process can create the necessary *content* from other resources, however, I am becoming more and more convinced that some content knowledge is advisable—especially in terms of competitive business strategy and organizational development.

Next, and as complexity reigns, we find ourselves more and more at the mercy of time. And because it takes time to move through process when no content is used, it becomes a luxury that may not be affordable by most people and organizations. This does not mean we drive coaching through content as it is almost always the case in athletic or performance coaching—where the pbc looks to the coach to provide corrective feedback and the answers to problems. Yet, a measure of content, at least industry specific, is, in my view, advantageous.

"In a conversation with coaches in a Fortune 500 company, they were asked by the employees of the organization when

*told they were coaches without industry experience, **"they
don't know our business, how can they coach us?"***

Sometimes, the beginner's mind is the way to go in coaching,
however, it requires such a high level of mastery in the pc that
most people using coaching as a methodology will be better
off with some content foundation—hence the continuum. We
can see that as we proceed along the continuum from process
to content there is hardly ever a point where the coaching is
strictly process oriented or primarily content driven.

I cannot say for sure that the situational continuum given us by
Hersey-Blanchard in terms of task and relationship orientation
may not have some importance to the continuum demonstrated
above? In terms of how much process and how much content
is used in each coaching situation, there may be other factors,
among them, the maturity of the person coaching as well as
the maturity or sophistication of the followers?

Obviously, time, in both instances, dictates how quickly we
move from process to content. This is a dilemma that many
coaches today, being trained in personal coaching, do not
understand. The organization, however, especially in an
increasingly competitive environment will constantly be faced
with the dilemma of resource allocation and time availability.

It would be wonderful to be in process and to allow the pbc
the flexibility to develop solutions on his/her own time,
however, due to the constraints of scarce resources, there may
be times when we are just unable to allow the process to move
through all of the stages in sufficient quantity as to allow the
opening to be fully explored in the coaching interaction.

This, by far, will be the most difficult call for the organization
as well as for the pc. The tendency will be--when cramped for

time and resources--*to provide fish rather than creating fishing opportunities.*

This is why a coaching system must be fully aware of the constraining resources—including time, as well as the leveraging resources--intention. If the organization designs and implements a CoachSystem™ as opposed to coaching on demand, then the ongoing relationships built through the coaching system can stabilize these issues of scare resources and constraining deadlines—in view of, and over time.

> *At times, the pc will leave the coach approach for other approaches, and it is important to understand this transition as another major reason why the pc will not often be a coach in terms of our previous definition. A pc is more likely to be able to shift from manager to trainer to leader back to the pc much more easily than a coach will be able to shift out of coaching. This is an important distinction to keep in mind as you develop your organizational coaching system!*

Let us consider yet another example. Let us say, an executive coaching interaction or relationship [interaction being defined as an event within a relationship] where we can see it will be important to use a great deal more of process orientation as the executive, in some cases, may be the expert. What is needed here is the listening process of the 4-R's referenced earlier:

receive, reflect, re-state and refrain.

In this case, the process becomes highly important and functional for the expert pbc. While it still may be a combined approach, it will be heavily weighted towards process rather than in a case of a high school soccer coach with a new player.

In all cases, we define coaching in organizations as the interaction to align personal and organizational right action--meeting environmental demands and creating desired business results—generating well-being, purpose, competence and awareness through a solutions based dialogue that values the person being coached.

In the case of the csr, improving performance at the customer interface is vital to the person and the organization. In the case of the executive, understanding the issues in creating effective leadership programs and as in the latter example, in helping the new soccer player to orient himself/herself on the playing field in the use of proper football technique in passing. In each case, the environmental constraints provide the cues for coaching and set the level of demand--in all cases the most effective coaching approach is defined by the situation, and the people in it.

Summary

What is clear about coaching is that it can be a methodology for achieving deep and profound change and development over time. What is <u>not clear</u> is what will be best in each and every situation. Truly, a situational approach will have the greatest efficacy over time, with the pc being fully capable of recognizing the need for content and the need for process—dynamically balancing the continuum. Being able to maneuver seamlessly along the continuum in view of organizational constraints will require mastery and system support. In the <u>Levels of Coaching</u> chapter we identify some clear levels of coaching in an organization that may help the novice pc reconnoiter along the continuum more easily.

Staging content versus process intervention will provide a safety net for new people coaching in organization. Starting out with pilot projects and providing a mastery track for the pc will aid the organization's integration of a coaching system. Learning the business system and culture is also central to lower resistance to coaching. As we move along the continuum from process to content and the organization becomes more fluid and capable, the pc can shift the coaching along the continuum from process to content as most effective in the interaction.

We need to be careful and proverbially, not throw the baby out with the bath water because coaching begins with a high content makeup, following perhaps a training impact session or when the pbc is not an expert. Coaching is a process where dialog is used to create an appreciative approach to learning and assimilation. It is, therefore important not to abandon coaching because of high content needs and low follower maturity or sophistication. If we are able to view coaching as a continuum of process to content and remember to engage the three C's, we can then gradually shift the interaction and the coaching system to fully embrace the Model II values prescribed by Argyris—out of a Model I values-set.

Coaching is the vehicle to get from where we are in organization (usually Model I, where defensive patterns create additional complexity and limitations—robbing us of energy and increasing effort) to where we need to spend most of our time—Model II, where advocacy, inquiry and appreciation for the views of others in a shared goal is more important than *saving face, holding our position at all costs or needing to win!*

Chapter 9

"Millions of items of the outward order are present to my senses which never properly enter into my experience. Why? Because they have no interest for me. My experience is what I agree to attend to. Only those items which I notice shape my mind--without selective interest, experience is utter chaos."

William James

Creating a Vernacular of Leadership

In order to talk coaching in the organization, we have to talk leadership and management. This subject is fairly controversial. I am often taken by surprise with the 850 or so definitions that Bennis and Nanus found while researching LEADERS, 1985- 1997. Yet, it is critical to establish some format for discussing leadership in coaching conversations. It is often crucial to the dialogue to speak in common terms— a shorthand of sorts—that creates inertia over time.

Since my first love is leadership, I began my own leadership journey by trying to discover what it was about leadership that was essential to use in coaching and how to create a vernacular that I could use with my clients. What resulted is a seemingly complex array of leadership babble, but it works. Once again, I resorted to what worked.

The following leadership vernacular was developed from my experience over time with many different kinds of systems and many different kinds of people. It seemed that some people faired well in some aspects of *leadership-making* while others needed more detail, less detail, more big-picture, more specifics, etc. To meet the needs of everyone, I developed what I refer to as <u>strategic intention</u>. Simply, strategic intention is "*what the heck we plan on doing*"--specifically!

Strategic Intention answers all the basic questions about strategy…and what experts often refer to as creating an essential *strategic architecture*--to use the term from Prahalad and Hamel's ground breaking book on strategy, COMPETING FOR THE FUTURE.

Strategic Intention (SI)

One of the most critical roles of a leader is centered in establishing "clarity of intention." Until intention is discovered by the organization, with help from the words and deeds of the leaders: trust, commitment, synergy, adaptation, performance, and satisfaction, it will not reach the potential that can be achieved.

High performing organizations are necessary for the future. To establish intention, an organization has little choice but to create a way of guiding the decisions made throughout the organization.

Peter Drucker, in an article penned in the late 1950s, wrote about strategic planning, and used the term "decision structure" to define an organizational decision-making hierarchy.

In order to create a strategic hierarchy around organizational intention, nine categories of intention have been identified as follows: assumptions, values and beliefs, vision, purpose, guiding principles, strategic objectives, key success factors, goals, and standards.

ASSUMPTIONS

Later on in the process of my own discovery with clients and organizations I found that we needed a central hub of assumptions that were woven into the eight factors. Assumptions we, and others make are critical to our ladder of inference as we use them to *interpret* the observable data through our senses. Assumptions are the *working mental models* that are applied to all of our behavior. By creating a strategic intention we *influence* the assumptions people make and help align the interests and needs of people and organizations.

The integration of these categories with assumptions into an evolving decision structure clarifies strategic intention and is one of the highest leverage activities in which a leader can engage. An example of an limiting assumption might be: *I better not bring the bad news to my boss as messengers are shot!*

The eight categories of strategic intention are briefly described as follows.

VALUES & BELIEFS

Leaders must establish a hierarchy of values and beliefs, and articulate what matters otherwise we leave room for the authoring of decisions, which may *devalue people and the organization and* lead us away from our core competencies reducing our competitive advantage. These *governing variables* as referenced by Argyris are critical to guiding meaning-making in the organization. However, values usually number from about 3-5 and often only one word, like *respect*—providing a guide for how people are treated in an organization for example.

VISION: Now, Near & Far

Energizing the organization with an overarching description of what the leadership sees the organization becoming is not an easy task. It is common to scoff at attempts to create vision in your organization. It is a lot easier to make light of the process than it is to really dig deep within the soul of the organization to find the ennobling causes that drive you to come to work each day to face the daily difficulties list.

Dividing vision into three components helps people to understand the complexity of our environment. Doing so, shifts our concern into several concurrent frames: *now, near and far.* With change and uncertainty occurring at such rapid rates, it may be too much to ask some people to make the intuitive leaps into the far vision when they hardly can see their future right *now*.

Holding a baby girl in your arms hardly helps you to understand the woman she will become in the years to follow—our vision would be for her to stop crying…

Defining vision in terms of now, near and far also allows a person to take a linear approach to the future—allowing them to focus on *now* in full view of near and far, keeping in mind what vision the leader has painted for the future, while not actually being able to see themselves in that position yet.

PURPOSE

The purpose statement is about the core competencies you intend to leverage. Whether it is "to provide nutritious meal solutions to elderly people in need" or any of a million purposes restaurants are created for in this life, the purpose statement is something that stakeholders must understand and practice. It does not mean that they will, but it needs to be clear enough that anyone can advocate it…even the leaders! You will find the core values and core competency enfolded into the purpose statement, usually 25 words or less.

Example Coaching Purpose:

> To facilitate the interdevelopment of the pc and the pbc through a respectful, confidential and masterful interaction towards personal and organizational right action.

GUIDING PRINCIPLES

This is an area that managers like to keep ambiguous so they can *make it up as they go*. If you start writing things down, the stakeholders will hold you to it and then you lose your advantage? *Wrong!*

Leaders use guiding principles to align, create trust, and to walk the talk by putting everybody on the same playing field. Energy is not sapped up in the politics of the organization because of different rules for each level of hierarchy at each given moment.

Principles are *no budge* sorts of things and create consistency and trust in a group. Let us remember that principles are the guiding forces behind the intention. They are closest things to the natural laws that govern the universe and provide the universal structure that people need to check-in with over time when they make important policy decisions.

Example: People have a right to due process.

STRATEGIC OBJECTIVES

Actually, taking the time to think through your intention and derive some overriding strategic actions will create the success outlined in the above categories of the decision structure. An example might be: "we will create a return to investment of 8%", or "maintain a commitment to training of 3% of budget." Real stuff—real action, and organizational building blocks that must be in place to clarify your intention and *derived right action.*

KEY SUCCESS FACTORS

These 3 to 5 driving forces form metrics on a time bounded *read out (daily, weekly, monthly)* and they are monitored like the gauges on the dashboard of your car. What 3 to 5 factors do you need to be concerned with as your business goes through its daily exercise? What about inventory turn, satisfaction, profit, etc.? What gauges need to be in your business dashboard?

GOALS

Clear, concise attention to intention—a selective experience as William James would state. Goals are stated in the first person in an affirmative manner that is empowering to those who live the goals. Unlike strategic objectives or key success factors, goals have definite beginnings and endings, are time sensitive and measurable.

Example: *We will add 10 salespeople to our regional sales force by June of next year producing 10% more revenue than this year.* (Very specific actions taken in light of strategic objectives.)

STANDARDS

These *minimum operating levels* describe what behaviors are acceptable throughout the operation during the execution of its duties. Obviously, care must be taken to not *limit* behavior to these minimum levels, but acceptable behavior must be clearly understood and practiced as a starting point, or there is no agreement on universal intention.

An example of a standard would be the manner in which a phone is answered, how many rings are ideal, what the opening statement is to be and in what manner of tone or facial expression. These basic building blocks of performance must be evident or you will find yourself depending strictly on the inference made from the data or experience viewed by others.

Answering the phone, for instance. How many different ways are there to answer a phone? It depends on the person's current frame of reference, conditioning, his/her view of organizational culture and the outcome currently desired. It is obvious that for every person there is a different way to answer the phone and while this seems petty and inconsequential, a *standardized* method provides the *caller* with a consistent interface regardless of who answers the phone.

LEADERSHIP & COACHING

As I stated previously, we need a leadership paradigm or fundamental way of talking about "leading" because we continuously coach leadership. Without a vernacular, you cannot move the process forward on all fronts. When I developed this process or vernacular, I did so in view of how could a line manager function in a coaching or leadership methodology and actually use it to get work done—right.

While a line supervisor or a fast food clerk may only be subjected to a narrow portion of the entire gamut of strategic intention, there still needs to be a strong thread of intention from the executive level to the line or customer level in order for everyone to be on the same page. Everything must be integrated.

The idea behind a CoachSystem™ is to create a free flow of ever-increasing sophistication throughout the organization. This evolutionary spiral of sophistication must scale and integrate the leadership initiatives from top to bottom. In order to do so, everyone in the organization must have as a reference of *right action*--the strategic intention—the answers to what and why we do what we do.

This right action agenda can only be integrated in real time-- whether by a jazz quartet or a symphonic orchestra--if everyone has the same music to play from. Not everyone may understand all the nuances of the intention—but they know their part--and in order for the music to move you, it has to be played in unison—hence the leadership agenda described by the strategic intention must under gird the coaching system.

HOW will WHO lead WHOM to do WHAT, WHEN--WHY?

Every part of this strategic model of intention is essential. You must have each piece *available*. Not everyone needs them all at once, so it is confusing at times to talk about purpose and vision, and values and key success factors, but taking the time to articulate these issues forces the powers at be—small or large—to help others decide what right action is in the organization—consistently and broadly.

While it is not the purpose of this manual to describe fully how to formulate and adapt a strategic intention, we have to provide a vernacular in order to communicate right action. Anyone in the organization can use this format to articulate what they intend. It can be simple or it can be enormously detailed and complex, depending on needs. It is scalable, and along with the model of coaching it fits like a glove around the focus on right action--for an individual person and the organization as a whole—and structure.

USING SI IN COACHING SYSTEMS

When I use SI in coaching, I approach the person being coached (pbc) with a sort of "fill in" the blank exercise to see what in the way of things they understand and how that fits with what they intend in the organization. (It is also a way to discover espoused values versus values in use!)

Often, all of the parts of the SI are in their head and those that are not, are often easily constructed—with the exception of key success factors. I find that area to be the most neglected because people do not understand how to generate a key success factor or critical success measure. The Balanced Scorecard is best for guiding this process and it is addressed in the *Coach-Wise Knowledgebase* and many other places on the Internet. [www.bscol.com]

When we discuss right action with a pbc, we have to understand what and how they got to where they got to—what worked and is working and what has not worked and is not working, and why. In order to do so, we have to climb the ladder of inference. Chris Argyris used this metaphor to describe how we come to act. By surfacing the strategic intention (espoused theory) including the assumptions people use to formulate intention, we can discover operational cues.

In other words, we know what they know, we hope to help them understand what they do not know that may be preventing them from arriving at the intended destination, and in the matter of course—what they don't know they don't know. Often, we can discover these clues through dialog up and down the ladder of inference developed by Argyris.

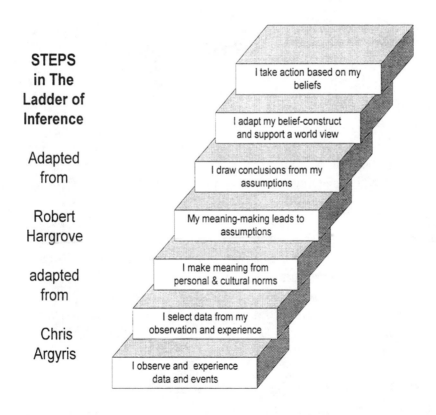

STEPS in The Ladder of Inference

Adapted from

Robert Hargrove

adapted from

Chris Argyris

- I take action based on my beliefs
- I adapt my belief-construct and support a world view
- I draw conclusions from my assumptions
- My meaning-making leads to assumptions
- I make meaning from personal & cultural norms
- I select data from my observation and experience
- I observe and experience data and events

The leadership vernacular described in SI helps us navigate through uncharted waters and to map the areas of knowing for the pbc. This can be done in a sophisticated manner for executive level coaching or a more straightforward process for line level employees, yet the two can be linked and integrated in the organization.

Let us examine why strategic intention and the ladder of inference are so critical to right action.

EXAMPLE:

- Take a viewpoint as a restaurant manager in a public restaurant.
- This is a fine dining restaurant in a fine hotel.
- The hotel has a new leader who insists the guest comes first. (SI)
- The season is Christmas and the restaurant is overbooked as usual.

In this example, the *system* has set up the restaurant manager to fail. In one case, the data or events (the overbooked condition) is going to be viewed in terms of the personal issues of the day by the manager: we are overbooked, the customers will be angry, the employees will be angry because they know customers will be angry and of course, this condition sets up a negative experience almost automatically as a pre-existing condition.

The manager views this data and events, reflects that against his/her experience from similar past events, draws conclusions about that experience (rather than allowing the event to actually take place in some cases), views it in terms of the organizational culture (seeing how much in conflict the SI is with practice) and proceeds to develop all sorts of conclusions from insolence to customers--to personal feelings of inadequacy.

In this simple example, the *system* created a disparity between the SI and actual practice. It places people in the position to fail almost as a preexisting condition because the SI has not permeated the entire organization in such a way that limitations are guarded against, and overbookings (in this restaurant case) do not occur as a result of structural design.

SUMMARY

The confusion between the interpretation of various levels of management and the lack of integration between the executive directive—the customer comes first—and the actual practice—overbooking, where the customers come when they come—blocks the system from achieving right action and *systems integrity.*

Integrating leadership, management and coaching is key to creating a system that is leveraged. You cannot expect a great coaching system to make up for and/or fix a *bad leadership and management system*—it will amplify it! Change must be integrated and it must be viewed in terms of systems integrity. Do not establish a coaching system without looking clearly at the leadership and management systems and establishing a clear foundation for coaching success with an articulated strategic architecture that is integrated to all levels of the organization.

An example of how to create an SI for a coaching system is included in the chapter on "creating a coaching system." If you have questions, please feel free to email me at si@coach2-the-bottom-line.com and I'll be happy to clarify meaning.

Chapter 10

If I ended the book here, would you have sufficient information about creating a coaching system? Here are three critical issues to remember.

Three Coaching Truths

Most Important

What is important to take away here is the basic Coach2 Model with three things in mind—Connect, Clarify and Commit. Any other skill, practice or even knowledge will *map onto* these three core competencies—no matter what you do in life. You can accomplish most anything if you connect with people—truly connect. You will accomplish more things if you clarify and of course, you can accomplish anything if you are able to create strong internal commitment.

Second

Remember the process model CIM *(Coaching Interaction Model)*.

If we always start with an opening and do not start coaching until we have one, it will be hard to make many mistakes. Why? Because in an opening, you have the opportunity with the pbc to discover and explore with trust and *openness led by the desire to learn and develop*. With an opening, you will always be in a voluntary situation, even with your children or your significant other. If we allow the pbc to set the agenda and keep content to a minimum, always allowing the pbc the opportunity to accept or discard our notions, a healthy pbc will always act in his/her best interests.

> *[One critical caveat. Coaching is above the line between health and pathology. Therapists can go below the line, coaches should NEVER. They should know when the line is being crossed and refer the pbc to another professional who deals with below the line issues like an EAP Program or Therapist!]*

Acting in one's best interests is usually very empowering and intrinsically motivating even when you can see that it might not be in their best interests for long. We have an amazing self-protecting mechanism--acting in our best interests—that prevails. In another case, when we act in what we think is our best interest and fail, we are more likely than not to seek help and to be *open* to coaching. Keeping these caveats in mind, you will see why it is hard to make a mistake when coaching through an opening!

The key to leveraging your openings is to co-generate possibilities. Sometimes this single thing will provide the motive force for the pbc to get unstuck, even though a solution to the immediate challenge is not forthcoming.

> *"You can't coach desire"*

Bill Bowerman, Oregon State Track Coach in <u>Prefontaine</u>—
the movie.

However, you can create the conditions to facilitate it by using the process model.

Do not coach until you have an opening. It is the biggest mistake I have made, and see made on a day-to-day basis. Some people do not want to be coached, others are not ready and for some, it would be a waste of your mutual effort. I really believe that half of coaching is "recognizing" when an opening is present. When it is, almost any technique will work as long as you let the pbc guide the process.

Following openings and possibilities, always help the pbc create some kind of plan. Some can do this blind-folded; others will need structural help to define their actions. Once the plan is made, preview it. What is likely to occur; what will happen when; who will be affected if we execute this plan; and how will you help the pbc discover and remove the barriers to success?

Hopefully, what will occur next is action. If the pbc fails to act then something went wrong in the process. If the pbc <u>does not own the action,</u> you may have been coaching in the gap!

> "A person won over against their will is of the same opinion still."

The Final Issue…

Is that there is not a final thing. Coaching, like everything else in life, is a journey. Let us remember that everybody coaching started somewhere, with some knowledge, skill and ability— even if it was bad. Do not hesitate to teach people slowly about coaching and let them learn the basics. Let them learn to connect and clarify in their own way towards reaching commitment.

Generate opportunities for people to develop along their own paths. Some people will not want to adapt or learn very quickly but may have other ways of contributing greatly to the organization that are not so fast and straightforward—be on the lookout for those subtleties. Give people the opportunity to fail in a safe environment at first, and don't hang them for it when they make mistakes! Blameless error is such a wonderful concept, but not easy to practice.

The very second that people *get* that coaching is <u>about</u> perceiving openings rather than gaps, your entire culture—inside and out—will change for the better. If you read nothing more than this part of the book, you will have the basic principles of a coaching system in hand. I hope that you will continue on, as what lies ahead will take you to the next level. However, feel free to take a few deep breaths, close your eyes and let this sink in—deeply.

Questions? Drop us a line at <u>questions@coach2-the-bottom-line.com</u>.

Part II

Coaching as a System of Change

What Employees Really Want

1. Recognition for competence and accomplishments.

2. Respect and dignity.

3. Personal choice and freedom. More autonomy in their jobs and to make their own decisions.

4. Involvement at work. People want to be informed, included and involved in decisions.

5. Pride in work - to do a good job.

6. Lifestyle quality. Time for family and leisure as well as work.

7. Financial security. People want to know they can succeed, even in bad times.

8. Self-development. Most people want to improve.

9. Health and wellness. As the workforce ages, more concern with long-term health.

Other important values:

- Having fun at work
- Making a contribution to society
- Improving one's standard of living
- Developing quality relationships

Not nearly as important as they once were:

- Loyalty to the organization
- Job security
- Making a lot of money

These trends in workplace values are from <u>Managing Workforce 2000</u> by David Jamieson and Julie O'Mara, Jossey-Bass Inc., Publishers.

Coaching as a Change Model

Coaching is a methodology or framework for change and learning—theory and practice. It is an approach that *helps* individuals, groups and organizations to develop a *predisposition as well as proactive nature* to change—one that is *effortless* in meeting the needs of a constantly changing environment. Coaching focuses on surfacing the personal defensive patterns that create resistance to change and resolving the difficult, complex, real-life challenges and opportunities that are critical to the well-being of people, organizations and society as a whole.

> *Coaching is a deep or profound change methodology that seeks to integrate leadership, management and learning into a coherent whole.*

In overcoming barriers to personal and organizational change, coaching does not simply focus on improving future problem-solving or decision-making skills. It does not concern itself with making only incremental changes (e.g., identifying opportunities; finding, correcting, reducing, or eliminating threats) even though that is part of the process.

What effective coaching promotes is a focus on looking inward, testing and developing new frameworks of evaluation, establishing new routines and mental models that create well-being, purpose, competence and awareness as a result of effective coaching interactions.

Coaching can and often does, follow impact training and learning; providing a methodology for integrating the principles, practices and concepts that are critical to performance, change and transformation.

In this portion of the book, we put the theory described in Part I to practice in creating an organizational coaching system. We add some reasoning and technique behind the COACH2 Model, but the primary focus of this book is to be an executive guide for the manager/leader who needs to know more about how to create a coaching system or effective coaching interaction in an organization.

There are literally *hundreds* of books, manuals and skill programs for developing the essential KSAs for creating competence in the coaching interaction. The beauty of the COACH2 Model is that as a source coaching model, these KSAs can be easily mapped onto the model to create added sophistication around the core competencies of connection, clarification and commitment.

In fact, each person will want to develop and use the specific set of KSAs that leverage their own intrinsic ability to relate to others in the coaching interaction. This section helps to apply the general theory behind coaching—using the COACH2 Model—to the broad competence required of a system designer or program implementer. This section does develop the C2 Model more in depth regarding the core competencies and the sub process, OPPOA (Openings, Possibilities, Plans, Outcomes, Action) in the context of how it fits into the overall coaching system.

However, the abilities of observation, listening, discerning, modeling and delivery are not covered in depth, except for delivery. This critical ability is covered in a chapter, later in this section.

It will always be important to keep in mind the *theoretical constructs* that tie everything together in the coaching system, however theory means nothing without the ability to apply it to personal and organizational challenges and to create organizational effectiveness and business results.

In the following chapters, the enabling practices and procedures are discussed along with some overriding knowledge, skill and abilities (KSAs) that support the COACH2 Model Theory outlined in Part I.

> *You don't create effective coaching from books; effective coaching comes from practice with intent to facilitate effective results from coaching interactions. Effective coaching comes from mastering essential abilities towards competence. Yet, awareness can come from books and out of that conversation, purpose and competence in coaching.*

Chapter 11

Uncertainty, turbulence and ambiguity are the norm.

Coaching as a Change Model

Nowhere to Now Here

> *Change is about constancy, moving beyond it and re-establishing it at a point of leverage. At its roots, coaching is about change. The coaching interaction is a change opportunity and at the minimum, the person coaching is a change agent.*

One of the key distinctions in coaching is between advocacy and inquiry. As pointed out in the chapter on differences, each of us has preferences and viewpoints that either dispose us to or limit our choice to advocate or inquire. In that continuum lies the opportunity to leverage, not only our own strengths, but those of the person being coached (pbc)—in harmony with the demands on his/her desires to align with them.

As we consider change and how to change, how to *learn to change* and how to change efficiently, *when coaching in organizations we must consider the effects of the coaching interaction on personal and system change, simultaneously.*

There is a lot that goes into creating a successful change effort. In the DANCE OF CHANGE by Senge, et al, we find described ten limiting processes that keep an organizational change effort from occurring successfully. I have paraphrased and listed them briefly.

Barriers to Change

1. Not enough time
2. Not enough help
3. No personal relevancy
4. Talk and no walk
5. Wasting time
6. Doesn't work
7. Only one right way
8. Nobody's in charge
9. Déjà vu (reinventing the wheel, again)
10. What is the right reason…?

The authors also go on to state the obvious, that leadership occurs at various levels, local, network and executive. This is very similar to Covey's levels of personal, interpersonal (network?), managerial and organizational. In either case, the change process MUST be directed at all levels. It must contain relevancy for each level and generate environments where customers, employees, stakeholders and leaders are likely to succeed, all in all, no short order.

One-to-One Coaching System

The person coaching (pc) essentially—in addition to their other organizational roles--becomes part of a *boundary spanner network*. In effect, the coaching system serves as a boundaryless organism that helps, in an appreciative manner, to connect and spread the innovations, learning and solutions-based processes across the organization.

One of the most interesting aspects of personal and organizational change is our adaptive response to change. It lies in dimensions of capacity and action, where some people are very adaptive naturally, and others not as much. The coaching system is the *compensatory* tool for personal and organizational change velocity. When we realize that we will not only have to *mass* customize our markets but our leadership and management system as well, coaching is the preferred *one-to-one* organizational intervention tool functioning at the *prime level of organization*.

Coaching allows us to customize our <u>change effort</u> just as a gardener produces an environment for each species of plant during cultivation. The one-to-one relationship in coaching provides the environment for isolating the effects of organizational and environmental change while reducing the overall complexity without fracturing the reality of wholeness. What is critical about this aspect of change is that change has leverage to the extent that it flows through an organization's resistances without being fractured.

Change can be seen as viscous and fluid, constantly attempting to permeate a personal and organizational pipeline. And to the extent that personal and organizational defensive patterns exist, resistance to personal and organizational change velocity is high.

Thus, the organization becomes slower to adapt and evolve, lessening the productive response to environmental challenges. In this respect, the universal laws of physics come to bear and the greater the change force and velocity, the more likely change is to occur. Therefore, by lowering resistance to change at the *prime one-to-one level*, we can leverage the resources of the organization more efficiently.

Efficient Change

Efficiency in system change occurs by enabling the reinforcing factors, and by removing the resisting forces. I was taken by a speech a decade or so ago delivered by a scientist whose name I cannot recall but the essential message was that by removing the forces of failure we could *"up the down side."* In biology, we know that there are two basic forces, reinforcing and limiting. In the dynamic balance between the points on this perpetual pendulum, we find the <u>potential</u> for coaching.

In coaching systems, we seek to remove limitations as we seek to add reinforcement, working both ends to the middle, never fracturing the whole. By seeking profound change, defined as the change that occurs both inside and outside—beliefs and behaviors—we seek to reinforce our strengths and remove our limitations. In some cases, that requires a different <u>match</u> between resources and outcomes, and in other cases, merely <u>redirection.</u>

Whatever the need, the coaching interaction is the least common denomination of change. At the interface of one-to-one, we find the leverage of change. As we move more and more towards a position *enfolded within* self-awareness and the interaction with our environment—perhaps towards enlightenment of sorts—we seek an opportunity to both change and stay the same—valuing who we are and who we are becoming.

Our internal forces are marshaled into constancy and rhythm. Yet, the external forces acting upon us seek to destabilize that homeostasis. Coaching provides inquiry into the need for change as well as the modus operandi for change. Not only what change is, but how to go about actualizing *efficient change*.

The greatest loss to organizational inertia is unsuccessful change. More time, energy and effort is lost due to inefficient and failed changed programs than to the work itself. In his book, *THE 80-20 PRINCIPLE*, Richard Koch indicates that "80% of all of our decisions are worthless." By contrast, if we view how change can be self-managed, we could consider *coached* organizational change as being effortless—a truly desirable state, yet how do we achieve it?

Achieving Effortless Change

Organizational Change occurs as a result of three inter-developmental factors:
- Personal benefit—WIIFM (what's in it for me)
- Collective Action spurred through communities of practice
- A spiral of success connected to bottom line performance where the change and likelihood of change is constantly reinforced through business results.

In the chapters that follow, we outline some basic tenets of the coaching system, how to interact efficiently with each business system and the reasons we would want to move from the inefficient world of Model I governing values to the more efficient and effortless worldview of Model II governing values. Again, an overview of these theories from Argyris are listed in Appendix E.

Summary

Basically, to create ongoing and effective change we must remove limitations created through personal and organizational patterns and enable the reinforcing behaviors of honesty, advocacy and appreciative inquiry to occur among one another. The dilemma resides, clearly, in our need for constancy and clarity in the face of increasing complexity in an uncertain, turbulent and ambiguous environment.

How do we lower our personal and organizational *shields* without giving over to others our only means of protection? If that belief is at the base of your inquiry, then we must look deeper in order to find out why we live and work in fear?

It is our fears that will set us free, not only our truth. When we personally and collectively are able to examine our fears and our beliefs that create them, we can begin a constructive dialogue about how to deal with the paradox of increasing complexity, and our heartfelt needs for constancy in a sea of turbulence. When we find the strength coming from a collective trust that our fears are no longer needed for self-protection, then the debilitating effects of defensive posturing can be limited, and adaptability, vitality, passion and the willingness to go the extra mile can be reinforced.

> *Luckily, people judge the credibility of human skills by evaluating what values they serve. This means that those who learn the new skills as gimmicks and tricks will be discovered. It means further that those who wish to gain credibility not only must learn the new skills, but also must internalize a new set of values.*

> Chris Argyris: The Executive Mind and Double Loop Learning, Org Dynamics, Autumn 1982, P.22

Chapter 12

First Ponder, then dare.   Helmuth Moltke

The Coaching Approach in Practice

How did we get here? You have been assigned to create a coaching system or coach approach in your work team or organization. You discern a gap or an opening either indirectly or directly, how do you know what to do?

For a coach or person coaching (pc) this is *the* question. Many times, the person being coached (pbc) or the organization leader/manager will come to you with a challenge or a circumstance that requires a solution based approach. This is a situation where the pc must potentially ascertain:

- What are the resources available, both for the pc and pbc?
- Is right action at issue?
- How familiar is the pc with the coaching process?
- What is the highest personal need?
- What is the business or organizational need (If not personal?)
- Is there an integrated approach available?
- What could be gained or lost?
- What forces are in play or will be called into play— reinforcing or limiting the possible effective desired outcomes?
- Is action supported for coaching by leadership?
- How is the culture staged for coaching intervention?

Stepping into a coaching system or a coaching interaction without consideration of these issues will often present contextual or possibly even structural resistance to accomplishing a positive result in the coaching interaction—personally and collectively.

In terms of preparing for the coaching interaction, depending on whether the coaching is deemed personal—outside of organization, or personal—inside of organization, or organizational, there are several things that need to occur.

Personal

In my view, the need to be in clear agreement, even to the point of a written constitution or intention as to what the coaching relationship is going to be—often a *scope of work,* is an ideal approach. A scope of work defines the parameters of what will be accomplished in terms of specific focus during the interactions in view of system goals. It also gives the pc the opportunity to pull things back into focus if the interaction, over time, begins to lose focus (starts to scale as a result of small wins) or loses contact with organizational needs. In the case where the interactions need to go outside of the scope of work, then the pc has the ability to reformulate the *agreement or intention of the coaching approach.*

This is a critically important caveat to the appropriate flows and focus of coaching interactions. A good deal of coaching fails (for that matter, any kind of intervention) without proper consideration of possible outcomes.

> *Often, the organization or pbc can be caught up in the need for performance when a developmental issue created the need for intervention.*

As you become more experienced, you will learn to do a consultation to assess what is needed versus what is being requested. In such cases you can either widen or narrow the scope of work to fit the intention of the pbc or the system mandate. In many cases, the C2 Model works ideally for this consultation in terms of connection, clarification and commitment. The universality of the model outside of coaching is clearly an advantage.

In other cases, you will simply identify coaching as a limiting force when considered collectively, or if system support is either non-existent or serving to create the limitations in the first place. In those cases, the decision NOT to coach can be the most effective commitment you can make to the organization. Develop the structural support before instituting coaching broadly across an organization.

Coaching can't be done in a vacuum. Obvious support mechanisms and structure must reinforce the coaching system. Otherwise, we have an isolated solutions-based approach that will not permeate the interaction of the pbc and the organization. This creates no leverage with the coaching system, as each action is unto itself, isolated and separate from the collective action. We have to create connections and conversations between these islands of knowledge and learning.

It may be appropriate to mention that change agents are often martyrs. While coaching may be seen by you as the most efficient and effective intervention, you may succeed and fail at the same time if the organization is not prepared to be *disturbed.* It may be best to isolate the causes and effects of a coaching intervention as a pilot project allowing it to stand on its own merit without bringing down the agents?

Organizational

A defined scope of work is also required in an organizational situation. It creates an opportunity for the pbc to see the C2 model in action as the assessment or consultation takes place. It is not as important when you are dealing with one person as it is when dealing with an organization of persons. Most of the time, the person setting scope of work is *not* the pbc in organizations.

Often, what the pbc needs and what the organization is willing to focus on is incongruent, e.g. performance and development. By having a clear scope of work agreement, either the pc or the pbc can go back to the originator of the agreement and request a widening, a narrowing or a transformation of the agreement. This creates clear and fair opportunities for the pc to renegotiate based on the additional scope.

In addition, a scope of work creates the forum for discussing pilot projects. A pilot project or prototype is often effective in bridging gaps where only cursory openings may exist, and success in pilot projects create leverage for wider openings, larger interventions, wider connections and boundary spanning effects.

These may seem like housekeeping issues with too much detail for an executive guide but they are absolutely necessary if you are to remove the barriers to effective coaching instead of creating administrative resistance that blocks positive outcomes. Obviously, you know by now that coaching is focused on several levels of the personal and collective action simultaneously. The performance issues ares merely symptoms of deeper change and transformation issues that require *different* developmental or structural approaches involving many organizational components and cross-boundary collaboration.

Components in a Coach Approach

- Capability
- Opportunity
- Efficacy
- Accountability

Capability is identified on two levels: pc and pbc. The pc must be capable of the scope of work and the pbc must be capable of meeting the goals of its intent—personal and organizational. Otherwise, <u>do not enter</u> into a coaching relationship.

Opportunity must exist, again, at the personal and organizational level. Setting people up to fail in a nice way through coaching is just as deplorable as setting them up to fail through a directly manipulative approach. An interventionist may eliminate the culpability by using a coaching system--thought of as being the right thing to do-- however without structural support and systems in place to buoy the changes required in the organizational systems—we end up going through well intended motions with ephemeral and inefficient results.

Efficacy is critical to the *transference* of capability to the pbc. Over time, the coaching interaction must create added ability in the pbc to become self-correcting and self-directed. Being able to obsolete the pc—from more direct to facilitating and supportive--is critical to the efficacy of the coach approach. In some cases this obsolescence occurs rapidly, in more complex situations it takes more time and resources. *Coaching is always a longitudinal intervention!*

Accountability is about who says go and who says stop and when. The scope of work defines these issues clearly at the outset and creates the metrics needed for the coaching relationship to either end or morph to a new level with a new *agreement*. It is crucial to establish measurements for the efficacy of the coaching intervention, either directly or indirectly and track them!

These four criteria are crucial to establishing effective coaching programs that are generative to individuals and organizations. *Do not tread lightly here.* Most coaching approaches fail due to one of these criteria not being defined at the beginning. Without an effective coaching agreement either implicit or explicit, the order of things will always degenerate in the face of Model I governance.

The most efficient way to manage scope and scale in a coaching system or interaction is to clearly define it at the outset. The appropriate resources must be outlined and a commitment made to interface and integrate the coaching system or interaction with other personal and organizational systems. Do it right up front and save everyone the lost time and problems of trying to fix it later on when it breaks down due to unclear objectives (ambiguity).

Environment for Coaching Success

Probably, the most important thing an executive staff can do when approaching a coaching system design is to research and develop those factors that contribute to coaching success. While most interventions are launched out of business necessity and require rapid implementation, coaching should only be introduced into an organization after careful planning and usually as a pilot project.

If you use the CIM model to develop the coaching system—openings, possibilities, plans, outcomes (scenarios) and action, in that order—and follow some simple guidelines, you will meet with success.

Creating Organizational Slack

Slack is referred to as the extra time and resources available to people in the organization. With downsizing and rightsizing and all of the reengineering that *has* to be done over time, we engineer out the *organizational slack.* This is certainly efficient and often drives short-term success, however, the organization of the future is going to contain a significant number of knowledge workers—if not already—and slack is required for learning and development as a matter of course.

> *Just as much emphasis should be placed on our ability to get better at what we do versus what we are capable of doing presently! Covey stated it as production versus productive capacity.*

Being able to get away from required meetings, deadlines and imposed agendas is going to be critical to organizational "fleet-footedness" in the future. This adeptness at the dance will be crucial to taking leadership positions in the marketspace as well as finding ways to dynamically balance personal lives.

> *Oh, you mean a person has a life outside of business? Well, in the future, life and learning are going to become integral components of the organizations commitment to success and well-being.*

Let us think about this.

If people can work longer periods of time in flow, the efficiency lost by increasing slack will more than pay off in terms of ROI. Learning and dynamically balancing personal life issues can be facilitated with the coaching system that leads directly to higher energy, innovation, more flow opportunities and higher levels of function and satisfaction.

However, to create and support coaching, the organizational leadership must understand slack and how to create it for people. *This is no easy task.* The executive is bound by ROI in many cases, so talking about creating time and resources for people to learn, which costs money in an organization, is not going to be an easy sell. On the other hand, if your focus is on the now, near and far vision of your organization, then you will find a way. [Even shareholders will begin to see the benefit of increasing productive capacity over time, rather than just riding a wave of production!]

The difficult part about slack is creating and maintaining it without letting loose the reins of the organization so far that gross inefficiency develops in response to poorly constructed standards and systems.

[Creating slack will quickly identify your organization's governing values!]

The benefits of slack—now—create opportunities for development of level II coaching in organizations (Model II) values and double loop learning to occur, which all require time for reflective learning.

As in all development paths there is almost an immediate drop-off in productivity. However, the resulting surge can be seen quickly if the appropriate measurements are in place at the outset before slack and coaching systems are created in the system. These are measurements that occur in the quadrant (balanced scorecard) of innovation and customer service (external) efficiencies.

It would be a good idea for anyone implementing a coaching system to find some way to measure, beforehand, the intangible effects of satisfaction—employee and customer—and innovation. These effects will not appear to be affected immediately but in the near and far terms, the effects of a well-designed coaching system will show up and be measurable!

Back to slack.

Slack is required for the reflective nature of double loop learning. It is required for effective coaching, as the work done as a result of coaching often requires the pc and the pbc to review and reflect on the issues at hand. We must have some time to do this without feeling that every single moment of our days are spoken for in advance and we end up going through a bunch of motion under the guise of development!

In some cases, the organization will have to mandate slack as some people will not be able to take the necessary time to do the reflective part of the work to achieve double loop learning, just as some people will not seek coaching relationships on their own.

[Part of this is due to conditioning and part to nature.]

When we understand structure and how it affects people, the executive must *structure* the slack and coaching interactions in order for them to occur within the system. An understanding of slack is critical to understand and to value, in order to create an environment of coaching success.

Principles not Recipes

There is a tendency especially when coaches are just beginning to move from something—managing, leading, facilitating, etc—to coaching, to need recipes and techniques rather than being guided by the deep intuitive "right doing" they sense coming up from within them in response to right action. To learn to trust these feelings takes time. Lacking experience with coaching, and in lieu of that inner trust built through practice, new and inexperienced coaches resort to the *tried and true* formulas.

When this happens, we often get *recipe coaching*. What I mean by this type of system is that we assemble all the necessary ingredients, follow the directions and wait for the results after an incubation (cooking) time.

While this type of coaching can work, it is also limiting because the coach must rely on their being round pegs and round holes! In most organizations, we have lots of round pegs and lots of square holes. When things do not fit too well, resistance increases dramatically, and we push a little harder. When resistance increases, coaching becomes full of effort, mistrust and misunderstanding. Frequently, a person coaching, or even an inexperienced coach will move toward *safe ground*—out of dialog—into assessment.

Assessments can be a wonderful tool for catalyzing openings and awareness, but when used in recipe coaching they can short-circuit the effects of the extraordinary results some claim to pursue through coaching interactions.

*Extraordinary results

Extraordinary results come from an attempt to appease the bean counters and bottom line people. And while we had better find some way to do that very thing, another avenue other than a panacea of *extraordinary* results will lead to greater indirect success. Anyone who has coached for a period of time--especially concerning adult development and transformation--knows that it occurs over time, is unpredictable and at best, anything but extraordinary.

While pundits claim they want extraordinary results, I find that is too great of an expectation for most coaching programs.

[While this may be a bad example, I think you can see the metaphor. In sports, only one team wins at the end, does that mean that all the rest were less than extraordinary?]

Moving from one level of development to another—a true shift in the nature of profound change—is often non-linear at best. It often occurs, when we least expect it, and although coaching provides the fuel for this shift, it does not fully take hold on behavior—not alone processes, practices and systems, for sometime. Even when one is able to shift beliefs significantly, it takes time to rebuild our behavior, because behavior is ingrained and highly unconscious.

We find ourselves moving from unconscious behavior to conscious behavior, back to unconscious behavior until awareness helps us through conscious behavior to recondition or replace those active unconscious scripts. And this is certainly extraordinary but difficult at times to directly relate cause and effect—a moniker of complexity.

With that admonition, it is important to separate our development from extraordinary results. The organization has needs, therefore in responding to those needs there is a tendency to overlook the human needs and time differentials in adult development towards achieving measurable results. This tendency is often fed by recipe coaching or assembly line training and coaching, coupled as an end all to learning.

We run everyone through the same process expecting similar results in terms of their developmental levels—their contextual frames. Yet, we have to realize that people respond to the recipe differently and on their own time and gratification sequence. The overarching need for people to develop from the organization's point of view becomes the driving force as recipe after recipe is regurgitated through the business system.

Coaching allows us to respond to differences in people on their own time and development sequences, helping to discover, explore and surface opportunities for development. Yet, what is normally the case, is that the *program/recipe* is *sold* to skeptical decision makers in terms of extraordinary results, and when they do not happen as a direct effect of the intervention, the program is discontinued, and in rolls the next *fix*—looking for the same extraordinary results.

> *Recipe coaching will damage the integrity and effectiveness of the coaching system.*

If we review carefully our commitment to establish coaching as a system, we can then move beyond the next, best recipe and intervention requirement. We can *structure* the coaching system to be integrated throughout the organization in a manner that removes the need for recipes. As a result, effectiveness will emerge from the conversations and interactions and will cause the system to change and adapt over time—achieving what some may call extraordinary results. COACHING IS NOT A QUICK FIX!!

Summary

A coaching interaction cannot follow a recipe. It can, however, be guided by principles that have been accepted as being universally relevant to natural organization. The same set of ingredients used with people in one case does not mean you will get the same outcome every time. If you use principles, the chances of reaching positive and effective outcomes are highly probable.

Using the COACH2 Model evokes the use of clear principles and not a recipe for coaching. The absolute best outcome is one that is co-generated from the process of effective coaching. It stands the highest probability of providing a high degree of *intrinsic motivation* toward commitment and right action. Understanding the central caveat that people are different, and as a result will respond differently to coaching, yields our best chance for positive outcomes for the person and the organization—concurrently.

Establishing, at the outset, clear guidelines of the coaching system or interaction outcomes is the best predictor of collective and organizational success. Take the time to dialogue about:

- Capability
- Opportunity
- Efficacy
- Accountability

Learn how extraordinary results can set the system up for failure and at the same time, *recognize the need for bottom line efficacy* of the coach approach. It is margin before mission, and at the same time mission before margin, a true organizational paradox. However, this paradox can be *managed* through a coach approach that is well thought out and integrated into the business systems of the organization.

Chapter 13

In organizational change, the boundaries between coach and player blur. Leaders must give as well as receive high quality help. One way to do this is to establish a cadre of coaches in which people can learn how to coach by helping others.

The Dance of Change, Senge, et al.

Levels of Coaching in Organizations

There are a number of complex circumstances surrounding the implementation of a coaching system in an organization. In most cases, the delivery of coaching in coaching interactions will be governed by many interdependent factors.

To establish a background for the different levels of coaching in an organization, we need to consider the aspects of situation and context.

There are a number of ways we can compare similarities between coaching and leadership. In leadership we see various *levels* of leadership, exampled by Stephen Covey's personal, interpersonal, managerial and organizational levels of effectiveness, or as in THE DANCE OF CHANGE with Senge, et al: local, network or executive.

In either case and in the case of levels we use in this book, what is being discussed are the same but different aspects of leadership and coaching at various levels and the role that these levels play in an organizational system.

Situational Leadership & Coaching

Hersey and Blanchard adapted a contingency theory of leadership that attempted to account for the different situations in which leaders find themselves in when leading. The situational aspects of this model concerned the maturity levels of the followers and the division of leadership approaches into four basic categories of leadership identifying the level of concern for task or relationship in each level.

- Telling
- Selling
- Participating
- Delegating

I point your attention to this model in order to create a basic reasoning for the coach system approach. It will depend on a number of factors that were also present in the determination of the Situational Leadership Model and is a good point of demarcation for the coaching approach in organizations. Hersey and Blanchard looked at three basic criteria for setting the standards of the leadership level with the maturity of followers:

- Achievement motivation of people involved
- Willingness to take on responsibility
- Amount of education and/or experience

Now, let us contrast these points from Situational Leadership with what noted author and organizational poet David Whyte indicated were the four central themes for personal and organizational well-being:

- Adaptability
- Vitality

- Passion
- Willingness to go the extra mile

In Whyte's version of organizational capability, the four factors above link all other actions of people and organizations into a framework of *conversational* effectiveness. What becomes obvious across any research or any theme, is that personal and organizational effectiveness stems from being able to perform, change and transform—proactively, as Covey states in one of his *seven habits*.

In the coaching approach it is sometimes easier to refer to the level of maturity--as does the Situational Leadership Model—as the level of sophistication a person being coached has in the context of the coaching interaction. Sophistication leads us to take into consideration certain aspects that also include *system* capability.

We have to remember Deming's admonition that performance is not always directly a result of just individual effort, but a number of interacting system components—often out of the direct control of the individual.

In fact, I believe Deming was reported to have said that if there was a problem with performance, it was most likely in the system rather than with the individual.

In view of your coaching approach, some people will be acclimated to very sophisticated human resource (HR) systems while others will not understand what the word means. As coaching becomes a choice for intervention—later, system integration--in organizations, the level of sophistication surrounding the coaching interaction will influence the coaching approach to performance, change and transformation.

Again, if we review the Hersey-Blanchard Model, we find four types of leadership based on the task-relationship dichotomy and level of maturity in followers. If we look at the issues from a coaching approach perspective, we find that the *level of sophistication* will put more or less weight on the coach to carry more of the administrative function during the coaching interaction—as it does in the situational leadership model.

This direction will come from *content versus a process perspective.* At some levels of the organization, development will be an indirect result because the focus will be on single-loop learning and performance, which is heavily content oriented. It is important to understand there is a place in coaching for all three: performance, change *and transformation at all levels of coaching.* However, the focus may be more direct on specific performance, change or transformation as sophistication increases in the pbc and the system. For example, a line manager may focus directly on performance and an executive coach may focus directly on transformation with the other forms of learning present, but indirect.

In many organizations, the HR system will setup and support the coaching system. This higher level of organizational sophistication will allow the person coaching (pc) to be less of a generalist (manager) and focus more on developing specific coaching KSAs while leaving the administrative details to the support system.

Since many of the coaching approaches are going to be situational I have attempted, in the following paragraphs, to describe them contextually, in terms of organizational needs and capabilities.

Coaching Levels

It is necessary to discuss the different levels in the coach approach. Whether we coach one person or create a coaching system there are certain aspects of the coaching approach that change when we design coaching systems versus a single coaching interaction. The real problem I see in practice today is people trying to implement *a one-size fits all approach* to all situational needs. While it is true we can use the same methodology, we can't use the same expectations, and that is the key—*expectations!*

Since the basic purpose of this book is to provide both the theory and practice of coaching in organizations, it becomes important to discuss coaching system design in organizations. These design decisions will become more and more important as coaching evolves from the individual interaction to a coaching system of interdependent interactions--integrated throughout the organization to create, sustain and evolve structural and cultural change.

The levels are designed as a progression in terms of how we move from a single interaction level to an integrated system of interactions that may take place, simultaneously, and in an interrelated fashion throughout an organization. In the same way that we concurrently view local, network and executive leadership in a change initiative as described by Senge et al, in The Dance of Change, we need to influence each level in the coaching system with relevance and timing of the organizational mission and required business results to leverage organizational effectiveness.

Coaching & Holograms

Something interesting to add here is that complexity has a way of creating many forms of interaction—often unrelated in terms of how each either builds or includes the other form. In a holographic system, each fractal (part) of the system contains all the elements of the system at large. Without making this concept anymore complex than it already is, please consider that the entire COACH2 Model is designed to scale up or down to create a methodology that can be holographic in nature, allowing each level of sophistication to scale up and down as needed in the interaction using the same methodology.

In other words, people using the model at the line level will use the same basic components that senior executives will use at the executive level. In this way, the various forms of the organization can be interrelated and integrated to create tracks of improvement and sophistication that are founded on and built on the same methodology. Each coaching interaction will be a fractal of the entire coaching system. Over time, this will be critical to remember as we use the coaching approach in organizations to sustain and complement organizational change that is not related directly to one-to-one coaching, e.g. future search, open space, appreciative inquiry, to name a few of the large system intervention tools used in organizational development.

It is also critical to remember that not all levels of the organization are on the same level of sophistication. Nor do they have the same needs. By creating a coaching methodology that is simple enough to use at prime levels and yet sophisticated enough to use at the higher levels of function, the organization gains synergy as people are able to move on and off the coaching superhighway at off ramps that are conducive to their own growth and developmental needs.

Each of these levels will need to be supported and integrated before moving to the next level in a process of coaching evolution towards structural adaptation and evolution. With the need to continuously evolve organizational structure to meet adapting environmental demands, coaching systems will have to evolve and change constantly--still maintaining the value of the individual interaction and connecting to the management/leadership system at large.

We will see a microcosm of individual change enfolded within organizational change--both occurring at differing rates and efficacies, yet connected and interdependent. The level of the coaching system in practice will determine the support for and capability of the organization to accomplish broad change and *improving capability* through these interconnected coaching interactions.

If left to their own design (to self-organize), the *edge* of the organization may appear to be blurred, as individual changes will be accomplished at different velocities. This may create limiting forces when integrated and related to organizational learning velocity as a whole. In some cases, this may be desired, in others, not so.

A coaching system must be designed, integrated and supported unilaterally across the organization for the organization change velocity and adaptability to increase. If we are able to integrate the micro-change with macro-change needs, then environmental demands will be met with higher degrees of success. The conditions Whyte referred to as *adaptability, vitality, passion and willingness to go the extra mile* will be in clear evidence.

LEVEL 0

At this level, no coaching is being done, nor is there any experience with coaching in the organization as a whole, therefore, the coaching approach may be the only intervention selected and it must stand on its own without support.

This is often the case when individuals are coached outside the organization or where the organization is a company of one. The pc and person being coached (pbc) are the system. All interaction in this level takes place between the pc and pbc. All evaluation of the coaching interaction is done between the pc and pbc, and all decisions made about whether the coaching interaction/relationship is a success is contained within this single relationship—single set of values.

As I write in 1999, most professional coaching, as we know it, is being done at this level. However, what I predict is that we will see an escalation in further movement among more sophisticated coaching levels, where more than one person is determining the success and further deployment of coaching in the organization and multiple value-sets are in vogue.

Executive coaching is usually done at level 0 and while the executive may be coached and supported by the business system, it is often the executive—his/her performance or success--that determines the efficacy of the coaching interaction. The actions of the executive will determine movement to adopt further levels in the organization in terms of structural change and the degrees of coaching intervention.

This level is not characteristic of specific values, as are the levels 1-3. In the case of individual coaching interactions, all levels of value are discussed and integrated into the interaction—not imposed by another person or system in *charge*. In level 0, the pbc is in charge, as is the case with all

1 to1 interactions. The level of values moves independent of the organization's commitment to structural change--it has to.

As more and more people reach higher levels individually, the organization will change as more and more people model higher levels of learning. This is consistent with the action science orientation promoted by Argyris containing Model I values and Model II values.

David Whyte also put it into context, in terms of his admonition that *no one has to change, but they have to have the conversation and change occurs from that conversation.*

Yet, it is clear that to compare the individual interaction as it moves with its own velocity with the often separate but related organizational change velocity—can, at times, be fool-hearty.

> *Individuals will respond differently to individual coaching both as influenced by the organization and towards influencing the organization.*

In order to begin system-wide structural change, level 1 will be reached by bringing into the organization coaching KSAs learned by members at level 0. Focusing on level 1 or (Model I) values, performance will be enhanced where possible and the stage will be set to integrate level 2 (Model II) values into the organization with the support system in place to sustain the required structural change.

> *A critical factor in organizational coaching success is the consideration of both the needs of the system and the needs of the person being coached concurrently. In that regard, we find ourselves truly in an organizational paradox of sorts as we consider that both the organization and the pbc must perform now as well as long term. This is why it becomes important to*

adopt the vernacular of now, near and far vision and how each of these pertains to a different set of circumstances that must all be addressed by the coaching system!

Level 0 Critical Issues

- Coaching is not introduced to the organization
- Coaching is being used as a management tool
- Coaching influences executives and executives influence the organization as a result
- Values at level 0 belong to the individual
- The focus of the coaching can be performance, change and transformation
- A coaching system does not exist in the organization
- Coaching is isolated from the organization
- *Expectations of coaching are indirect, geared toward improving individual performance, change and transformation, or repairing people.*

LEVEL 1

The nature of the practice will be different at different stages of learning. During the early stages, you should be able to make errors without a high cost to you or to the organization.

Chris Argyris, <u>The Executive Mind and Double Loop Learning</u>, Org Dynamics, Autumn 1982

At the basic level of a coaching interaction, organizations will seek to create immediate gains—now-- with coaching interventions. Since coaching—like every other investment--must contribute something to the bottom line in order to be continued, the coaching interaction in this type of situation will have to be carefully structured in order to survive.

One strategy in this particular situation will be to introduce coaching KSAs at the level of line manager and to focus on directly influencing unit or process performance through performance change with single loop learning.

However, this is not common as coaching is see as something reserved for the elite. Usually, organizations begin coaching at the top levels hoping for a trickle-down or *influence effect.* We coach the top because they have more *effect* on the organizations decisions, yet, in my view, this is typical of a backwards intervention and typical of traditional mechanical thinking.

It would seem we should introduce coaching at the line levels where the interaction at the customer interface is occurring, rather than two or three, perhaps four or five levels above, where the benefits of changing from advocacy to inquiry and resolving personal and organizational defensive patterns affect our customers?

Yet, very little justification can be made to spend hundreds of thousands of dollars on the troops, when executives are in *charge!* And that is the key behavior to notice, that is, who is in charge, the executives or the customer?

[Author retreats quietly from soapbox.]

If by some rare opportunity, the organization implements a coaching initiative either simultaneously at all levels in the organization, or at the customer interface, the single loop learning around performance can often provide the leverage for double loop learning to be launched into an organization--a much more sophisticated approach—requiring *more resources* and significant organizational slack. This can and should be done on a pilot basis, but the thrust should not be only at the executive level, but at all levels in an effort to integrate the structural change required.

Back to Level 1

In this introductory level there are two factors that need to be kept in mind. One is that coaching must immediately create an impact, and two, is that coaching in level 1 should create an opening for coaching in level 2—double loop learning. A strong foundation of interaction, along with *transparent* system sophistication must accompany movement to level 2 where the coaching interaction seeks long term structural and cultural change success through double loop learning.

Again, in my view, the concept of now, near and far vision makes the most sense as we must segment the future in terms of possibilities and capabilities.

One of the difficulties in designing a coaching system is that people are different. What this means is that people will respond to coaching--over time--differently. In some cases, people will be open and receptive to change. However, if the organizational culture is closed and mechanical with many personal and organizational defensive patterns--those organizational patterns will have permeated individuals--people will respond to the coaching intervention with personal defensive patterns according to those demonstrated by organizational norms.

Many coaches are approaching these kinds of organizations without a proper understanding of the ingrained dynamics of a dysfunctional organization. Coaching is not a panacea, nor it is going to be the answer to poor and dysfunctional structure. In my opinion, effective coaching--at times--may fragment the current structure (especially if it is primarily Model I) as the various levels of difference in the organization respond differently under coaching creating more questions than the organization has answers for in terms of why are we doing this, when we could be doing that more efficiently. Once people begin the journey to testing assumptions in Model II, all hell can break loose!

When a coach approach is being considered in an organization, adequate time should be taken to examine the current organizational situation. If we look carefully at the CIM, we can use the process to evaluate the potential openings, possibilities, plans, outcomes and action required in order to implement a coaching system in the organization.

Level 1 Critical Issues

- Coaching is systematized in the organization
- Coaching is designed to increase performance
- Coaching performance leads to change
- Coaching lays the groundwork for transformation to Model II
- Coaching is designed to get results in single loop learning NOW.
- Coaching is supported by other change initiatives and training
- Coaching has created a path of coaching evolution
- Coaching is being integrated into other structural systems

- Coaching is facilitating the openings for level 2 coaching
- *Expectations of coaching are centered in performance*

LEVEL 2

Creating the Open Double Loop

No, it is not an acrobatic maneuver but it sounds like one. Many learning loops are closed. In level 0, coaching in an organization, the benefits of executive or personal coaching are often closed and the effects of coaching are distilled through leadership—not at all a bad thing—but it is diluted through lack of system integration. Argyris refers to a condition where the loop is closed as *self-sealing*.

In level 2, coaching systems, we find support from other systems for the coaching interaction to permeate the entire organization, at every level—therefore creating the *open loop*. Perhaps an example would be good here. If we integrate tightly the financial system, human resources, customer service, leadership and rewards systems with coaching, then each interaction that takes place would have almost a direct effect on another system's capacity for improvement.

Lowering personal defensive patterns leads to better levels of collaboration, opening doors to innovative change across boundaries. In effect, we are deliberately promoting conversations across many communities of practice and out of that, comes change. It lies true to course that as personal defensive patterns change so follows the change in organizational defensive patterns and vice versa. The organization begins to move as a whole—although fractally—to higher function. It all sounds so simple? It is, IF and a big

IF, we allow conversation and interaction to carry the weight of the change! If we connect the islands of knowledge and create conversations across boundaries, then we will in effect, spread the weight of change across a broader area of the organization—this can be good and bad if we are structurally unprepared for the degree of chaos created through this destabilizing force of conversation. Can too much innovation be bad?

In level 1 we gain a feel for how coaching KSAs have been introduced, adopted and integrated into organization. There is an ongoing program of support for coaching, and managers at every level are being supported to integrate single loop performance throughout the organization. At this level, it becomes necessary to introduce movement to "Model II" concepts throughout the organization. In levels 0 and 1, we have introduced coaching interactions and Model I learning as a <u>now</u> benefit. [Remember in Level 0, individuals and not the organization is being coached—using all aspects of learning, performance, change and transformation.]

[A good example of what I mean by this level of new learning is described in Appendix E under action science. Several authors, researchers and practitioners led by Chris Argyris have developed an "Action Science" methodology that seeks to create organizational learning around double loop learning systems. The action science research is well summarized in Appendix E by Tobias Brown.]

Double loop learning arose out of a systems thinking vernacular that identifies how people and organizations learn. In the level 2 coaching approach, it is necessary to strategically introduce "Model 2" values to the entire organization and support that movement in structure with individual coaching interactions designed to bring each individual to these practices.

The following comparison illustrates the difference between Model I and Model II values according to Action Science parameters and the several ways in which a coaching system can bring these values and theories of action to the personal and organizational level.

The diagram is taken from:

> Chris Argyris, <u>The Executive Mind and Double Loop Learning</u>, Org Dynamics, Autumn 1982

Model I Theory-in-Use

Governing Variables -

- Control the purpose of the meeting or encounter
- Maximize winning and minimize losing
- Suppress negative feelings
- Be rational.

Action Strategies -

- Advocate your position in order to be in control and win
- Unilaterally save face—your own and others

Consequences -

- Miscommunication
- Self-fulfilling prophecies
- Self-sealing processes
- Escalating Error

Model II Theory-in-Use

Governing Variables -

- Valid (validatable) information.
- Free and informed choice for all concerned.
- Internal commitment to the choice

Action Strategies -

- Advocate your position
- Combine with inquiry and public testing
- Minimize unilateral face saving

Consequences -

- Reduction of self-fulling, self-sealing, error-escalating processes
- Effective problem solving

In a coaching system that moves organizationally from level 1 to level 2, it becomes important to provide support and integration of the coaching system in order to leverage the change that will occur as a result of this *movement*. The movement from a performance-based level 1 to a deep change level 2 requires a number of key variables to be in place:

- Slack
- Blameless error
- Openness
- System support
- System integration

People will not respond the same to these central changes in structure, therefore, it will become the responsibility of an integration between other organizational systems and the coaching system to support individual differences and non-linear change during the structural changes created from level 1 to level 2. These can be severe and chaotic if not led.

It is also important to remember that coaching alone will not provide the structural support required for sustaining the organizational change to Model II or Level 2 systems. It must be integrated with all management systems in order to provide the individual capability required to mitigate the differences in response among the organization to the new structure.

Level 2 Critical Issues

- Coaching is integrated into the organization
- Increasing performance and the ability to perform is the goal of the coaching system.
- Creating a pro-activity towards change through coaching is enabled
- Coaching is directed through performance (now) to changing values (near) from Model I to Model II
- Incremental improvements are matter of course; real focus is on increasing innovative responses to challenges
- Coaching is fostering authority to the individual and people are becoming self-correcting and self-led
- The systems of change are integrated deeply into the organization
- People are their own authorities as quality information flows freely

- New people are sought for their predisposition to Model II governance in recruiting and promotion
- *Expectations of everybody being on board are high and expected.*

LEVEL 3

Far Vision

At this level in the organization, all systems including management, coaching and leadership are integrated—systems integrity is a key enabling factor for adaptability in *zero time*. Model II values promote fast adaptation in the organization and new employees are attracted, effortlessly selected and integrated into the system as all systems support the Model II learning system values from beginning to end. The coaching system has integrated organizational learning into individual coaching interactions. As a result, it spins off high function and operational leverage in the organization.

While the organization may not be perfect in terms of its responses to the environment, it will be very quick to adapt, often in *negative or zero time* because the information about the customer of its customers is known and studied. Managers have access to and continuously learn additional coaching KSAs, integrating them into the daily interactions they have with subordinates. Single loop learning is guided by double loop learning as more and more work is evidence of an examination of how things are getting done and why.

Organizational right action is occurring regularly from individual interactions that permeate the right action of the organization. Continuous testing of the basis for right action is occurring respectfully within the organization.

Utopia or Pollyanna?

It is often premature to expose the constructs of Level 3 coaching systems before one has experience with coaching, so if you are reading this and do not have the slightest clue of how to get from where you are to here, please understand that it takes time to move to an understanding of this level of *organizational consciousness.*

For those of you who are interested in moving to more advanced levels of understanding of consciousness and how unified many of the theories are becoming in terms of how development, consciousness, and change towards a sustainable future are becoming, I encourage you to read the essay in Appendix J. Here is an excerpt of an email message from Richard Brodie (Author of Virus of the Mind and developer of Microsoft Word) to a mailing list explaining his three levels of consciousness:

Levels of Consciousness

> "**Level 1** of consciousness is instinctual and animalistic. Level-1 operators do not live by conscious philosophy. Abstractions such as economics and physics are foreign to them. They live with the hand they were dealt, not making much use of learned philosophy.
>
> **Level 2**, where most educated people operate, makes use of conceptual tools to map out life and plan results for the future. Religions, the scientific method, and all academic learning are examples of Level-2 structures. In Level 2, one's picture of the world gets clearer and clearer. Often people will not break through to Level 3 unless and until they have a life experience that

invalidates and shatters their world-view.

Level 3 is characterized by the ability to flex your *meme-space* on the fly--to use multiple models depending upon your purpose and priorities. It's possible to gain an intellectual understanding of what this means from Level 2, but probably not possible to really feel the impact of the difference in life experience. The Level 3 mind has a great capacity to hold dissonant, contradictory beliefs. (Einstein was said to have this ability.)"

After a couple of years of looking at this message, I noticed how these three levels (fully described in Appendix J) are germane to single loop, double loop and *triple loop*--described by Hargrove in *MASTERFUL COACHING*--learning. We can see how the levels of coaching in an organization fall into similar patterns not unlike these levels of consciousness described by Brodie above. This patterning occurred naturally as we attempted to explain the similarity in development between personal and organizational systems.

I believe that an organization can have a consciousness, perhaps not in the same way we think of individual consciousness does by *being aware of itself*, yet, in my view, the collective consciousness of individuals creates the ability for organizations to behave independently of any one person.

As organizational consciousness moves to higher and higher function through the development of individual function, we approach a synergy with each other that is only available to us in and through organization.

And in my opinion, this is evidenced by the ability or capacity of people to perform as a group in a manner that is NOT the sum of their parts. Having experienced this at times in my athletic career and in special project teams where things *just clicked*, I am often struck by the ability of others to be in unison and behave at a higher level of synergy and function—*at level 3*? Perhaps a study of championship teams and effective workgroups would yield a similar conclusion?

What is even more interesting is the adult development theory by Kegan, et al being applied by Catherine Fitzgerald, Robert Goodman and others to executive coaching. At the outset, it would appear that my reference to organizational consciousness is in keeping with the level of consciousness seen in adult development theory. I think they parallel each other sufficiently enough that they can coexist within a personal and organizational framework simultaneously at different levels—*the key being to bring into alignment higher levels of personal consciousness towards higher levels of organizational consciousness in practice to meet environmental demands.*

I admit not being able to fill in many of the blanks, but to perhaps to stimulate a dialogue about these concepts among various types of practitioners in an effort to advance what could be a unified theory of personal and organizational consciousness surrounding development. This is a fertile area for observation and growth in coaching!

Obviously, the coaching interaction, personally and organizationally, provides the medium for this alignment and development. While it may appear to some that these highly *personal* issues have no place in an organizational environment, I think you will find more and more evidence to the contrary as we seek what David Whyte referred to as personal and organizational *adaptability, vitality, passion and willingness to go the extra mile.* While this book is not the forum for further discussion into the alignment of personal and organizational consciousness, the opening does appear to exist.

Level 3 critical issues are:

- Observation of Model II governing variables in force
- Innovative inertia woven into all responses
- Higher levels of individual harmony
- Development occurring as a matter of course
- Responses to demands efficiently in zero time
- People are self-generating and self-authoring
- The organization moves *as one*
- The quantum leap is a regular exercise
- The organization understands level of development and acts accordingly to leverage these factors to the benefit of the individual and consequently the organization
- *Expectations have been replaced by knowing*

Summary

In some cases, the movement of coaching interactions in conjunction with right action is in concert with individual and organizational consciousness. Clearly, the coaching interaction provides the forum and the *appreciative methodology* to align and advance consciousness, individually and collectively over time.

It is this alignment in consciousness and development that creates the opportunity for well-being, purpose, competence and awareness to each one's need. We design the coaching system to reflect these individual and organizational needs and concerns. Concurrently, we must also create a dynamic balance between performance, change and transformation-between levels 1, 2 and 3—now, near term and far off. All levels will occur simultaneously in the organization, often in parallel dimensions. The organization will change from the inside out and from the outside in—two critical dimensions added by an organizational coaching system.

Each individual change will affect the organization's change velocity. In the DANCE OF CHANGE by Senge, et al it was reported that if during an organizational change you can change 20% of the people, you could, over time, modify the organizational structure.

Coaching is precisely the methodology to promote the structural change that is required of our modern day, turbulent environments, in both individuals and organizations.

Understanding that you will NOT want to embark upon a level 3 intervention without first laying solid ground with levels 1 and 2 is the critical issue. To integrate all management systems before creating level 2 and 3 expectations remains the most important issue in an organizational coaching approach.

Chapter 14

> *"Every manager is primarily concerned with generating and maintaining a network of conversations for action—conversations in which requests and commitments lead to successful completion of work."*
>
> *Terry Winograd and Fernando Flores, Understanding Computers and Cognition*

Structure and The Coaching Interaction

In this chapter, I want to give you my ideas on structure in the coaching interaction between the person coaching (pc) and the person being coached (pbc).

[Please note this is called <u>structure</u>, and it should not be confused with organizational structure]

There seems to be an impetus—coming from instructional design or pedagogy—on creating a linear or rigid structure for the interaction between the pc/pbc.

I think, in the beginning, it is probably necessary for the pc to adopt a simple set of guidelines in order to move the interaction to the commitment stage, however, in practice—in respect of differences—*structure is emergent*. What do I mean? If you know anything about sales, you would have seen the sales process divided into structural bits, however, most good salespeople—those who are successful in selling—do not follow a *set procedure* but rather find ways to guide the interaction in response to their expertise in surfacing client needs.

In speaking, another example of structure is: "tell 'em what you're gonna tell 'em; tell 'em; and then tell 'em what you told 'em." In the COACH2 Model, we use only connect, clarify and commit, as structure. Why? Because coaching although based in science, is an art. While painters and artists do have structure in their work, their best work—emerges through intention towards outcomes and so does coaching. It is important to keep in mind the sub process of the COACH2 Model:

Coaching Interaction Model (CIM)

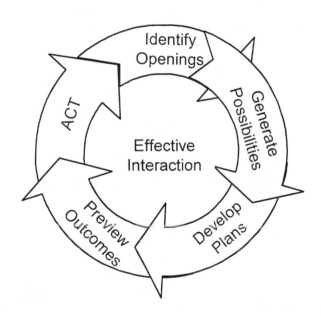

OPPOA
- Openings
- Possibilities
- Plans
- Outcomes
- Action

Please note that this is NOT a linear structure. You can, at anytime move directly to commitment to action and you should, if the opening dictates that emergent possibility. The coaching interaction need not take all day; in fact, it could take less than 1 minute. Here is a simple example:

[Notice how the interaction emerges and the underlying structure of Connect, Clarify and Commit. Also, take note of how the sub-process enfolds and emerges for the pc/pbc interaction]

Pc: (passing pbc in hall): Hi John

Pbc: Hi Janet

Pc: What's new?

Pbc: Our team is stuck on getting our latest software release done in time…

Pc: What's happening…?

Pbc: We have two developers at each other's throats and I have been trying to coach them…

Pc: Any luck?

Pbc: Not much, they hate each other…

Pc: Do they realize what's at stake?

Pbc: Apparently not, they are insisting on doing things only one way.

Pc: Wow, I guess everyone will suffer…

Pbc: Hmmm. I guess you're right, I wonder what would happen if I set up a meeting with the team…

Pc: I thought you had regular meetings?

Pbc: No, I mean a meeting where we just tried to surface the problems between these two, perhaps a dialogue where everyone could talk about what is going to happen if we let these two keep at odds…you know, what no one wants to talk about—the undiscussables!

Pc: How soon will you try to do it…?

Pbc: Tomorrow!

Pc: Good Luck, I hope everything works out.

Pbc: I'll let you know, thanks Janet.

Pc: See you John.

Of course, the interaction was simple but I think you can see every element of the COACH2 Model guiding the sub process along the way.

There was no real attempt by the pc to "fix" the problem, only to stay in process and use the right delivery method at the right time. Can you see how feedback, ideas, questions and challenges moved the interaction?

If not, just go back and reread this simple exchange. The real issue is that it was real and it happened. The names have been changed to protect the innocent.

Coaching as an Emergent Structure

What creates opportunity for the pc is having at their disposal the coaching KSAs so that the coaching interaction can emerge without feeling processed! The worst possible thing to do is to try to manage a process such as coaching in a linear fashion. It could have worked, perhaps, between two people who were very connected and in very similar cognitive patterns, but anytime the patterns are different, the linear process will create resistance to the effortless flow of what feels right. If the goal of the interaction is right action then the COACH2 Model will facilitate that happening in an emergent conversation or interaction.

The coaching KSAs such as observing, listening, discerning, modeling and delivery will all emerge at the right time as long as the focus is on the pbc with the intention of the outcomes clearly in the minds of both pc and pbc. What is needed will *become* apparent at the appropriate time based on your level of coaching development. Often, two different people coaching will arrive at right action through dissimilar paths. This does not make either right or wrong but only tells us that meaning making is different in each case. In fact, everybody's right, and if you don't believe me, just ask someone. <grin>

Summary

All of the issues discussed in differences will interact to create different meaning for different people at different moments in time. What is important to understand is that allowing flexibility in process will be okay in terms of right action.

People can arrive at the same place at different times and through different means. The arrival demonstrates there is not only one right way to accomplish these ends. *The less structure framing an emergent process, the better.* If we become rule and procedural bound, we will spend too much time worrying about the rules of structure and not enough time using our natural coaching KSAs.

This is the key. Organizationally, we must create the environment and opportunity for the coaching KSAs to become natural through exposure, learning, experience and practice. These KSAs do not come easy at first, especially if the person coaching is new to the coaching KSAs— *and is still dancing with the person who brought them to the dance!*

Over time and with practice, each of these KSAs will find a natural fit in a person coaching and contribute to the emergent process of the coaching interaction. Structure is critical to the coaching interaction, but the emergent structure will always be more important than defining a structure with too many rules and procedures.

I would caution you again that an *opening* creates the opportunity for successful interaction. Without it, the interaction will be filled with resistance and effort. The personal defensive patterns that the pbc has been conditioned to use in the face of threat or coersion will keep the pc from *connecting with* the pbc.

When an opening is present, the pc can dance with the pbc in order to surface the right action known by the pbc. An opening, a connection is more important than structure. The rest will emerge as long as the focus is on the pbc and not the agenda of the pc.

Think: connection, clarification, commitment to right action.

Chapter 15

"Change just 20% of the people in your organization and the structure of the organization will change..."

Bill O'Brien, quoted in The Dance of Change

Creating a CoachSystem™

The primary aim or purpose of this book is to provide the methodology for creating a CoachSystem™ (CS) in an organization. As a leader or decision-maker in your organization, it becomes your responsibility to integrate a coaching methodology into the leadership and management systems that exist to achieve *better or desired business results!*

> *Our vision is to create a methodology that supports those with desires for development, promotes those who are able and willing to develop and encourages those who are not—towards well-being, purpose, competence and awareness at every level, as the organization embraces performance, change and transformation.*

Production Work to Knowledge Work

A CS is designed to integrate into every area of the organization and to provide a methodology for tapping into the richness of your human resources. The CS is designed to promote well-being, purpose, competence and awareness throughout the organization at *every* level.

Many executives enjoy the *privilege* of being coached due to the phenomena described by the 80/20 rule. This is probably consistent with most leadership philosophy from the 20th Century. However, as a new age of knowledge work dawns upon our organizations, we find that providing a CS throughout the organization can help mine the hidden ore that exists in human resources.

The essential difference between the knowledge worker and the worker of the past is that it will be *impossible* or at least highly improbable that knowledge work can be improved merely through experience alone. Knowledge work often requires significant investments in learning as well as experience.

It used to be that for a machinist or fabricator to learn their trade or job tasks, an apprentice-like or experienced-based training period was provided. In the matter of a few short weeks, the worker was prepared to execute the job duties and get more proficient with each iteration.

In today's world, a knowledge worker may require years of learning and experience in order to be prepared to execute his/her job duties, and even at that, may require a process of ongoing learning and experience in order to fully maintain that degree of skill as the job evolves quickly in light of new information.

An accountant, surgeon, corporate lawyer, web designer, financial analyst and hundreds more job titles are representative of this process. And still, the integration of the support jobs that are critical to supporting this type of knowledge work—bookkeepers, nurses, legal clerks, programmers, customer service representatives—all require continuous learning, development and experience.

Organizational Value

A CoachSystem™ that integrates into every facet of the organization provides development along with the learning and experience activities that must occur in the modern day learning organization. The CS is representative of the organization's responsibility to provide for its own evolution and adaptive response to the environmental demands or *be obsoleted.*

In the coming years, we will see many organizational forms die because they are no longer efficient frameworks for the exchange of value. In order to succeed, any organizational framework must include development of its human resources so that those resources *adapt* the organization and maintain its efficiency.

Each organization competes with itself as well as other organizations in order to attract, retain and develop the highest quality human resources. This continual lifelong process is important to the individual in that organization and to the organization's ability to maintain its exchange potential in the marketspace. This book is not about organizational forms, but *about value.*

> *How can we, as organizational leaders, over time, account for the longevity of our organization in terms of its ability to create high value for the constituent parts—namely our employees and our customers?*

One solution offered in this book is the CoachSystem™. It is an approach which satisfies the obligations an organization has to itself and its people for development of value. The following example depicts the generic intention of a CoachSystem™.

As you read through the example, it will become obvious to you that there will be different assumptions to make and different principles to use. However, what I have done here is to lay out a *format* to help you outline *an intention using the strategic leadership architecture (outlined in chapter 9)* in terms of how a CS can be described, what are the necessary components and from that point who would be involved in your organization for implementing it and safeguarding the critical aspects of the system.

Coaching Assumptions

What we will do in this example is to create for you the opportunity to develop a methodology that will be unique to you--respecting your individual and organizational differences--and provide some common guidelines about the heuristics (rules of thumb) described in this book about coaching and coaching effectively in leadership roles.

Many times you will find yourself flying by the seat of your pants as you encounter situations you could have never imagined, yet, if you follow some basic guidelines you will never find yourself not knowing what to do, what to say, or knowing when to observe and listen.

Probably, the best place to start to frame the coaching system or methodology that you will develop, will be to talk about principles, or one step further back--the assumptions/beliefs that effective coaching is based upon. Assumptions provide a window into the construction of the methodology and upon what beliefs the coaching principles are based. Without the assumptions or *mental models*, there is often a *gap* between what is intended and what is understood.

A quote from a wonderfully updated treatise on management in organizations would serve to introduce the assumptions of the coaching methodology. The excerpt is from MASLOW ON MANAGEMENT, by Abraham Maslow, updated from his earlier book *Eupsychian Management*, written in the early 1950s. In this quote, Maslow and Douglas McGregor, who wrote the HUMAN SIDE OF ENTERPRISE in 1960, were said to have discussed these very assumptions during one of their debates (P.15, <u>Maslow on Management</u>) or meetings.

QUOTE

...that day the great debates began. Both men died imploring every leader to look into the mirror and question their assumptions. Their questions, a half-century old, still seem a great place to begin:

1. Do you believe that people are trustworthy?

2. Do you believe that people seek responsibility and accountability?

3. Do you believe that people seek meaning in their work?

4. Do you believe that people naturally want to learn?

5. Do you believe that people don't resist change but they resist being changed?

6. Do you believe that people prefer work to being idle?

Our answers to these questions affect everything that we do. We've asked groups of executives these questions. Surprisingly, we've found that many of us have never really taken the time to analyze our assumptions about people.

We often recommend that managers and leaders spend time in groups discussing the questions mentioned above. Debate and dialogue over the answers should be encouraged. Perhaps organizations should state their assumptions about people for everyone to read and discuss. We feel they are as important as mission statements and corporate values.

END QUOTE

Imagine these words being discussed almost 40 years ago! How time flies, yet how everything stays the same. How many times have you seen corporate policy dictated without a clear examination of the assumptions underlying those decisions? Would it not be more effective to surface and test the underlying assumptions and beliefs about people, your organization and the ways you do business in response to environmental demands? It is, if you intend on moving your organization to a Model II governing variables.

In developing a coaching system one of the key points to remember is the desired outcome of developing self-correcting and self-led people. Clearly, not everyone has the same capacity or desire to be self-directed, yet the potential of the organization and one's own personal life depends to a large extent on one's ability to be self-led or self-authoring—a high level of function and consciousness.

This is not to say that we should become self-driven in spite of others but in collaboration with others, which is another key assumption. NOT EVERYONE will want to move to higher levels of function and that must be acceptable to the organization in terms of selecting those who are most willing and able to perform organizational tasks and matching people with job responsibilities that are mutually best.

This may be difficult for some to enfold, however the organization has a duty to itself, in concert with its duty to its people and customers, to adapt and prosper. By establishing a CS, the organization provides a path for all people, which is *right for them.* It effectively promotes opportunities for higher levels of function for those who seek development and appropriate job matches for those who do not. We must accept the fact that people are different and that every organization will be a composite of those people as well as desires in various stages of function and development.

I believe this is the answer to those who would ask the question, "what is different about a coaching system, isn't it just another management by objectives scheme?"

CoachSystem™ Intention

In tying together coaching and the other aspects of leadership and management systems, it will be helpful to make some assumptions about the coaching heuristics (rules of thumb) that are presented in order that you can formulate your own coaching system. Here are the basic assumptions guiding these generic coaching *rules of thumb*:

COACHING ASSUMPTIONS

- Coaching is about performance, change and transformation--*user defined*
- There are many paths of well-being, purpose, competence and awareness
- Our chief want in life is for someone who can help us do what we can (Ralph Waldo Emerson)

- People are different and consequently desire to be treated as individuals
- Because people are different they see the world differently
- People do things for their own reasons
- People act to gain a benefit
- Behavior is controlled through inference
- Inference is controlled through mental models
- Collaboration improves results over time
- Structure needs to be adaptive and flexible
- W. Edwards Deming's five factors contributing to performance (noticing that only ONE of them is directly controlled by the individual!)
  - The innate ability of the individual
  - **The effort given by the individual**
  - The selection, training and orientation given to the individual
  - The variability in the system in which the individual works
  - The variability in the interpretation of system performance
- effective coaching is defined as interactions that increase development
- effective coaching improves the productivity of knowledge workers
- effective coaching reduces degenerative effects such as conflict in organizations
- effective coaching creates the openings for success and happiness
- effective coaching is not about rightdoing or wrongdoing
- effective coaching is generative in nature, creating expansion and abundance
- effective coaching in organizations must impact the individual and organizational bottom line simultaneously

- effective coaching identifies coachable issues vs. labeling and generalization
- effective coaching focuses the interaction with the pbc (person being coached) on the pbc

While there are many more beliefs and assumptions that could be listed, the real key is to discover what your assumptions are and what beliefs do you base your coaching system upon? It is your responsibility to adapt and add to the list in your CS design!

GOVERNING VALUES of this model

As we move forward with developing your coaching system, it is time to pause and list some key values that will govern this process.

- RIGHT ACTION
- RESPECT
- CONFIDENTIALITY
- DEVELOPMENT
- MASTERY

There are many more sub-values that can be tucked underneath of these major categories, such as safety, continuous development, fairness, and honesty, yet you will find that these basic values guide the development of the heuristics in <u>this</u> example--effectively.

COACHING VISION

As we gradually build a foundation, we keep an eye on the future. The future we envision as an ideal description of the outcomes we desire, which lead to well-being, purpose, competence and awareness—both individually and as an organization. We also accept the fact that this vision will change and be required to adapt over time as we move along the path now, near and far. We take time, however, to augment and recreate our vision in order to understand what really matters to us.

[A vision of these heuristics or rules of thumb about coaching follows, however YOU will want to spend some time creating your own vision of the coaching process you will use towards developing others in your organization.]

The Sample Vision

[This vision is written to reflect many of the sensory aspects of perception]

We see a place where people have the right to fail as well as learn, without blame. We think about organizations where people are happy, collaborative and generative. We feel a world that is constantly connecting and expanding to provide for the care and sustainability of continuous development and change--respecting the rights of individuals to be rewarded for and to practice that change at rates they choose.

We experience a world where differences are valued. We hear a world that speaks to the future sustainability of all kinds of life and we feel a part of a world that generates harmony, opportunity and well-being through its quest for expression. We know that the bottom line counts and our efforts are focused to create value for our customers and one another.

[This may be too touchy-feely for some, but it is written to express the altruism of a higher function—profit is a natural result, as people understand margin and mission are parallel.]

COACHING PRINCIPLES

[Principles as you recall, are the guiding forces behind the intention. They are closest to the natural laws that govern the universe and provide the universal structure that people, over time, need to *check-in* with while making important policy decisions.]

1. **Co-generate opportunities for developing people**.

We must understand that an outcome of effective "leadership" coaching must be to develop people individually and the organization as a whole, simultaneously. Clearly, in today's organization and in the organization of the future, the choice of work by people through which to make a contribution is a noble way. We must, however, examine that contribution and understand that competition for scarce resources does exist, and that to see our fair share of those resources while generating the opportunities for others to seek those resources, is a noble cause. As such we must realize that seeking to improve, expand and make more abundant the opportunities for the development of individuals is at the core of this coaching system.

2. **Facilitate sharing in collaborative environments.**

It may be debatable but certainly not wrong to foster sharing and collaboration among individuals, organizations and community. While the differences in individuals will govern the extent of each individual's wish or even preference to collaborate and to what extent, we see and promote the need for collaborative environments as being conducive to the formation of a generative culture over time. We seek to create conversations across boundaries in our organization to join the common vision.

3. **Value and promote individual differences.**

People are different. We each have an inborn (nature) and acquired (nurture) differences that make us unique representations of the collective intelligence. These differences create conflict and promote individuality in our world. However, when the organization shifts to encompass our differences and creates the space for us to actualize those different gifts (potentials) towards a generative culture, we achieve the leadership goals of creating opportunity and respect for all in view of our unique gifts.

4. **Create opportunities for change during coaching**.

In organization, in life and in community, the mere existence of life causes us to choose. In the gap between stimulus and response, which Stephen Covey describes in *7 HABITS FOR EFFECTIVE PEOPLE*, is that space where decisions are made. These decisions and this life of choice constantly challenge us to perform, change, and transform to meet environmental demands—individually and as a collective organization.

Coaching is designed to facilitate those shifts towards: what really matters, development, better choices and better lives and communities. The coaching interaction is germane to change as change is to life--never forget what your role is when coaching--*creating opportunities for performance, change and development through appreciation of individual potential--towards what really matters.*

5. **Focus on inquiry versus advocacy.**

Encompassing the previous four principles, we move from being directed outwardly to being directed inwardly. We use the coaching interaction to seek understanding rather than to be understood. We strive for ways to understand and through understanding to promote *openings for development* through the coaching interaction. We listen to understand what really matters. We choose compassion. We seek to become that which is reflective of the best in us.

6. **Connect coaching success to organizational success.**

The bottom-line.

If success in coaching cannot be seen through improvements in performance, change and transformation in people and organizations, then we have failed to connect the human experience to organizational outcomes. We exist and live through a framework of organizations, whether they are spiritual, community, business-related or family. Without an improvement in these frameworks, coaching is an enigma-- better played in our spare time. This dialectic between success and happiness, development and stagnation, between self and other; must be approached in parallel--concurrently-- not in lieu of or in competition with one another.

Life seeks life. The pressures of resource allocation will always be a paradox, yet through the practice of leadership and coaching, we, as a people--in family, community and organization--can live virtuously in pursuit of potential, sustainability, abundance and well-being.

> **[Granted, these principles may contain too many soft aspects for your organization, so modify them to represent the best in your organization.]**

COACHING PURPOSE

To facilitate the inter-development of the pc and the pbc through a respectful, confidential, and masterful interaction towards personal and organizational right action.

> *[Notice how the purpose statement (25 words or less!) integrates the values described above]*

STRATEGIC OBJECTIVES of COACHING

- effortless change [Not without work, but with less resistance]--increased organizational change velocity
- facilitate development of others to increase organizational response to challenges--innovate
- create expansion of resources through coaching
- create a safe environment for interaction (respectful & confidential) enfolding *blameless error*
- seek measurable mastery in coaching KSAs
- improve organizational success and sustainability
- achieve bottom line results and measurable ROI

KEY SUCCESS FACTORS IN COACHING

- ROCE (return on capital employed in coaching) above market rates
- Improved innovation, adaptability—individual and organizational
- Improvement in customer satisfaction
- Improvement in employee satisfaction
- Improvement in individual & organizational capability and speed of response to challenges (growth)

COACHING GOALS

This area is to be designed by each individual or organization employing a coaching methodology as a part of their organizational practices, however for the purposes of this example the goals are specified in order to guide expectations.

The coaching system will be deployed throughout the organization by Jan 200.?

Each manager or pc (person coaching) will be trained during a 3-day coaching makeover seminar.

All graduates of the makeover sessions will receive 1 day of training/experience per month in basic coaching KSAs. The following coaching skills areas will be used to guide monthly training experiences: listening, observing, action science, systems thinking, knowledge management, appreciative inquiry, organizational learning.

Any employee will have the opportunity to be coached by someone other than someone in the employee's direct chain of command.

Human Resources will integrate coaching, assessment activities, EAP (employee assistance programs) and appraisal into a coherent system of employee development.

Human Resources will contract with external coaches to provide coaching to those persons not able to be coached under system rules, e.g. executives—who control chain of command.

[Remember, these are just examples of how the system typology would appear. These broad goals could then be taken and used as guidelines for

departmental goals and so on. However, it is important to guide/coach the system development as well as the system itself through expressed intention.]

COACHING STANDARDS

- The following core competencies will be central to all coaching systems. [List them]
- Any person holding a supervisory or management position will be required to know and practice the basic methodology outlined in the coaching makeover.
- Persons coaching in the organization will be given opportunities to develop their coaching sophistication on a regular basis in addition to regular training, at a minimum of 4 hours per month.
- Assessments will be controlled and administered by only those effectively experienced in their use and application.
- Varying levels of competence in coaching KSAs will be continuously promoted and assessed—providing a system of checks and balances through *regular* appraisals connected to organizational and business system goals.

[These are just some examples of some overarching guiding standards that can be integrated with individual standards required of those "operating" the system. You will notice that it is important to "integrate" the coaching system—over time—with all management systems in place otherwise the effectiveness of training people in the coaching process is "pigeonholed" in the organization, and does not have the leverage we need in organization to produce business results through coaching systems.]

Summary

If you made it this far, you can see that developing a coaching system in an organization is not a "slam dunk," so to speak. It requires leadership, **dialogue** and a clear strategic intention that cannot be just slapped on the organization like a coat of paint. Yet, what you can also notice is that by stating the intention to establish a coaching system at every level in an organization, you can really *effect performance, change and transformation* in people and the organization, just with this process.

Tying coaching to appraisal will create structural change in itself. The mere implementation of a basic methodology that is taught to people at all levels and reinforced through continuous exposure and conversation will provide, at times, the structural change required to *un-stick* the organization. If the coaching system is promoted effectively and not as the flavor of the month, the real change will occur subliminally as people in the organization begin to relate differently over time.

Coaching—broadly speaking, is not a quick fix. It takes time to develop relationships, openings and the willingness for people to look at *what they don't know they don't know*.

What coaching can do with the leadership and management system in an organization is to create the necessary structural change to *open* the organization to further development of its people.

If we revisit the socio-tech model of organization, we see that this fundamental organizational form stands on three legs— people, structure and technology. If we substitute methodology for technology, it will be easy to see how coaching can affect structure in an organization, and in turn affect people, who in turn affect methodology in a spiral of performance, change and transformational success.

[The aspect of technology in socio-tech model of organization is being integrated into ALL of the three areas listed in the model in the explanation preceding. It may be where this model needs to adapt as a source organizational model?]

Again. Who, what, when, where, why and how we connect, clarify and commit governs our developmental velocity individually and in organization. If we consistently remember that well-being, purpose, competence and awareness are both deserved and valued through the coaching methodology, we can alter structure and create as a result, opportunities for personal and organizational success.

Chapter 16

Successful organizations do something different or better than other organizations to be successful. We can call this "something different" or "something better" a "competitive advantage," a "capability" or a "core competency" depending on our conceptual framework or our discipline. Regardless of what we call them, these distinct abilities are highly valued and guarded by the organizations that have them, and highly sought after by those that do not.

> Global Business Culture Study Group,
> November 1998, by Mark Hannum

Connection, Clarification & Commitment

Connection

In connecting, the following aspects of the interaction or relationship are enhanced:

- Rapport
- Trust
- Credibility
- Comfort
- Openness
- Curiosity
- Willingness to explore
- Internal commitment to discover
- Control
- Assurance

- Responsiveness
- Esteem
- Safety

Clarification

Clarification provides a procedural path to help surface the following things between the pc and the pbc:

- Unmet needs
- Unknown needs
- Below surface (unconscious) desires in the realm of work
- Level of development in the pbc
- Needed KSAs (knowledge, skills and abilities)
- Desired level of performance
- Key motivational leverage
- Situational demands
- Environmental challenges
- SWOT (strengths, weaknesses, opportunities, threats)
- Sense of urgency
- Sense of importance
- Incoherence
- Incongruities

Commitment

These factors arise out of commitment to action:

- Self-correction
- Self-management
- Self-awareness
- Emotional intelligence

- Internal well-being
- Performance
- Change
- Transformation
- Intrinsic motivation
- Achievement
- More iterations
- Faster error detection
- Shorter cycle times
- Harmony
- Impersonal attribution
- Solutions-based versus problem solving
- Valuing others
- Positive business outcomes
- Individual growth
- Adaptability
- Vitality
- Passion
- Willingness to go the extra mile

Summary

The reasons are clear and simple to pursue competence in these three areas. Let us remember that no one has to change but everyone has to have the conversation. The mastery of that conversation and the integration of organizational systems in support of those conversations are critical to coaching success.

Merely increasing the number of *respectful conversations* in an organization will increase learning dissemination, collaboration and innovation. Using a coaching interaction to increase the number of conversations will over time, increase organizational change velocity faster than any other method.

These three core competencies are vital to any coaching system or methodology. What is easy is listing the various component parts, what is difficult is authentic practice. Where the competencies are formed is in the key abilities in the next chapter.

Chapter 17

In our work with exceptionally talented leaders and coaches, we've discovered that they make dozens of intuitive judgments daily about how to work with their people. Sometimes they focus on removing barriers to performance. Other times they immerse themselves in a situation and exert a great deal of influence on the way it turns out. There are times when they help people work through personal or performance problems, and there are times when the only requirement is to provide straightforward information. In some situations the coach is the dominant figure, while in others the team practically forgets he or she is there.

A PASSION FOR EXCELLENCE, Tom Peters & Nancy Austin

COACHING: The Key Abilities

We have listed the attributes of the three core competencies of Connection, Clarification and Commitment. To create high levels of mastery in these core competencies, we need ability. In the COACH2 Model the essential abilities are:

- Observation
- Listening
- Discernment
- Modeling
- Delivery

Delivery is so powerful for coaching mastery that I have dedicated an entire chapter for the executive/manager/leader to use in creating effective coaching systems and interactions. This is not to say that the four other *key areas* are not critical and perhaps more important, but the initial component that provides content to the pbc in the coaching interaction itself is delivery—the **medium of the conversation--**the thoughts, beliefs, ideas and assumptions to and from the coach. It is the articulating ability of the person coaching (pc) to enable and leverage the other four abilities.

Most other programs geared to intervention, cover listening as a skill. We will spend the least amount of time on this ability, as it is the most talked about and common to training programs anywhere in organization. The abilities <u>observation</u> and <u>discernment</u> come with experience and practice, and the ability to <u>model</u> comes with your own conscious awareness and personal commitment to your own development.

Let us begin with a description of the first four abilities.

OBSERVATION

Why is observation so critical to effective coaching interaction?

Because most of what occurs around us is NOT through the spoken word. Research indicates that about 7% of communication occurs verbally. In some cases, our observational ability is limited by the medium, such as phone or email through which many of the non-verbal cues are hidden.

Email has become more and more interesting as a coaching medium because more and more organizations develop, use and integrate email into their operations. When used for coaching, it requires careful administration and higher levels of trust. And when used as a coaching medium the powers of observation become even more complex. I will, however, leave that subject for another time. Please check the knowledgebase that accompanies this book for insights into the use of email in coaching interactions.

Let us just remember that **any** conversation becomes a medium for a coaching interaction. Allow the medium to carry the weight of change and address yourself to the conversation—the nuances and inferences—in order to guide the relationship.

In observing the coaching interaction both as a participant and as a *witness* to the conversation, the person coaching must begin with an openness that allows two things: *free expression* by the person being coached (pbc) and *without prejudice*. Both of these two issues require an awareness of our own limitations, and filters towards inference. The ability to use clarification whenever our barriers to understanding are blocked through something said or done in the interaction is triggered through astute observation.

We have to remember that we have our own defensive patterns and coaching without them getting in the way requires us to have a good sense of our own worth as well as the intrinsic worth of the pbc. If we can, during the interaction, set aside our own ego needs, we can bring more energy and attention to the present moment, allowing us to approach the interaction without ego—quite impossible, but figuratively the ideal condition for the successful interaction.

Observation requires us to notice what is happening for the pbc and what is happening as a result of the interaction. We must help the pbc to identify patterns of dysfunction in terms of personal and organizational defensive patterns. This can only be accomplished through observation of what is being said and what is NOT being said by the pbc.

Using our competence in clarification, we passively as well as directly, observe openings, gaps and inconsistencies in the words, actions and behavior of the pbc. We must test the observed assumptions, beliefs and conditions that may or may not be influencing the performance, change and transformation desired by the pbc and the organization. This is aided through:
- direct observation,
- observation indirectly through others, including assessments—properly developed and administered, and
- observation of the consequences of the behavior of the pbc, in terms of observable results and consequences.

Applying our coaching KSAs in all of these areas helps us to observe the true conditions that may or may not exist to help the pbc now, in the near term and towards the far vision held by the individual and organization. We observe differences, misalignments, inadequacies, inconsistencies and failures to align espoused theories and actual theories in use in the pbc as well as in the environment.

The degree to which the pc gains and uses his/her experience in the powers of observation will make seeing and coaching through openings that much easier. The ability to generate possibilities—alternative futures—prepare plans and preview outcomes or scenarios with the pbc create much higher levels of commitment when the pc is astute and skilled in observation.

LISTENING

> *"To be able to really listen, one should abandon or put aside all prejudices...When you are in a receptive state of mind, things can be easily understood...But unfortunately, most of us listen through a screen of resistance. We are screened with prejudices, whether religious or spiritual, psychological or scientific; or, with daily worries, desires and fears. And with these fears for a screen, we listen. Therefore, we listen really to our own noise, our own sound, not to what is being said."*
>
> Krishnamurti

Listening through our own noise is the most difficult thing we will ever practice. It begins with our own awareness of our filters, our prejudices, inferences and beliefs. To really hear the pbc requires us to literally set aside much of our own agenda and that is one clear reason why it is almost impossible for a manager with authority, responsibility and accountability to quiet his/her mind enough to really hear the needs, openings and inconsistencies in the pbc among his/her own internal chatter in the coaching interaction.

To the extent that our listening is filled with our own agenda, we are disabled in our attempts to help the pbc find his/her own sense of right action. It all boils down to what we hear, what we see and how we process that information. To really listen requires practice.

After becoming aware of our own sense of right action, the needs of the pbc become clear. When we can become a witness to those needs and agendas without bringing them to bear upon the pbc in the coaching interaction, we can quiet the noise. Without a doubt, this will be the single most difficult aspect of mastering effective coaching for anyone.

Our own desire and drive to satisfy our direct and indirect needs will unconsciously influence the interaction to the extent we are unable to set them aside and be in the present moment with the interaction. *As we know it,* much of coaching is direct.

The power of listening is the first key to becoming less direct and learning to evoke openings and commitment from the coaching interaction. In the beginning, more work than with any other ability should be done with learning to set aside our own needs. Delivery will be the easiest to study and learn, but knowing *when* and *what* to deliver will come from our ability to listen and to observe.

DISCERNMENT

To discern: to discover with the eyes or the mind.

Discernment becomes an *integrating ability*. We cannot discern (feel/know) without sensory data obtained from observation (the eyes) or listening (the ears). Our ability to take in information comes purely from our ability to set aside our personal agendas, and to become open to the pbc in terms of alignment with their inferences.

The ladder of inference is effective as a discernment tool because it is closely aligned between the observational powers of the pc and the ability to clearly understand the inferences being made by the pbc, thus the key to enabling discernment.

Discernment is to see clearly what is the opening and why the opening is still a gap—only noticed by the pc. Once we can open the pbc to a realization that an inconsistency is blocking his/her performance, change and transformation, we create leverage in the interaction. The combination of observation, listening and discernment allows us the procedural process to help the pbc uncover, surface and become aware of inconsistencies and defensive patterns that block performance.

These barriers may be limitations in the form of their own capability versus the requirements of the job, limitations in orientation or training. Being able to discern this incoherence is critical to finding the point of opening or leverage. At times, the opening is impersonal. It is NOT, usually, the direct cause of the person's desire or direct behavior. It is, usually, a response to a system flaw or process limitation.

This creates the fully appreciative approach allowing us to help the pbc discern that the limitations to his/her performance, change and transformation are not always a personal *malfunction*, but a response to a system cue either perceived incorrectly or in all likelihood, a structural condition that leads to his/her response.

It also helps us, as system designers to understand that when these system flaws and inconsistencies are identified, we should be able to find solutions that are effective in removing the incongruities between the system and the pbc.

Becoming aware of the incorrect perception or structural inconsistency promotes an impersonal attribution where high value is retained for the pbc. This feeling of worth and value achieved through appreciative interaction is critical to maintaining personal leverage for the pbc.

Our attribution that something is not wrong with US, but that our system of inference is either miscued or misdirected is valuable to the pbc in terms of ***moving forward with a sense of worth and value***. If you get nothing more from this book than this, you will most likely succeed in your coaching interactions.

Maintaining, surfacing and promoting self-worth and value through an appreciative coaching interaction holds more leverage than any knowledge, skill or ability that might be created for the pbc through the interaction. Adaptability, vitality, passion and the willingness to go the extra mile, they all stem from our sense of belonging and self-worth.

Discernment is the enabling element, the trigger for the appreciative approach. It requires the pc to set aside personal agendas and needs, and to focus *through* the interaction into the needs, beliefs, assumptions and behaviors of the pbc.

Through discernment we are able to leverage our connection, utilize clarifying methodology and to promote commitment to performance, change and transformation as a result of the effective coaching interaction.

MODELING

The highest leverage ability of the coaching interaction comes from this area. The reason why, is that most of our learning comes from vicarious modeling. Do you want to know what kind of culture an organization has? Observe behavior.

Why is modeling so critical to becoming effective as a person coaching (pc)? Because, if nothing else happens in the coaching interaction, the pbc will be observing your actions and behavior. If your behavior is modeled, would it be leveraging for the organization?

If that were the one test of an effective coach, it would be enough. For all of the other abilities and competencies would be observable through the pc. In this act alone, we influence others around us in terms of how we act, what we place importance on, how we manifest abilities through our behavior. This one key element alone makes you successful in the interaction as long as you model effective behaviors—the power to observe, listen, discern and deliver right action.

Listen in on this summary from the First Edition of <u>A First Look at Communication Theory</u> by Em Griffin, McGraw-Hill, Inc., 1991. as he discusses social learning theory by Albert Bandura.

---*Begin Summary*

…Northwestern psychologist Donald Campbell calls these tendencies "acquired behavioral dispositions," and he suggests six different ways that we learn to choose one option over another: using a gun and butter as the objects.

> 1. *Trial and error experience* is a hands-on exploration that might lead to tasting the butter and squeezing the trigger, or perhaps the other way around.

> 2. *Perception of the object* is a first-hand chance to look, admire, but don't touch a pistol and a pound of butter at close range.

> 3. *Observation of another's response to the object* is hearing a startle or a contented sigh when someone points the gun or spreads the butter on toast. It is also seeing critical frowns on faces of people who bypass the items in a store.

> 4. *Modeling* is watching someone fire the gun or melt the butter to put it on popcorn.

5. *Instruction about the object* is a verbal description of the gun's effective range or of the number of calories in a pat of butter.

6. *Exhortation* is the National Rifle Association's plea to protect the right to bear arms or Willard Scott's commercial message urging us to use real butter.

Campbell claims that direct trial and error experience creates a deep and long-lasting acquired behavioral disposition, while perception has a somewhat lesser effect, observation of response even less and modeling, less still. *Exhortation is probably the most used but least effective means to influence attitudes or actions.*

Stanford psychologist, Albert Bandura agrees that conversation is not an effective way of altering human behavior, but he thinks that classical learning theory's preoccupation with trial and error learning is shortsighted: "Coping with the demands of everyday life would be exceedingly trying if one could arrive at solutions to problems only by actually performing possible options and suffering the consequences." His social learning theory concentrates on the power of example.

Bandura's major premise is that we can learn by observing others. He considers vicarious experience to be the typical way in which human beings change. He uses the term *modeling* to describe Campbell's two mid-range processes of response acquisition (observation of another's response and modeling), claiming that modeling can have as much impact as direct experience.

… because it is simple, distinctive, prevalent, useful, and depicted positively.

Bandura adds that we store events in two ways—through visual images and through verbal codes. He is convinced, however, that major gains in vicarious learning [modeling] come when the observer develops a conscious awareness of the technique involved. These insights are stored verbally.

---End Summary

In other words, as the coaching interaction unfolds, the pc and pbc become aware of the use of technique, in this case, observation, listening, discernment and delivery to actually reinforce the learning [modeling] experience.

What actually takes place is that a transmittal of these abilities occurs first through the display of them and subsequent, unconscious observation by the pbc of these abilities. In time, the pbc will learn how to develop these abilities as the nuances are enfolded into the interaction and longitudinal relationship—the key modeling influence.

Summary

Delivery is covered in the next chapter. To summarize the four key abilities discussed here: observation, listening, discernment and modeling, we have shown how critical they are to each other. We have also stated before that these key abilities align very closely with our senses: sight, sound, touch/feel, taste, and speech.

In connection with the basic senses we use these abilities to integrate what is occurring for the pbc in regards to inference, belief and assumptions about what is happening in his/her life. This is contrasted with what appears to be happening in the organization as viewed by the pbc and the pc. These assumptions [mental models] are tested through clarification methodology.

We examine our espoused theory, what we say we do versus our theory in use, what we actually do, and try to find ways to align them by discovering why they are not aligned. This discovery is based on observation, listening and discernment.

Modeling is used to demonstrate high function by the pc helping the pbc to unconsciously assimilate, learn and develop. In the next chapter we discuss how to deliver feedback, questions, ideas and challenges in the interaction.

Chapter 18

"I have heard what the talkers were talking...the talk of the beginning and the end, but I do not talk of the beginning or the end.

There was never any more inception than there is now, nor any more youth or age than there is now; and will never be any more perfection than there is now, nor any more heaven or hell than there is now.

...I am satisfied...I see, dance, laugh, sing..."

Walt Whitman

Coaching Delivery

One of the most difficult things to master in a coaching interaction is delivery. By delivery, I mean the way in which we offer any form of content to the person being coached (pbc). Through other abilities such as observation, listening, discerning and modeling we integrate much of the interaction through our own system of discovery, and at some point need to deliver some form of content during the interaction. In the following paragraphs we will explore five basic forms of delivery:

- Feedback
- Questions
- Statements
- Challenges
- Ideas

Of course, it goes without saying that we *deliver* content through the perception of the pbc's interpretation of any movement, gesture or even lack of action, and those issues become very important when engaging in a coaching interaction. Often, the pc and the pbc learn a great deal and perceive a significant amount of information from these non-verbal cues.

I believe the ratio is 7% of what we say, 38% of how we say it and the rest—around 55%--are non-verbal cues. Therefore, when we do deliver this very small portion of the total communication in words, it needs to be designed to evoke a response or reaction in the pbc that moves the developmental process forward, or at a minimum over time, causes a degree of reflection and consideration.

Coaching in various mediums require different sorts of skill and ability combinations. The combinations that might be effective for face-to-face (f2f) interactions would be somewhat ineffective over email, or perhaps even the telephone, where the interaction is more heavily based on what is said and how it is said as opposed to how what is said is represented through non-verbal cues. Each level of coaching from fully synchronous (FSC) to fully asynchronous coaching (FAS) requires concentration on a different delivery combination.

In today's modern organizations, we communicate in a number of different mediums and in every case, each medium becomes territory for a coaching interaction. Here is a list of some of the mediums we deliver content in during and towards a coaching interaction—ranging from FSC to FAS:

- F2f
  - Personal
  - Interpersonal
  - Group

- o Intergroup
- Meetings (where more than one person is present)
- Speeches
- Telephone
- Voice Mail
- Email
- Written Memos

The five forms of delivery can often be delivered with a *charge*—positive or negative—and centered in the past or the future. Some delivery methods are for the most part about the past, such as feedback, or mostly future oriented, such as ideas. Statements, as a delivery choice, fall mostly in the median between past and future and it is probably the most effective method for dealing with the present. The following diagram indicates this in a more visual way.

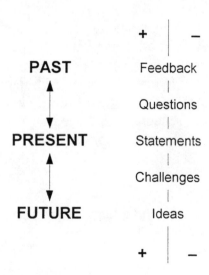

Basic Considerations

Charge

Charge is a general characteristic of all communication and must be clarified first. Charge, as it is meant in this framework, is the emotional constituent evoked by delivery, both by the pc and pbc during the interaction. It can be positive, negative or neutral. In coaching, a focus on delivery in the neutral or positive state is required. In an appreciative approach, little negative charge is used, however, a negative charge may often be interpreted regardless of intent by either party.

Charge is perhaps the most difficult nuance of the delivery because the difference between what is intended and what is actually interpreted can be great among people. Mental or cognitive set, condition of mind, structural organization, level of attention and even transmission of non-verbal cues all play a role in defining charge. In many cases, a reaction or response from the pbc will often be the result of *perceived* charge. In the following section, we can see how easily it might be to misinterpret charge in a conversation.

Inference

Interpretation of data, events and intent is often very complex even though it seems simple. The differences in people *influence* our ability to make meaning in terms of our own preferences, styles, conditioning, level of development and cognitive organization. The diagram that follows illustrates how simple the process really is…to make things very difficult!

A Person's Intention is usually private	becomes	A Person's Action	becomes	A perceived effect with meaning made by B
A's Intention		A's Action		Effect on B
A's Private Intention	A encodes	Observable by anyone	B decodes	B's Private Effect
Must be inferred by B				Must be inferred by A

It is easy to see how much latitude there is in terms of interpretation and inference from this simple model of an exchange between two people in a coaching interaction. For that matter, it is also easy to understand from this model why so much confusion and pain exists in our daily lives—realizing that we all perceive the same event through our own system of interpretation and inference.

Argyris stated these four steps in his *ladder of inference:*

- Data in a conversation—relatively direct
- Perceived through culturally understood meanings
- Filtered through our *theories in use*
- Leads to our interpretation of the meaning of the data

This ladder is shown with more steps as adopted from Hargrove's *MASTERFUL COACHING,* in turn showing inferences made about Argyris' original data:

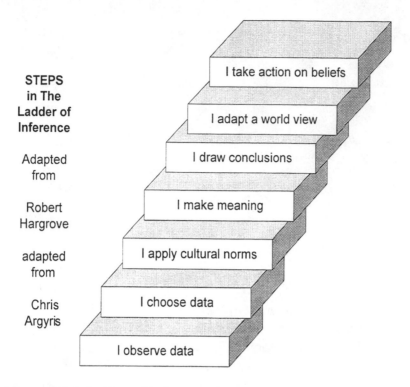

STEPS in The Ladder of Inference

Adapted from

Robert Hargrove

adapted from

Chris Argyris

I take action on beliefs

I adapt a world view

I draw conclusions

I make meaning

I apply cultural norms

I choose data

I observe data

Now, which ladder of inference do you prefer? The one taken from The Executive Mind and Double Loop Learning, by Chris Argyris, or the one above synthesized from two iterations after?

We see that inference and meaning-making—a component—is a very complex issue, often oversimplified. If we happen to have all the same preferences, conditioning, cultural norms and are witness to the same event, perhaps the way we and the person we share those similarities with—understand each other? However, imagine if you have NO similarities…?

Languaging

This topic is a whole lifetime in itself. Our entire cognitive apparatus stems from "languaging" thought. It is, undoubtedly, one of the most important things that can make or break a coaching interaction. Frankly, it does not come easily to those who have a great deal to offer coaching, yet it must be learned and practiced continually. Languaging is a form of communicating our thoughts, attitudes, beliefs and intention.

It would be possible to spend a great deal of time on the skill itself. As a decision maker, it would help you to explore this aspect of skills training with your coaching system. The few short paragraphs devoted to languaging here, are not enough to develop any skill. Content delivery occurs through languaging. We will provide information on the delivery methods using languaging as a basis.

Languaging is the manner in which we relate our thoughts to others through a delivery method. Languaging is not easy to learn although some people do have a *knack* for saying the right thing and not saying the wrong thing, however the subset of these people is small. When you meet someone like this, it almost seems like heaven! The clarity of their delivery leaves no room for subjective interpretation.

So how do the rest of us manage? Simply, through learning and practice. Developing this skill is often representative of something Sam Walton said during his Wal-Mart building era. When asked by a reporter one day on how he did it…he told the reporter that it was through good judgment and luck. The reporter, not satisfied with these remarks, inquired further, "how did you arrive at good judgment?" Walton simply stated—*experience*. Still unsatisfied, the reporter probed, "how did you get experience?" Walton replied: --*bad judgment!*

The message here is that in order to get good at something, we must first be bad at it and know why. For most of us, the challenge is to be bad at something without destroying our careers!

Aristotle once said that the goal of wisdom is experience and reflection. In the coaching interaction, we will make mistakes in languaging AND if we learn from them, the experience will help us become more adept at languaging our thoughts and observations in a way that becomes generative for us, and the pbc.

Methods of Delivery

Feedback

Feedback is the most commonly used and misused form of delivery. In the coaching makeover that we present to clients to expose them to languaging and delivery of content, we stage an exercise that helps people to experience first-hand the challenges of using feedback to improve results and gain positive outcomes. The revelation to most people is that in the workscape we use mostly negative feedback! "You shouldn't have done that…."

There are two forms of feedback, positive and negative. Feedback is always about past performance thus its limitations. However, the first thing anyone speaks about in coaching is feedback. Feedback, when used in Maslow's paradoxical statement as a panacea for everything—"he who is good with a hammer, thinks everything is a nail"—is very limiting in the coaching interaction.

In great part, coaching is concerned with the present and more often than not, the future—development and performance of individuals and organizations.

Feedback is an essential tool, but it is often used in a negative rather than an appreciative sense. Here are some examples of negative feedback:

- You shouldn't have…
- That's not what we want…
- People in your situation should be more…

In each of these statements about the past, the implication is that something has been done wrong. Of course, we need to be able to advocate a position through negative feedback, it is an effective learning tool, however, it is not THE TOOL as often used by a person coaching.

I remember my days in athletics and I think that for many people coaching, negative feedback was the preferred selection of delivery. In terms of this book's definition of coaching, they were certainly not coaches although they thought they were. There are other ways to evoke performance—and more effective—than using negative feedback as your only tool in the coaching interaction. Ken Blanchard referred to this as the "Leave alone, ZAP!" theory.

Similarly, positive feedback is used many times to evoke performance, change and transformation. While appreciative, we need to be careful to use it in such a way that it remains credible. People using only positive feedback fall prey to what appears to some as using syrupy or happy talk. In my experience, a few people are this way naturally as their lives are full of optimism. They do take a little getting used to sometimes.

We should point out that a good deal of positive feedback is technique and when it feels like technique, it evokes the opposite of performance—resistance! Our personal and organizational defense systems kick in—commonly known as a BS Detector, and we find much of the content being filtered into the recycle bin of our minds. Positive feedback is NOT happy talk. It is specific and direct to a particular situation or circumstance that is observable when most effective.

It NEVER hurts to tell people they are doing well or to praise someone when you *catch them doing things right*. Yet, at times, spreading positive feedback over all situations becomes less effective the more it is used.

One thing people want is praise. Research has shown that it is critical to high functioning work places. As a person coaching, you can deliver positive feedback very specifically during structured interactions that means something to the person being coached. However, be certain that other people hear the praise for the pbc as well. This is certainly motivating to the entire organization but do not stage it. Like anything else, the use and languaging of this method of delivery is critical to effectiveness.

Examples of Positive Feedback:

- That was a good idea…
- I liked the way that you…
- You were right to have…
- The way you handled that was…

Positive feedback, used correctly, can be highly effective in the coaching interaction. It can be part of an appreciative approach and focus on assets rather than on liabilities. Using it correctly requires practice and allowing your own positive feelings to surface and be communicated. Frequently, the best guide to knowing when to use it comes from the heart.

Questions

Questions can be in the form of discovery, exploration, probing, challenging, rhetorical, including non-verbal communication. A great example of a rhetorical question comes from Wu Wey's short "ghetta" (please excuse the spelling). Wu Wey asks the question, "why are you not happy?" "Because 98.98% of what you do is for yourself and there isn't one." Rhetorical questions like metaphors, stories and statements are effective ways of relating abstract concepts and beliefs that one can apply to one's own situation.

Questioning must never take the form of interrogation. If it does, then the defensive patterns we all rely on for our own self-protection are triggered and the interaction becomes full of resistance and effort for both the pc and pbc. Another important thing to understand with questioning is that the type of question and its charge can be both effective and debilitating to the interaction. Knowing when and how to charge a question is critical to evoking *movement*—toward development or action--with the pbc.

Let us understand that when the student is ready, the master appears. This metaphor applies in both cases to the pc and the pbc. Using clarifying questions are a very important part of any interaction and the time spent in clarification is later on rewarded through commitment. In the past decade or so, a new form of inquiry has been promoted. In Appendix D, references are provided for further exploration of the method of *appreciative inquiry* as a dialogue tool.

Inquiry is a much better term than questioning, which often has a pejorative connotation. Inquiry, in itself, is a very effective form of accomplishing all three-core competencies: connection, clarification and commitment. Inquiry in the form of building rapport, genuine compassion, understanding, empathy and achieving agreement contributes to all three competencies. In fact, all of the delivery methods contribute to the core needs of the interaction.

Inquiry is part science but more often than not, art. In one of his talks David Whyte made the statement that "a true conversation does not have an agenda or a point where it will arrive…." I found his statement to be profound. And to a great degree, it separates a person managing and a person coaching. When the agenda of the pbc is unknown and the nature of the challenge confronted by the interaction is unknown, only then inquiry provides us with a guide along that journey to the unknown.

> *Whyte also said: …"conversation takes a person to the frontier of their conversation with self…what is begging to be asked…what is not being spoken?"*

In inquiry, in conversation, we can explore the links between the individual and the organization in a way that creates a bridge across the perceived gaps between the two entities. Through inquiry we discover, explore, value and generate commitment to movement, to motivation, to uncover and surface that which is *begging to be asked.*

Statements

The power of statement. There are many "jargony" terms in the coaching industry surrounding statements: truth-saying, truth-telling, speaking your truth, telling it like it is, laser informing, etc.

All of these have one thing in common: they are all statements. A statement is a communication of a thought, belief, action, idea, advice, observation or what may appear to be a truth as you understand it. (Often not really a truth at all.) You might say I am wary of people stating their truths. Very often, our sense of right becomes conveyed as a universal right. There are few universal truths. With the complexity of today's life we see a truth and state it as such without having all the data or knowing the many forms of consequence and pretense that frame the circumstances.

I very much like the idea of stating an observation. When someone states an observation rather than a perceived truth, it is usually contained within an appreciative frame.

Here are some examples of statements:

- Here is how I see it…
- This is what I have observed…
- Here is an idea that came out of my seeing…
- I really liked how you approached…
- When I do that, this often happens…
- Here is what I'm feeling…
- I'm feeling…
- I've observed…
- Here is what I make of it…
- Say more about that…

You can see almost all the methods of delivery contained within these statements. The statements declaring your truth as you see it, do not seem to be righteous. A statement to a coach is like a scalpel to a surgeon. When we take an action to create a statement we are, in effect, seeking to cut through the opening into the frontier of conversation. A statement is something that the pc uses to guide the process not unlike the other forms of delivery, but more so in terms of the control being shifted to the pc in the moment of delivery.

The pbc is cueing off of what the statement means to him/her in these circumstances. A statement becomes a method for delivering stories, analogies and sensitive information. The statement has a great deal of power in that it is always perceived based on the meaning given to the person delivering it, in terms of the credibility they have with the pbc. Just as in a statement by a powerful "who said" in our life, someone who has a lot of reverent power. If the statement comes from a powerful *"who said,"* then the reactions and responses triggered can leverage the interaction or stall it.

The art of the statement is simply *timing, tone and circumstance*. All three work to provide cues of when to make a statement, so to speak. You must be careful that you do not use a statement to *direct* the pbc. As a manager or leader, we tend to rely on our *expert* status in the interaction to motivate the pbc. As a pc, when you direct, you can close or fail to see the opening that may exist.

In terms of direction, it is best to use a question, challenge or idea to guide the process rather than a declarative statement affirming a truth. This is the difficulty for managers who people expect to be coaches for it becomes another way to manipulate the pbc into YOUR agenda. In order to develop, change and transform the pbc, it is necessary to guide rather than direct. Using one of the next two methods can help you do that effectively while not dis-empowering the interaction.

Challenges

Stretch, Speed and Integration: the battle cry of modern organization in a global environment. Yet, how do we get people to stretch…fast? The essential component of actualizing this outcome is, coaching. One, it provides an empowering, appreciative approach; two, it creates a direct link between individual and organizational development; and three, the coaching interaction is the ideal ground to explore possible openings for stretch opportunities—in the safety of trust and challenge.

Challenge is very personal. What is challenging for one is impossible for another. How we create enough tension through challenge is an exciting part of the coaching interaction. It requires us to *customize* our approach to the individual differences of the pbc. It is so much better than issuing a broad—mass challenge—to the entire workforce without the power to distill the challenge into personal, manageable small bites.

One of the biggest problems I see is in how people respond to challenges—personal and organizational. With there being so many layers of complexity in a person's life, even the same challenge at a different point in the person's life becomes impossible due to the constraints we all experience from time to time. However, the coaching interaction with its ability to address concurrently, these personal and professional issues, is ideal to promote the type of challenge that leads to high motivation and commitment throughout the organization.

How do we use challenge as a delivery method?

Good question. Challenge can be offered according to need, difference and situation: [note a + or – to indicate possible charge.]

- by using feedback:

- Learning all we need to know from that mistake we made will really help us in the future to solve other similar dilemmas in another division.

+ The way you were able to gain commitment on that project was simply amazing. We have some other projects that need a leader like you.

- By using questions:

+Can we get the same performance from your team that we are seeing from Pat's team?

- By using statements:

+We need 25% improvement in gross sales margin in the next quarter. It is important that we achieve this goal in your project.

- By using ideas:

+What if you could beat your last month's forecast by using three more people moved over from order fulfillment to support the sales team, could you do it?

In all of these simple examples, we can see how a challenge can be evoked to create stretch. All the approaches are appreciative and offer to create an opening for the pbc. Yet all of them are delivered by the pc to initiate some movement or motivation to meet a challenge.

The other form of challenge in the coaching interaction is based upon a discrepancy or incongruency between some action the pbc has taken or is taking, and which appears to be creating, unconsciously, poor performance, poor outcomes or results. In this case, the pc has little choice but to help the pbc become *aware* of these openings. In fact, at times these openings will be so hidden from the awareness of the pbc that the pc will have to make a challenge in order for the pbc to become aware, or switch to a reflective mode that helps him/her become self-aware.

Here are some examples:

- By using feedback:

- Julie, the last project you did was 10% over budget and it would be impossible for us to complete another one in that fashion.

+ Jim, I really like the way you handled yourself in that "Barnaby" Situation, now we need to list the things that we learned about this experience so we can make it even better next time.

- By using questions:

+ What is it about the current situation that is not working for you?

- Does the way you are going about your relationship with your team really produce the effects you are intending?

- By using statements:

- I observe a real incongruence between how you say you are acting and what you are really doing.

+ I once had a situation very similar to yours in which I had to change how I thought about the situation and what actions I took when it came down to it.

- By using ideas:

+What if you took some time to write down how you feel everyday in a journal when things like this occur and after awhile take a look to see if there are some patterns?

-What do you think would happen if instead of feeling angry, you tried to look at that situation from the other person's point of view?

In these cases, the delivery was used to create a challenge to the person's way of being and acting. The delivery method dictated a challenge or challenging situation that required the pbc to stretch out of the acceptance of his/her current modus operandi.

Challenging is challenging!

In order to create a wider opening in the pbc rather than closing the opening down to coaching, we have to take into consideration the differences, preferences, success opportunities and possibilities at hand.

How much of a challenge can some people take and still be motivated to a commitment to perform, change or transform? With regard to understanding this opportunity, we need to know a little bit about what motivates people.

Let me conclude this method of delivery with a challenge to you the reader, the executive, leader or manager. Challenge is NOT a one-way street. You just don't go around challenging people; you have to challenge yourself. As director of systems and as resource allocator, it becomes critical for you to examine YOUR role in the challenge and stretch the goals you put forward.

1. Have you done due diligence in removing barriers to performance?
2. Have you looked to the system for integrated opportunities?
3. Have you prepared people with KSAs to take on these challenges?
4. Do you have appropriate reward systems in place?
5. How are you going to objectively measure performance and change?
6. Have you communicated the *right reasons* underlying these requests?
7. Have you walked a mile in the moccasins of your reports and followers?
8. Have you made clear what needs to be clear in terms of purpose and principles?
9. Are you personally prepared to get involved and stay involved? How will you model this?
10. What kind of commitment to stretch and challenge have you made?

Some things to consider. These are clearly times for leadership as well as coaching based on purpose, competence, awareness and ultimately, well-being. The challenge is to integrate what we do with who we are—personally and professionally—and not separate our lives, one from the other.

The clear challenge is to embark upon a system of integration that permeates all of our organization, our systems and our people.

Ideas

My favorite part of delivery, for sure. Some of us are naturally like this and others, well, we could not come across an idea even if we were wearing it. Part of what makes coaching a challenge is to become complete. In my own journey, being far from complete, I have noticed a special dispensation to using ideas. For most of my life, I figured that was the way everyone approached things until I began to become a little bit more aware of differences.

Using ideas can be a very effective way to promote performance, change and transformation as long as they belong to the pbc. Now, it does not matter where they get them from or who gets credit for them—*you would be surprised at how much gets accomplished when nobody worries about who gets credit*! But essentially, ideas do not do a lot of good until the opening is realized. Just using ideas can de-motivate some people as much as using only positive feedback.

In my view, the power of an idea is directly related to the timing of the need for the idea, and the delivery of the idea in the coaching interaction. Before or after that, it is just another articulated thought taking up space. Ideas do have a place in the repertoire of people coaching. In fact, ideas often become strategies, both short and long term and they can be essential to evoking high function in the pbc.

The best idea is the one the pbc identifies. Many people coaching expect an idea to become an action on behalf of the pbc; another valid reason why people with responsibility, accountability and authority over the pbc are not coaches. On that fine line, it must be the pbc who embraces and accepts the idea. This ownership powers the commitment to action that is sorely lacking in personal growth and development in today's organizations.

Use ideas sparingly, listening carefully for the fertile openings where the idea can be planted. Brainstorming is fine as long as it is what the pbc has agreed to do, otherwise it becomes a flood of information that finds no resting place. In fact, it destroys focus and leads the interaction into inefficiency.

While some may say that conversation is important, it is the interaction that takes place during the coaching relationship that produces leverage. Allow ideas to serve the interaction and not the other way around. If all you do is brainstorm, perhaps you are not, really, in a coaching interaction?

An idea, at the right time, can move mountains. Our modern day success is based on the power to innovate and so should the coaching interaction. Personal innovation in how we think, belief and behave is critical to development and the power of ideas are a force in the right direction—used timely and appropriately.

Summary

The pc needs to become aware of the use of all of the methods of delivery, each to their own time and circumstance. Working towards understanding how and when to use each method provides mastery to the coaching interaction—not withstanding efficiency!

Languaging of each method is critical and must be practiced. When in doubt, deliver less! Allow the pbc to guide the delivery and to create the opening through interaction that beckons the *right action* on your behalf. In order to know when and how to deliver the *right thing, in the right way, at the right time,* you will have to observe carefully, listen attentively, discern through experience and inner knowing, model the opportunity to learn, grow and develop and understand the *right reasons* for doing so.

Chapter 19

"The true alchemy lies in the human potential to create far beyond our imagination, to manifest answers to seriously complex organizational dilemmas and to solve market paradoxes with the greatest of ease. All you have to do is to help them have the confidence to land."

Coaching Alchemy

Alchemy is the art of combining simple ingredients into something of value. I heard the term spoken at a seminar I was attending and while the person who spoke about the term cloaked coaching in the mysterious realm of *alchemy*, I thought to myself at the time that this person did not really understand the principles of coaching.

Coaching is alchemy. In fact, I would venture to say that alchemy describes coaching better than art or science. For example, when you feel a shift occur or a revelation spring up from out of nowhere, is it often a result of some scientific process? When the light turns on, is it a part of an artistic moment? Most likely, it is not. Usually, it occurs randomly and without prediction. Even when we try our hardest to *get* something, the effort against the internal resistance of a linear paradigm just does not bring forth that moment of realization.

As an alchemist, the person coaching (pc) can use very simple ingredients of observation, deep listening, discernment, modeling and delivery to fashion a reaction that is often transparent to the person being coached (pbc). Knowing when to add a little of this and a little of that, or to withhold a portion of this or refrain from adding some of that, explains the true mastery behind coaching.

I was practicing the C3 model last evening as I was talking with a person who I had met earlier in the day. Through the course of the conversation, the person announced the "arrival" of a revelation. When describing it, I noticed it was modeled along a personal story I had related regarding my own journey down life's road. The connection made by this person to that story caused an alchemic reaction. This person also said that it was a minor revelation but important and thanked me for helping it to arrive through our dialogue.

Many times I feel that coaching is just about connecting with people and offering them a small plate of simple ingredients, listening and, perhaps presenting a clarifying question to center the dialogue. However, the pbc often performs the mental gymnastics to arrive at the landing, so to speak.

My children were very active in gymnastics and as they grew in competence, the coach always remained close by, not doing much, but close by, while they did the work—always seeming to come together for the landing of the dismount. The confidence the children derived from knowing that the person coaching would be close by and offer help if needed, seemed to be enough to cause them to do very brave things on their own. This metaphor is appropriate to understanding that once the connection and clarification have been made, the commitment arising out of the interaction flows naturally. It almost seems like alchemy.

In my own career and in the writings of Csikszentmihalyi on *flow*, there appears to be a connection between the ability to attain the state of flow that is connected with right action and the sense of confidence that is transparent in terms of a process during that flow state.

This same state seems to be related to the alchemy achieved through a connected, clear and committed coaching interaction. The two become one in a dance of alchemy, neither fully art, nor fully science, yet complete and confident allowing for shifts in consciousness and the manifestation of something of value from really nothing at all—alchemy?

So, leaving all mystery aside, how would alchemy and the state of alchemy lend a hand to coaching performance, change and transformation? Quite clearly, it is related to the four outcomes we desire from effective coaching: well-being, purpose, competence and awareness. When these constructs are woven together in the right combination, the states of flow and change become active and allow us to access the sources that are always available to us to see the purposeful connection we have with the change or shift.

When I ask people how they would define a shift, I receive a variety of answers. Yet, for each of us, being able to see something that was not clear before is probably close to a meaning of shift. The shift can occur in very small increments or in huge revelations where our lives bifurcate and change forever. A person coaching facilitates these shifts according to the nature of the pbc. The pc does not just try to shift people become the process becomes the pc's agenda and not the agenda or timing for the pbc.

This is why process is so important. If we continue to stay in process allowing for the alchemy of it to emerge when it is needed without resorting to a recipe, we can provide the tools and the confidence for the pbc to *land*. As a pc, if we stay open as to what is going on for the pbc and quiet our own noise and inferences—publicly testing our assumptions through clarification—we can serve as a guide along the path of alchemy for the pbc.

Any person coaching can be successful with very little training if they remember these things:

- Allow the pbc to define their agenda
- Offer the pbc your full attention
- Understand the simple process of COACH2
- Use the CIM to guide the process
- Use the simple coaching skills of observation, deep listening, discernment, modeling and delivery to walk with the pbc and help them land.

Over time, the practice will help you to become more efficient, but you will NEVER be more effective than when you just begin—without the arrogance of experience. The coaching interaction is a simple process to guide the natural wisdom of the pbc. The pbc will move at a speed different from you and being sensitive to the needs of the pbc rather than your own needs to instruct, impress, *fix* and improve the pbc will be your hardest task.

Alchemy is a reminder that coaching is simple. If you try to solve problems you are coming from science, if your try to illuminate the client, your art is showing. If you proceed on process gently nudging, testing, clarifying and challenging the pbc when need be, then the pbc will shift in his/her own time.

My greatest fear, and always fed by my observations of "people coaching" in organizations, is that the organization and the pc have an agenda or hidden agenda that is manipulating the coaching interaction between the pc and pbc. As an executive and a leader in your organization—create the agenda for everyone through leadership—allow the coaching to create outcomes that are consistent with effective coaching—well-being, purpose, competence and awareness—and the results will take care of themselves.

We certainly have a role in leadership to articulate the vision of the organization, its purpose and the key objectives that must be obtained in the now, near and far terms, however, the coaching process follows the path of alchemy allowing the arrival of each pbc to occur on time that is suitable for him/her. No coaching is NOT a performance tool, although it will promote performance. No coaching is not a change tool, although at the very least—change will occur. Coaching is a transformation tool, however, it will not occur directly, but it will occur out of the coaching interaction--over time and in time—and the host of conversations that occur as a result of the coaching system.

Most people use coaching as a direct tool. We learn this from our athletic and academic experiences, but try and remember one time where a coach made a real impact on your life and see that it was a direct tool?

I remember one time when I came off the football field and threw my helmet into the bench—at that moment being quietly *apprehended* by a coach who said very little to me and was not my position coach—but made an impact on me to this day. He pointed out to me that champions do not throw their helmets. He was so aware of who I wanted to be and where I was at that moment his *gesture* has stuck in my mind to this day—thanks Joe Benson!

You see, he wasn't interested in finding blame or pointing out the mistakes that caused me to be upset. He merely stated the obvious in the only manner that I was open for this idea. It was not direct, yet the shift that he helped me land, changed my life forever.

Coaching is often indirect and not direct concerning the performance required because coaching recognizes that most things are inferred from the deeply held convictions we hold from childhood. To affect those deep levels of belief and not be barred by defensive resistance designed to protect our "self," it is often the indirect approach—the non-threatening approach that reaches the deepest.

How many times have you felt a revelation when no one was pushing? How many times has the comfort of being with someone, non-threatening, allowed you to be open and in a flow state cognitively? My guess is that we reach more shift experiences through indirect methods than by direct challenges.

Using a coaching system to directly cause performance limits the ability of coaching to surface real change and innovation. The coaching system is alchemy. Most times you cannot direct the products of alchemy; they just show up through guidance.

In this way, and through this metaphor, the executive or leader of the system can understand the best way to use coaching—by creating systems of guided conversations. Through the systemic and direct structural integration of organizational systems and the benefits of great numbers of conversations occurring simultaneously the organization will come alive with innovation and performance.

I am continuously enamored with the poetic structures created by David Whyte and his poignant remark that "no one has to change, but they have to have the conversation—out of conversation comes the change." In this statement he simply provides us with the reasoning for the indirect, almost alchemy of the coaching interaction.

If we try to force people to change, they resist. Change must come on our own terms and in our own time. The quote I often use to describe this condition is "a person won over against their will is of the same opinion still." Even though we force people to change, we create a "self-sealed" person because inside, his/her resistance prevents him/her from fully showing up with all of their cognitive and emotional potential, bound by their own sense of right and wrong and the resistance of the *imposed* change.

The more people try to structure coaching in terms of using it to cause change, the less likely change will come effortlessly. The more rules we make for performance, the less likely performance will come effortlessly. If we were all the same, we could perhaps construct a system with all the rules, yet it should be clear to us by now that we are not only different, we are different at being different.

The coaching interaction is the prime conversation in organization that must be facilitated by the organization. There are other conversations, those arising out of communities of interest—often referred to as the grape vine—but these are not often facilitated by the organization. They occur in spite of the organization.

Many years ago, when I started studying coaching, I was impressed with organizational communication and how most of it occurred informally, through the grapevine. It was fast, efficient, and only went to those that needed the information.

WOW! I thought. An organization designed like a grapevine! Coaching in organizations functions as a communications tool for promoting conversation, much in the same way that the grapevine promoted contact. It is personal, trusted and non-threatening.

As leaders, we have the opportunity to facilitate conversation in much the same way. It will be through alchemy, of course, as you have no way of structuring the outcomes. But by taking simple ingredients, and combining them with a structure that promotes, supports and learns to use coaching to create conversations—meaningful conversation that is, you can provide your organization with the tools to create performance, change and transformation beyond your wildest dreams.

> *The true alchemy lies in the human potential to create far beyond our imagination, to manifest answers to seriously complex organizational dilemmas and to solve market paradoxes with the greatest of ease. All you have to do is to help them have the confidence to land.*

Part III

Where I think the real challenge for companies lies today is the place where they are trying to implement sophisticated, multidimensional, complex, third generation strategies with their newly de-layered, de-staffed, horizontal, networked, second generation organizations; but they are trying to do all of that with essentially first generation managers.

What I mean by first generation managers...managers at all levels—top management, the CEO, people supporting the CEO, folks in the senior level in the middle, heads of divisions, heads of sectors, heads of functions on a world-wide basis--all the way the down to the front line, people managing specific business, specific product lines, specific activities in particular markets, right across the board.

They're trying to do all of this with managers whose sense of their own value-added, whose personal skills and competencies, whose relationships inside, whose definition of their role in the company have been shaped by an earlier model. This is where I think the real challenges are. It is this process of evolution that brings me down to that level of managers...and therefore inevitably to the topic of management development.

Sumantra Ghoshal, <u>Keynote</u>
<u>1997 Global Leadership Development Conference</u>

Coaching: Where it's headed…

In this brief excerpt from Sumantra's keynote delivery, he essentially substantiates the underlying *raison d'etre* for creating a coaching system in an organization. Organizational evolution creates complex adaptive requirements for the leadership and management system. As people, structure and technology advance in light of demand requirements—a combinatorial effect (Kaufman)—we find the modern organization, as Ghoshal states, *trying to meet third generation demands with second generation organizational models filled with first generation management.*

This is probably the most critical challenge for an *integrated leadership-management-coaching system.* And it is driving the need for performance, change and transformation among the individual and in the organization. To merely continue to perform is not enough. We need to change what we do, how we derive solutions and promote the capability of each individual to function in a complex environment, or at least find leverage to do so.

This final part of the book attempts to--along with the included appendices—create openings for development of this order among individuals, business and organizations. We are at the frontier of a conversation, be it personal or organizational and that requires us to see things differently.

The expanding edge of chaos is becoming wider and pulling our organizations into pieces—pieces attempting to explain and deal with broad complexity—as the organizational leaders attempt to hold on to a fragmented whole.

Our leadership, management and coaching strategies must evolve as well to create opportunities for each fragment—torn from the whole—to be reunited, at a minimum, as a fractal of the whole, to represent the vision, the values, purpose and principles of the whole while *achieving business results*.

Through leadership, we attempt to achieve strategic objectives concurrently, which encompass our reason for being—efficiently. This will become an even more difficult task for the person framed in older mechanical models.

The older business models are less capable of dealing with complexity in real or *zero* time, less capable of morphing themselves to environmental demands and creating adaptive responses to accelerated change and unending turbulence. Without question, the organization must evolve to become self-directed, self-correcting and self-generating amidst the confusion at the edge. Coaching performance, change and transformation will be one strategy to meet this evolutionary need in organizations—appreciatively.

The following chapters identify some of the areas where coaching and organizational evolution are taking us today on the edge of coaching.

One final comment that has been eluded to in the remainder of the book, but not specifically stated, is the role of coaching coaches in this kind of atmosphere. As our coaching system becomes more advanced and sophisticated, we need to add an additional connecting layer in levels 1, 2 and 3 coaching systems and that is coaching the coaches—boundary spanning.

We need to establish a specific organizational learning cycle around the islands of coaching knowledge that will have a tendency to form functionally. By that, I mean that we need to connect the coaches into a community of practice and commitment in order to harvest the knowledge gained from the *perspectives* created through coaching in organizations.

As I write, there is not much actual data on this but taking examples from anthropology and knowledge management, we should be able to devise a system capable of leveraging this coaching knowledge to coach the coaches.

If you are more interested in this topic, send an email to coachingcoaches@coach2-the-bottom-line.com. You'll receive regular updates on our research progress regarding this interesting phenomena in organizations!

We can't lose any opportunity to increase connectivity and conversations at any level, specifically those levels that are boundary spanning levels. Critical to organizational learning, these boundary spanners unite the innovative capability among organizations into a cohesive strategy that directs innovation and change.

Executive MUST understand these critical roles and must do everything in their power to facilitate sharing among these communities of practice. Every encouragement has to be made in order to structure and connect the knowledge contained in our functional silos and various layers of activity.

We must begin to embrace zero and negative time, understanding our customers customer as what they want our customers need, so we create competitive advantage through organizational awareness and learning.

Read the next couple of chapters and the appendicies with an open mind, coaching is developing abilities to create development at all levels more effectively and it will integrate many different disciplines to do so. The most exciting thing that will happen in our lifetimes is a synthesis of the human mind, ability and heart to create more flow and opportunities to learn and grow in our workscape towards a sustainable future with one another.

Chapter 20

"A major issue that is getting practically no attention in the management literature is the reality in many cases the chief executive officer does not have the conceptual capacity to grasp the degree of complexity that he or she must now confront. In short, they simply do not know what they are really up against and what is happening to them and to their organizations, let alone knowing what to do about it. They simply can't absorb the range of information they should and organize it from multiple sources and focus it on the organizations' problems in a way that would both become vision and strategy."

Harry Levinson, <u>Why the Behemoths Fell</u>,
American Psychologist, May 1994

Coaching as Art and Science

I would like to acquaint you in this chapter with some issues that are making the art of coaching truly into more of a science. Adult developmental theory, being led in part by Robert Kegan of Harvard, et al holds many interesting clues and cues to development in adults, whether it be through a coaching methodology, counseling or pedagogy. Kegan's 1982 book, <u>THE EVOLVING SELF</u> outlined some key issues in adult development that are germane to effective coaching systems.

One of those keys--validated in my own coaching practice--is the issue of development. Einstein is reported to have said that the level of thinking required to solve problems is not the same level of thinking that created them. I believe Einstein was talking to the person coaching.

Somewhere in the literature, and I have forgotten who, it was indicated that in school we ask students to solve problems at one order of development when they are at a different level. We do the same thing with performance management without coaching. If we see an environmental or organizational challenge, we mechanically outline a plan to meet it and move to problem solving rather than discovering what has worked in the past and doing more of it—a solutions-based approach.

We cannot solve developmental challenges through management by objectives. I think most of us are beginning to understand that issue. It is like a gardener hollering at their plants to grow rather than seeing to the cultivation of an appropriate growing environment.

In developmental coaching, we help the pbc identify and remove barriers to growth and development rather than insist on fixing his/her problems, as it is so easy to do in management.

Often, in management systems in the past, and since time is a constraint, we have taught people to come to us as leaders and managers for answers—consciously and unconsciously. Because, we found in the short term, it is a process often safe for them and easier for us. In doing so, however, we stunt their growth in the long term and then wonder why they cannot solve difficult and ever more complex challenges?

Although a novice when it comes to developmental coaching, I believe we all need to start paying more attention to the keys adult developmental theory brings us in the form of more and more research about learning and growth in adult development. In my opinion, many of the clues to reenergizing our human resources lie in that realm. As we approach the whole person concept of leadership and management, we create the fertile framework for people to perform, change and transform their own lives and their organizations as a result.

Inner Coaching

Probably, the most difficult aspect of coaching is coaching oneself. Many people react most unfavorably to the prospect of self coaching, however, we will have to illuminate the concept in this section of advanced coaching methods.

As you become more experienced at coaching and more cognizant of your own personal role in development, you will find an ability to separate yourself from your behavior, or in other words, become a witness to the coaching. I am not a psychologist nor someone fully experienced in adult developmental theory, but from what I have pieced together while observing myself--my own development--and the literature, it becomes prudent and desirable after a time, to become self-authoring and self-coached.

This is not an excuse not be coached. Another person's perspective is always *critical* to further growth and development. However, one should begin by becoming aware of the issues that are important to reach our desired states. Some of these states will be easier to achieve than others, yet an awareness of the opportunity for using the coaching KSAs on (our) "selves" will be important to the process.

Our observation, listening, discernment and conversation with (our) "self" is just, if not more important, than any other conversation we have with others. In that conversation, we become aware of the discrepancies, feelings and incongruities—as well as the coherence and flow—we experience on a moment-by-moment basis. This becomes increasingly important for people in high stress positions and in leadership positions where they are pulled apart by paradoxical dilemmas that confront them daily—individually and organizationally.

Being able to distance oneself from the cacophony of our thoughts and those issues that have no *right* answer, allows our *self* to remain vibrant and able to find constancy while addressing a turbulent environment.

In itself and at first, this is a feat not easily accomplished without a net, hence the reason we need coaches. Yet, understanding and allowing ourself to come to terms with the need for someone else to help us guide our development is not always a welcomed proposition for a leader or executive.

The Heart Aroused

Inner coaching should be tested against a capable and compassionate person coaching. Actively seeking to "self-coach" yourself is a viable way to "*have the conversation and to allow change to come from that conversation.* "

Here is a poem on the matter of waking up and saving our lives, given by an old Native American elder. The poem is in the form of a story handed down from generation to generation, the kind of story an elder would tell to a young girl or boy whose own life depended on the question, *What do I do when I'm lost in the forest*. David Wagoner, chair of poetry at the University of Washington rendered it beautifully into modern English.. The poem is called "Lost."

> *Stand still. The trees and bushes beside you*
> *Are not lost. Wherever you are is called Here,*
> *And you must treat it as a powerful stranger,*

Must ask permission to know it and be known,
The forest breathes, Listen. It answers,
I have made this place around you,
If you leave it you may come back again, saying Here.
No two trees are the same to Raven.
No two branches are the same to Wren.
If what a tress or a bush does is lost on you,
You are surely lost. Stand still. The forest knows
Where you are. You must let it find you.

Excerpted From THE HEART AROUSED,
by David Whyte

Clearly, as coaching advances and our own developmental needs advance, we have to use all of the tools at our disposal. Inner coaching happens to be one of those tools. Becoming self-aware leads to higher levels of emotional intelligence. It is critical to leading complex adaptive systems, including our own!

Chapter 21

This principle of structural tension—knowing what we want to create and knowing where we are in relationship to our goals—is the most powerful force an organization can have.

Robert Fritz

Structural Coaching

This form of coaching was developed as a result of studying the principles contained in the philosophy of Robert Fritz. His latest book, *THE PATH OF LEAST RESISTANCE for Managers, 1999* contains the structural philosophy that this coaching practice is based upon. This kind of coaching has particular relevance to executives, leaders and organizational developers.

In this chapter's opening quote listed above, the <u>structure</u> named is the tension created, much like the creative tension described by Peter Senge in *THE FIFTH DISCIPLINE*— tension as a result of the attractive forces of a stretch goal and current reality.

In adapting these philosophical underpinnings for structural coaching, I felt it was important to use these principles to fully under gird the concept.

In Senge's Foreward to the book by Fritz, he uses a metaphor of people in their flying machines and the following quote emerges as he speaks about their many attempts to fly like birds using bird-like *structures* in the early days of flight:

It doesn't matter how hard people try, how good they are as people, or how lofty their aspirations are. There is nothing people are going to do to create the results of which they are potentially capable given the structures that predominate. And worst of all, very few people are even aware of the problem.

What caught my attention, besides Fritz's first book, *THE PATH OF LEAST RESISTANCE* a few years ago, was the emphasis on structure. The COACH2 Model overlays the concept of people, structure and technology (the socio-tech model).

Where technology is fully integrated into people, structure and methodology, coaching becomes an essential component of the helping function in facilitating the integration of the three issues based on the Socio-tech model of organization.

On the next page, a diagram of complex networks of structure overlayed onto one another (top down view) demonstrate the structural forms that are taking place in the following areas:

Levels of Complexity	Graduated layers of Attention	Levels of Intention
5	━━━━━━━━━━━━	Practice
4	━━━━━━━━━━━━	Ksa's
3	━━━━━━━━━━━━	Methdology
2	════════════	Business System
1	════════════	MarketSpace
0	- - - - - - - - - -	Environment

Layers of Structure

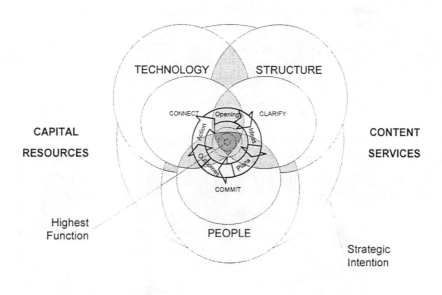

This graphic is not the best but what it does show is that layers of complexity create varying levels of structure and complexity that must be dealt with simulataneously. The question then became, what is it about structure that affects us as human beings, not just the organization?

Clearly, James Flaherty pointed out in his recent book on *COACHING: Evoking Excellence in Others,* **structure of interpretation** is the key issue in behavior:

I recommend that we account for behavior by understanding it as what follows from the way the world is showing up for someone. In other words, it's not events, communication, or stimuli that lead to behavior, it is the interpretation an individual gives to the phenomenon that leads to actions taken.

He goes on to conclude that *"Our job as coaches will be to understand the client's structure of interpretation, then in partnership alter this structure so that the actions that follow bring about the intended outcome."*

Clearly structure has a multidimensional meaning but can be distilled into the cognitive organization of perception, thought and judgment that is unique to the pbc (person being coached) at any point in time. When we consider the structure of this organization, it becomes clear that the structure itself becomes a determinant of behavior in the pbc. When we include in *that* structure, the environmental organization (super-ordinate structure) surrounding the cognitive organization of the pbc, we can easily see the complexity of behavior and why it is not so easy for people to change the results of the convergence of these structures.

[Clearly, this one principle, the principle of multiple conversations, with self, among others and between others—with all of the structural norms and principles involved—*creates a rather defined difference between personal coaching and coaching in business and organization.* Dealing with multiple sets of constraints at the same time ***in a multidimensional*** focus (where organizational needs are as important or more important as personal needs), is much different than dealing with a person as a central focus having multiple constraints.]

Simply, if we can understand what the pbc and the organization really wants to accomplish, help them to understand where they really are--in terms of current reality and desired futures--and to co-generate a plan of action from that tension, we as *helpers* stand an excellent chance of being helpful. Fully, in my view, this is a process that falls well within the realm of coaching KSA's.

Towards that end, I offer the following discussion on structural coaching.

The coaching interaction referenced by the COACH2 (C2) Model fully integrates an opportunity for structural coaching to take place. If we review the process of the Coaching Interaction Model (CIM): Openings, Possibilities, Plans, Outcomes, Action, we can establish a clear path towards assessing structure in the pbc. Using the appropriate delivery method (feedback, questions, statements, challenges and ideas), we can guide the pbc through the process of discovering what they really want, or what really matters to them—in other words—right action in full view of organizational demands.

When we have brought into full view what is important to accomplish, we can then create the tension needed to generate the *pull or attractive* forces that are indeed effortless in terms of what Fritz terms: *The path of least resistance.* Even though effort is required, the path chosen becomes effortless in terms of cognitive and emotional struggle about right action to decrease the tension between current reality and our desired future state.

What has to happen after the tension is created is for a plan of resolution of the tension to be created. Usually that is where the pc/pbc connection generates emergent solutions or synchronicity as some would call it. In terms of clarification and real commitment, once the tension is created with the proper ends, the means can be created more easily. *Once we know where we are going, it becomes a lot easier to get there.*

If we review the CIM, we see that the opening itself is the key again to establishing the *needed* discrepancy between the results we are getting and the results we want. In this opening—brought about by awareness of incongruence--lay the roots of creative tension. If the pbc views this as an opening, then it is clear that the opportunity for creating attractive forces leading to powerful commitment exists.

One thing that is becoming more and more clear to me as I view the difference between gap and opening is a passage from Fritz's book: *"A gap suggests an empty space between something and something else. Instead of an empty space (the absence of something) there is a tension (the presence of a powerful dynamic force)."*

This also helps to explain the esoteric meaning of attraction that is often so difficult to understand fully in the context of coaching. If something is there—this tension that Fritz states—then there is an attractive force, although weak and unknown if the discrepancy exists. It is the opening— awareness of incongruence--that clears the way for us to "stretch" the attractive force already present (making it a strong force), develop it and make it stronger by identifying fully the desired state and the current reality of the pbc— leading to commitment.

Only then can we move to the next steps of generating possibilities leading to a plan of resolution—powering the attractive force of commitment and action. Here are some of the questions to ask at' each stage of the CIM.

Openings:

What is evident here?
What are the discrepancies that are creating the opening?
What is the attractive force? Is it weak or strong?
What is compelling the pbc to sense and offer the opening?
Why is the desired state unachievable now?
What is compelling about that future state?

Possibilities:

What is clear about the alternatives?
What delivery is bringing about the greatest amount of tension?
How can we explore the discrepancies in light of options?
What possibilities generate the greatest amount of enthusiasm and passion?

Plans:

Do we know the result that is of highest value to the pbc?
Is the result quantified in terms of desired vs. current?
Is the client using the same comparative terms for both?
Do these plans create results or fix problems?
Are the plans clear and specific?
Do they achieve a why, or is the plan about how?

Outcomes:

Does the plan provide the reference for creating the outcomes desired?

Is the picture of the plan and what it will produce clearly in line with the desired state?
Does the plan take into view the whole picture?
Is the plan objective?
Preview the plan in terms of the scenarios that are likely to occur—do they match?
Is the plan doable or is it too pollyana in terms of the capability of the pbc?
Is current reality clearly stated or is it exaggerated?
What are the barriers to completing the plan?
What is the level of enthusiasm for the plan?

Action:

Do the action steps match every aspect of the desired state?
When the plan was previewed, was the desired state reached through action capable of being taken by the pbc in the current state of reality?
Are the action steps clear, concise, time specific and measurable?
Is the pbc absolutely clear on what is expected of them in terms of the plan they have devised?
Can every action step be measured in terms of success?
Does the pbc know when they are finished and the tension is resolved, or is this merely a continuous struggle with effort?

Summary

Structural coaching, what is it? The process where the pc and pbc discover the attractive forces residing in the creative tension between what is desired and what is currently being realized—developing a clear, committed plan of action to resolve the tension created through the structural difference.

[Structural difference can be inherent in developmental levels of the current and future realities, the differences in governing variables between Model I status in the organization and Model II in the pbc, or vice-versa or a mismatch in values or principles inherent in the individual and in the organizational role they are in. This also applies to family and community organizations as well.]

This simple yet effective technique can work for a pbc, an organization, a team or a project. I recommend the book by Robert Fritz as a means to fully explore how to map structural tension in a complex organization and how to use structural tension to engage a pbc or an organization along the path of least resistance—*effortlessly.*

Chapter 22

The emphasis that I place on citizen action and initiative is not intended to diminish in any way the importance of leadership.

An alive, aware citizenry will not lessen the need for leaders; it will ensure better leadership. People get the leaders they deserve.

Effective leadership is essential to cope with the inertia present in any social system. Systemic inertia is characteristic of all societies, but especially true of this nation.

Our system of checks and balances dilutes the thrust of positive action. The multiplicity of interests inherent in our pluralism acts as a powerful brake on significant public initiatives.

The system is designed to grind to a halt between crises. James Madison constructed it in such a way that it simply will not move without vigorous, driving leadership.

I've often wondered why he didn't say so. Having in mind his brilliant contemporaries, I suppose it just never occurred to him that the day might come when leadership would be lacking.

It's more than a question of leadership at the top. We'd all be better off if we stopped looking for a savior. We need leadership at every level and in every segment of society -- not only in government, but in business, the professions, labor, the universities, the minority communities.

We need leadership that will move vigorously to keep each of those special worlds abreast of the swift social changes that are wracking the nation and the world. But even more, we need leadership that has some understanding of how all the special worlds fit together into a functioning society.

John Gardner on Leadership

Coaches & Leadership

What is clearly in evidence as I move through my own coaching development is why coaches—people coaching—must be strategists in leadership, business development and global competitiveness.

In business interactions, we notice gaps between what is required from the environment or business system and the current capability of the person being coached. These *variances* or gaps lead to openings at some point, but nevertheless, the discrepancy and incongruity between the challenge and the solution exists. These openings through which people coaching can create a conversation arise out of this dissonance between *what is and what needs to be.*

While it is the purpose of coaching to co-generate development in this opening, my reasons for generating this part of the discussion are:

Incongruity between

- level of development required and current development
- knowledge of what is and what could be
- skills and abilities of current and future needs
- strategic view of now, near and far vision
- current EQ and future EQ (Emotional Intelligence) required
- espoused theory of action versus theory in use
- orders of consciousness--now and future
- level of current and future integration
- current policy and future innovation
- level of cognitive organizational models—local vs. global

Coach Outside-In?

...make a clear, compelling reason for change, especially to people who are accountable for other parts of the system. Work from outside-in by focusing first on meeting outside market demands, then on internal, personal aspirations.

Excerpted from Audio-Tech Business Book Summaries, Richard Lalich, Editor, from THE DANCE OF CHANGE, by Peter Senge, Art Kleiner, Charlotte Roberts, Richard Ross, George Roth & Bryan Smith

What is interesting about the quote—taken out of context—is the implication that some other *way* rather than inside-out—a popularization by Stephen Covey about individual change—is called for in organizational change.

The dichotomy of outside-in and inside-out is a paradox that concerns us all. Rather than being able to rely on an inside-out movement—championed through personal change rhetoric--we now are being confronted with the complexity of the evolving organization—required to meet environmental demands—and the need to change from a direction of outside-in.

Review the quote again.

The key point made is in the order of attention to intention. In order to change *an organization* of individuals, we MUST consider meeting the demands of the organizational constituency (the customer—internal and external), then *satisficing* internal demands.

This is quite contrary to much of the present thinking in personal coaching! It is also the key point of demarcation— against our own self-declaring sense of importance—or bifurcation, if you will of personal and organizational coaching.

In the case of personal coaching—inside-out--and organizational coaching—outside-in, we find the creative tension, openings and awareness of multiple goals.

- The importance of the organization to the individual
- The importance of the individual to the organization.

This is merely the proverbial tip of the iceberg. The challenges that this paradox represents will be debated ad infinitum with no clear truth arising—one can't exist without the other—all other things being equal.

Peter Drucker in his recent book, MANAGING IN TURBULENT TIMES, describes a situation in family businesses with succession challenges, where he indicates "the family must serve the business and not the other way around."

This resolute ambiguity will constantly create friction among individuals and organizational constituents. The good of the few or the good of the many—the ultimate question of self-protection we all have to face. Those of us in leadership and management coaching straddle the fence between you and the organization.

Coaching is the boundary spanning methodology. The ability to value the individual and the organizational needs as one and as separate truly the separate horns of a dilemma.

> *As coaching in organizations moves forward to meet these challenges, the executive must live in ambiguity around need and value, around personal and collective and find ways to bridge the gaps with integrated leadership, management and coaching systems.*

EPILOGUE: Insights so far

As I *right* this, I realize that I have only scratched the surface of coaching. It would be nice to say that this is a definitive work, but that hardly is the case. As I think through the process that will take me further along the path, I am thankful that I live when I do. If I were a monk (not likely) somewhere writing this by hand on papyrus, knowing that it would take a number of the brethren to even gain a copy or two, I could not engender the thoughts I have now of continuing to research and write additional chapters which will be easily added via the web-based and on-demand publishing I am using with this book.

> *Be sure to send in your comment and registration form or visit the website and request your membership number so you can keep up with the game.*

I guess what I would like to leave you with are the insights I have had thus far. Many of them are scattered throughout the book but I've tried to summarize some of them here hoping to reduce the rhetoric to a few key take-aways and come back-tos. I again extend to you my invitation to come to one of our coaching makeover sessions (most likely they will be free intro sessions) or to sign up for our COACH2 coaching program. The schedule of these sessions can be found on the book's website http://www.coach2-the-bottom-line.com.

Thanks again for reading or just picking up the book.

Happy Trails!

COACH2 *Insights*

(Read the best of the book here!)

"The time has passed that we are able to command the world's markets and our employee's time, life and existence. A fragile, yet dynamic balance is coming into vogue where we must—for the right reasons—conduct ourselves individually and collectively in harmony with one another and our environment."

"The difference between personal coaching and organizational coaching is that in personal coaching, the pbc is figuratively the center of the universe in terms of focus. In organizational coaching, there are at a minimum, **two** universes of intention and attention, the individual and the organization. There may indeed be others as role complexity increases dramatically in organization."

In the simplest terms, **a coach is someone who uses coaching knowledge, skills and abilities (ksa's) without responsibility, accountability or authority over the outcomes of the *person being coached (pbc);* while seeking to co-generate well-being, purpose, competence and awareness as a result of a coaching interaction.**

A person using coaching ksa's is not necessarily a coach and should not be considered a coach unless they meet the specific criteria above. A modern day illusion is that everyone is a coach, as many pundits have indicated. Often an organization failing to recognize the following distinctions sets up people— they call coaches—to fail.

The following distinctions will frame the theory more clearly:

1. A *coach* normally has many years of specialized training and experience; a person coaching is often not formally trained as a coach, only in coaching ksa's.
2. Coaching is practiced through openings, management coaching through gaps
3. Leaders, managers, mentors, counselors and teachers all practice coaching but are not coaches.
4. The significant issue differentiating coaches and people coaching is agenda; *a coach does not have one*, or the RAA to see that the person performs or achieves a specified outcome.
5. A coach, as stated previously has no RAA over the performance of the pbc, while a pc often has at least one and often all three.
6. A *true coach* practices in a strictly voluntary environment.
7. Almost anyone can and should develop and use coaching ksa's, however it often takes many years of practice to become masterful at coaching.
8. The difference between personal coaching and organizational coaching is that in personal coaching, the pbc is figuratively the center of the universe in terms of focus. In organizational coaching, there are minimum two universes of intention and attention, the individual and the organization. There may indeed be others as role complexity increases dramatically in organization.

In short, here is the remainder of the theory surrounding the COACH2 Coaching Methodology. Any kind of coaching has in common at least one and more often than not, all four critical coaching outcomes—personal and organizational—in all cases.

- An improvement in well-being
- Purposeful behavior

- Higher levels of competence
- Increased awareness

However, there are three *core competencies* that under gird **any** coaching process, methodology or system. Any other system of coaching can be mapped onto the COACH2 Model creating enormous personal and organizational leverage, but all must attain competence in three key areas:

- Connection
- Clarification
- Commitment

Without all three of these competences evident in the coaching methodology or technology, it will be difficult to achieve the stated and desired outcomes of well-being, purpose, competence and awareness or organizational effectiveness.

In regards to outcomes and core competencies, there is a host of other ksa's that contributes toward fulfillment of these significant virtues. Many processes are involved, triggered and co-created during coaching interactions but all have five important sub-processes in common. They are:

- Openings
- Possibilities
- Plans
- Outcomes
- Action

The action portion of these five characteristics is stated as key abilities that must be continuously developed and improved. Those abilities are:

- Observing

- Listening
- Discerning
- Modeling
- Delivering

These five abilities in concert with the five key subject areas of openings, possibilities, plans, outcomes and action create the realization of the three core competencies and resultant desired outcomes listed previously. What is also interesting is that the key abilities are directly represented by our five senses in one-way or another: *Sight, Sound, Feeling, Action and Speech.*

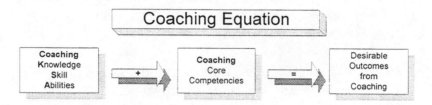

This equation assumes that a coaching interaction is based on these basic values:

- RIGHT ACTION
- RESPECT
- CONFIDENTIALITY
- DEVELOPMENT
- MASTERY

There are literally hundreds of ksa's available to coaches, all of which have there place and their time, however they must all flow-through these essential components of the equation in full view of governing values or variables.

To complete the abridged version of the COACH2 Methodology, there are two remaining factors to consider as central to the model. A coaching conversation, approach or interaction basically consists of two things: content and delivery. Delivery is but one aspect of communication, but is central to coaching. You will notice that all five action abilities: observing, listening, discerning, modeling and delivery are all required components of communication.

We know that coaching occurs in every discipline and in every possible situation, at times. Content is often created about and through those unique circumstances, but delivery methods a person coaching uses can be categorized as feedback, ideas, questions and challenges. Every one of these methods can be charged positive or negative and occur as such to the pbc. Effective coaching to promote the agenda or--when the agenda and desired outcomes are not the same—the desired state of the pbc can masterfully use each method.

Effective use of timing, placement, force and focus of delivery all provide the appropriate impact on the interaction or relationship. To evoke excellence in others requires the effective use of coaching ksa's and practice. In order to co-generate well-being, purpose, competence and awareness requires our coaching to be humane and compassionate, clear and courageous and empathetic and masterful.

Summary of Coaching Guidelines

To close this overview of COACH2, here are some simple, yet elegant guidelines:

1. People are different--seek understanding of those differences with a beginner's mind
2. Spend the *appropriate* amount of time connecting with the pbc.
3. When in doubt, listen deeply and ask a clarifying question: "Say more about that?"

4. Coach through openings, use coaching ksa's to create openings out of gaps.
5. Coach the pbc where they are with an eye on their desired future.
6. Challenge the status quo of the pbc when they are stuck.
7. Use the C.A.R.E.S Model to guide the coach approach:

   - Control – Assurance – Reliability – Empathy – Safety

   Provide the pbc with all of these in the interaction!

8. Ask for commitment to action
9. Embrace the concepts of *blameless error* and successful failure.
10. Smile a lot and enjoy the interaction with the pbc.

"Coaching is a deep or profound change methodology that seeks to integrate leadership, management and learning into a coherent whole."

"You don't create effective coaching from books, effective coaching comes from practice with intent to facilitate effective results from coaching interactions. Effective coaching comes from mastering essential abilities towards competence. Yet, awareness can come from books and out of that conversation, purpose and competence."

"Since the basic purpose of this book is to provide both the theory and practice of coaching in organizations, it becomes important to discuss coaching system design in organizations. These design decisions will be more and more important as coaching evolves from the individual interaction to a coaching system of interdependent interactions--

integrated throughout the organization to create, sustain and evolve structural and cultural change."

"A person won over against their will is of the same opinion still!" (Author unknown)

"He who is good with a hammer thinks everything is a nail." Maslow

"A manager is seldom ever a coach and shouldn't be, yet should master coaching KSAs."

"If you connect, the interaction will likely be effortless and fun."

"Understanding differences is probably everyone's biggest challenge."

"When we *do* understand others, our attributions are mostly impersonal."

"Coaching is about commitment."

"Development is a business term for the path to enlightenment—that we might dare."

"Compassion and dispassion are the true noble friends of a coach."

"*Person coaching* is a better term to describe the coaching system in an organization rather than using the term coach generally."

"Coaching employs process and deploys content sparingly."

"It's hard to hear what the person being coached is saying when you are talking."

"Conversation is a medium, seldom a learning tool."

"The medium (conversation) carries the weight of change."

"The simpler, the better, yet integrating complexity will require integration of a number of simple concepts— concurrently."

"Seeing complexity as layers is sometimes easier to understand and model."

"Different problems require different solutions."

"Assessments will do MORE harm than good in the wrong hands."

"Instead of labeling people, we should discern their basic differences."

"Prediction using assessments is folly and almost certainly guarantees that you will fail some of the time."

"The criticality of our success as persons developing and maintaining an effective coaching system depends almost entirely on our ability to leverage and value differences among people."

"Here's the real learning in studying differences in my opinion. Attribution. Can we attribute the interpretation, meaning making and behavior a person displays to something other than their personal affect? In other words, can we attribute the way someone is different towards a reason other than a personal motivation to harm us, discredit us, show us up or become a threat to us?"

"Some people should not be coached."

"Coaching through openings beats coaching in the gap any day!"

"You will seldom ever make a mistake coaching if you coach through an opening."

"Stop trying to articulate every thought you have, instead be with it for awhile."

"PLEASE, don't make your managers coaches—give them coaching ksa's and opportunities to use them with their subordinates, but DO NOT CALL THEM COACHES! It will always do more harm than good."

"No coach should ever coach someone whose outcomes they are responsible for!"

"Fully integrate coaching into your leadership and management systems"

This by far will be the most difficult call for the organization as well as the pc. The tendency will be--when cramped for time and resources--to provide fish rather than creating fishing opportunities.

Clearly at times, the pc will leave the coach approach for other approaches and this is important to understand this transition and another major reason why the pc is not often going to be a coach in terms of our previous definition. A pc is more likely to be able to shift from manager to trainer to leader back to the pc much easier than a coach will be able to shift out of coaching. This is an important distinction to keep in mind as you develop your organizational coaching system!

In all cases, we define coaching as the interaction to develop personal and organizational right action that meets environmental demands—creating well-being, purpose, competence and awareness through dialogue.

"Understand that the organization exists to provide value on both sides of the equation and continuously renew its capability to do so by developing people and customers."

"Give people opportunities they want not what you have."

To the extent that our listening is filled with our own agenda we are disabled in our attempts to help the pbc find their own sense of right action. It all boils down to what we hear, what we see and how we process that information. To really listen requires practice *after becoming aware of our own sense of right action, the needs we seek to satisfy* and reaching a place where we can become a witness to those needs and agendas without bringing them to bear upon the pbc in the coaching interaction. This will be the single most difficult aspect of mastering effective coaching without a doubt for anyone.

"Hire good people, don't try to fix them."

"If you're going to use internal coaches, get them out of the direct chain of command."

"Provide coaching opportunities throughout the organization not just to executives."

"When you create a coaching system, do it deliberately and don't try to make everyone coaches at once. If you change 20% of the people in your organization, they will change the other 80% over time with nothing less than a guiding vision to do so."

"Just because people aren't sophisticated doesn't mean they and the organization won't benefit from a good coaching program."

"Give line managers coaching skill development opportunities—regularly."

"Create a culture of coaching through continuous development of coaching ksa's."

"Mastery comes in small bites."

"Don't lose faith when coaching programs don't immediately work wonders, it takes time for people to develop and change."

"Always include a coaching program with an impact training program."

"Coach all your managers to become teachers and all leaders to articulate their teachable points of view--often." (Research from Noel Tichy)

"Most of us learn by doing and watching, not talking—always take coaching to the next level—that of modeling."

"Always coach to the person, not as a result of a preformed process."

"Understand situational coaching, what it is and what it is not."

"Coaching with courage requires restraint and timing."

"Coach from here to there."

"In order to become more effective as coaches we have to understand how people develop in terms of consciousness and higher order thinking. As more and more of what we do as a pc becomes centered around increasing returns—an ability to improve at improving—our ability to help people climb developmental ladders quickly in spite of their age or experience, can make drastic improvements in the business system and organizational effectiveness."

"Understanding our role as part of the "business system" and what as the person coaching our role is in improving the organization helps us to meld the various differences and potentialities of our human resources into an interconnected whole."

"Maintaining, surfacing and promoting self-worth and value through an appreciative coaching interaction hold more leverage than any knowledge, skill or ability that might be created for the pbc through the interaction. Adaptability, vitality, passion and the willingness to go the extra mile all stem from our sense of self-worth."

STAY TUNED

FOR OUR COACH2 The Bottom Line: An Executive Conversation on coaching knowledge, skills and abilities in organizations—coming soon!

Don't forget to fill out your feedback and registration form!

The Final Word

Coaching and Enlightenment

First I want to say that I am not in a position through enlightenment or experience to be offering advice to anyone. Yet, I would like to state a position. As I dove into this project years ago, discovering layer after layer of complexity, I became confused with all of the models, concepts and protocols of leadership and coaching. Fortunately for me, after a time, the confusion settled and I began to see patterns and threads of commonality among the various models.

It seemed the more I learned the more evidence the research provided. As I put into practice many of the methods you have read about in this book over time, a few things have surfaced and became clear.

Coaching in one form or another is about enlightenment. If I would be permitted to define enlightenment as becoming aware, then coaching is about becoming aware.

There is a lot to me that is unclear, but what has become clear is that all of us are provided through nature and nurture-- uniquely reinforced--a set of default values. Without getting too spooky, I have began to see evidence of a common thread- -discussed for centuries by various spiritual leaders--all leading to the same place. As the coaching interaction takes place, there are many possibilities, the most important of which is awareness. Awareness of who we are and are not…awareness of our purpose…awareness of our limitations and how all of those open a door to realizing competence-- effortlessly…awareness of the essential common thread of all human being and doing…the undisputable force that lies within all of us for well-being and the pursuit of happiness.

Yes, life is confusing and mixed up at times—too fast and too complex—and we make it so. Wo/man's search for meaning is a cacophony of doing and yet in the silence between our thoughts lies the peace and well-being that has always been there—a dear friend has help me realize this dream.

Coaching is about enlightenment, for each of us a different view, a different tune, perhaps a different life, yet in those unique differences lies a common thread of well-being. It is ours to find, ours to explore and ours to nurture through our life and works. Coaching in all of its methods, technologies and mystery provides a process for the co-creating the openings for that, which has always been.

I don't know your answers, as the journey is yours.

However, if you will take to heart the principles and practices in this book, wherever you are, whatever language you speak, your journey will be one of significance, if to no one other than yourself. We can not control what happens to us, yet we have the awesome power to decide our attitude about it. Life is what you make it, we have the power to create that which is around us for the kingdom of GOD is within us—we have in the final end…choice.

I hope that something in this book has helped you to **imagine** the future that you dream of, will **inspire** you to take action, help you **innovate** your own coaching methodology and **integrate** it into your life and organization, however YOU will have to **initiate** action to become that which you desire.

It is after all about the bottom line…yours!

Mike R. Jay, 1999

Afterthoughts

Whimsical notions and Weird ideas?

IS IT POSSIBLE TO COACH AN ORGANIZATION?

In coaching an organization, is it possible to forget about "the who" issues when the organization is tied up in knots? Specifically, dysfunctional organizations that have merged two separate cultures, or organizations that have a cancerous core that only spends its time on happy talk, or not upsetting any one?

Instead of *playing to the obvious interpersonal issues,* focus on creating the structural tension required by where we want to go versus where we are, as objectively as possible and hold everyone's feet to the fire for setting clear action plans based on the tension?

Sounds like managing or leading?

If we were to strictly focus on the structural tension and continually focus the organization on where we need to go; what current reality is objectively; and the action plans required to resolve the tension, would it be possible to *transcend and transform the organization at the very same time?*

If people had to focus strictly on the matters at hand and look past whatever differences there were in terms of subjective means, could the *organization*, through structural conditioning heal itself in the short run and cause the interpersonal issues to subside?

The implementation part would not be coaching, but perhaps the coaching could be done through the combined or doctor/patient model in terms of the organization as an entity in itself—in view of the dysfunctional interpersonal systems.

This of course, would not be recommended as SOP (Standard Operating Procedure) but as a *if we don't do this the organization will die* (maybe it should<grin>) or in times of transition where we KNOW the organization needs to die unto itself—an old biblical term I think—and be reborn.

However, in today's world, that may take too long to save the organization, the jobs and the means to the end. Food for thought and discussion.

(Send comments to me at <u>dysfunctionalorg@leadwise.com</u>).

BIBLIOGRAPHY

Argyris, Chris, Schon, Donald A., - Theories In Practice:
Increasing Professional Effectiveness, Josey-Bass, (1974)

Autry, James - The Art of Caring Leadership , Morrow, New
York City (1991)

Benton, D. A., - Secrets of a CEO Coach, McGraw-Hill,
(1999)

Bennis, Warren; Nanus, Bert, - LEADERS, (1985, 1997)

Berquist, William, Merrit, Kenneth, Phillips, Steven, -
EXECUTIVE COACHING, Pacific Soundings Press, 1999

Brodie, Richard, Virus of the Mind: The New Science of the
Meme (Integral Press, 1996)

Buckingham, Marcus & Coffman, Curt – First, Break the
Rules: what the World's Greatest Managers do Differently,
Simon & Schuster (1999)

Collins, Jim - Turning Goals Into Results, HBR, July-Aug,
(1999)

Cook, Marshall, J., - EFFECTIVE COACHING, McGraw-
Hill, (1999)

Covey, Stephen - Principle-Centered Leadership, Summit,
(1990)

Crane, Thomas G., - The Heart of Coaching, Using Transformational Coaching to Create a High-Performance Culture, FTA Press, (1998)

Csikszentmihalyi, Mihaly – Finding Flow: The Psychology of Engagement with Everyday Life, Basic Books, (1997)

Downey, Myles, - Effective Coaching, Orion, (1999)

Doyle, James S., - The BUSINESS COACH, A Game Plan for the New Work Environment, Wiley, (1999)

Drucker, Peter - Managing In a Time of Great Change, Plume. (1998)

Edwards Demming, W. – The New Economics, MIT Press, (1995)

Flaherty, James, Coaching: Evoking Excellence in Others, Butterworth Hinneman, (1999)

Fritz, Robert, - The Path of Least Resistance for Managers, Designing Organizations to Succeed, Berrett-Koehler, 1999

Gilley, Jerry W., -- START COACHING, How Performance Coaching Can Enhance Commitment and Improve Productivity, McGraw-Hill, (1996)

Hanna, David P., - Designing Organizations for High Performance, Addison-Wesley, (1988)

Hargrove, Robert, Masterful Coaching, Josey-Bass Pfieffer, (1995)

Hersey & Blanchard - <u>Management of Organizational Behavior : Utilizing Human Resources</u> by Paul Hersey, Kenneth H. Blanchard, Dewey E. Johnson

Hudson, Frederic M., <u>The Handbook of Coaching</u>, A Resource Guide to Effective Coaching with Individuals and Organizations, Hudson Institute Press, 1998

Jamieson, David & Julie O'Mara - <u>Managing Workforce 2000</u>, Jossey-Bass Inc., Publishers.

Kaplan, Ann R., – <u>Maslow on Management</u>, John Wiley & Sons, (1998)

Kegan, Robert – <u>The Evolving Self</u> , HBR Press, (1982)

Keidel, Robert, W., - <u>Seeing Organizational Patterns</u>, A New Theory and Language of Organizational Design, BK Publishing, (1995)

Lahey, Souvaine, Kegan, Goodman & Felix, – <u>A Guide to Subject-Object Interview</u>, Its Administration and Interpretation, 1998

Luthans, Fred, <u>ORGANIZATIONAL BEHAVIOR</u>, Sixth Edition, McGraw Hill, 1992

McGregor, Douglas – <u>Human Side of Enterprise</u> (1960)

McKenna, Regis, <u>Real Time</u>: Preparing for the Age of the Never Satisfied Customer, HBR Press, (1997)

Mink, Oscar G., Owen, Keith Q., Mink, Barbara, P., - <u>Developing High-Performance People</u>, The Art of Coaching, Persues Books, (1993)

Motsett, C.B., - <u>If it Wasn't for People…This Job Would Be Fun</u>, Coaching for Buy-in and Results, St Lucie Press, (1998)

Peat, F. David, - <u>INFINITE POTENTIAL</u>, The Life and Times of David Bohm, Addison-Wesley, 1997

Peppers, Don, Rogers, Martha, - <u>One to One Fieldbook</u>, The Complete Toolkit for Implementing a 1to1 Marketing Program, Doubleday, (1999)

Peters, Tom & Nancy Austin - <u>Passion for Excellence</u> (Summary from the First Edition of Em Griffin, <u>A First Look at Communication Theory</u>, McGraw-Hilll, Inc. (1991)

Pralahad & Hamel – <u>Competing for the Future</u>, HBR Press, (1994)

Schein, Edgar H., - <u>Process Consultation</u>, Vol II., Lessons for Managers and Consultants, Addison- Wesley, (1987)

Schwarz, Roger M., - <u>The Skilled Facilitator</u>., Practical Wisdom for Developing Effective Groups, Josey-Bass, 1994

Senge, Peter; Kleiner, Art ; Roberts, Charlotte ; Ross, Richard ; Roth, George ; Smith, Bryan ; <u>The Dance of Change</u>, Currency Doubleday, (1999)

Smart, Bradford Ph.D – <u>TOPGRADING</u>: How leading companies win by hiring, coaching and keeping the right people, Prentice Hall, (1999)

Stone, Florence M., - <u>Coaching, Counseling & Mentoring</u>, How to Choose & Use the Right Technique to Boost Performance, AMACOM, 1998

Stowell, Steven J., Starcevich, Matt M., - <u>The Coach</u>, Creating Partnerships for a Competitive Edge, CMOE Press, (1998)

Tannen, Deborah Ph.D. – <u>That's What I Meant!</u>, Ballantine Books (1986)

Vaill, Peter B., - <u>Learning as a Way of Being</u>, Strategies for Survival in a World of Permanent White Water, Josey-Bass, (1996)

Whiterspoon, R. & R. White – <u>Four Essential Ways that Coaching can help Executives,</u>, Center for Creative Leadership, (1998)

Whitmore, John, - <u>COACHING for Performance</u>, 2nd Edition, Nicholas Breasley, (1999)

Whitworth, Laura, Kimsey-House, Henry, Sandahl, Phil, - <u>Co-Active Coaching</u>, New Skills for Coaching People Toward Success in Work and Life, Davies Black, (1998)

Whyte, David – <u>The Heart Aroused</u>, Currency Doubleday, (1994)

Whyte, David – <u>The House of Belonging</u>, Marc Rivers Press, (1997)

Articles

Argyris, Chris - <u>The Executive Mind and Double Loop Learning</u>, Org Dynamics, Autumn 1982

Hannum, Mark – <u>Global Business Culture Study Group</u>, Global Human Resource Institute, November 1998

Keynote Speeches

Sumantra Ghoshal, Keynote at the 1997 Global Leadership Development Conference

Whyte, David, The Frontier of Conversation, 1999 Linkage, Inc. Boston, MA

On Line Articles

Articles available on Harvard Business School Publishing website
http://www.hbsp.harvard.edu/hbsp/prod_detail.asp?92105]

David S. Taylor, School of Education, University of Leeds at
http://www.cbl.leeds.ac.uk/~edu/inted/icu/compete1.htm

Bandura,Albert (TV Violence)
[http://www.afirstlook.com/docs/Bandura.html]

Frost, Robert: *Two Tramps in Mud Time*
[http://redfrog.norconnect.no/~poems/poems/02139.html]

Audio

Audio-Tech Business Book Summaries, Richard Lalich, Editor, from <u>THE DANCE OF CHANGE</u>, by Peter Senge, Art Kleiner, Charlotte Roberts, Richard Ross, George Roth & Bryan Smith

Appendix A

Glossary of Definitions

Blameless error: a situation where error detection and correction does not include assessing blame in a learning environment.

Boundary spanner network: A network of people whose role it is to integrate connections they make across the organization and learn from them in order to be more effective in integrating the initiative with a total connected change effort across boundaries.

Coach: a person participating in a mutually voluntary interaction with neither responsibility, accountability or authority over the outcomes of the person being coached towards a result of mutually desirable performance, generative change and development of the whole person.

Coaching: an interaction that occurs between people that produces desired performance, change or transformation in consideration of personal and organizational awareness, purpose, competence and well-being.

Core competence: addresses the collective learning of an organization. Prahalad and Hamel, cited below, introduced the concept and said three tests can be applied to determine a core competency: First, a core competence provides potential access to a wide variety of markets...Second, a core competence should make a significant contribution to the perceived customer benefits of the end product....Finally, a core competence should be difficult for competitors to imitate.

And it will be difficult if it is a complex harmonization of individual technologies and production skills.

[If you apply these to coaching and substitute some words, you can get a feel for why connection, clarification and commitment can be core competencies for a system of coaches.]

Double Loop Learning: also a term coined by Argyris meant to depict a change in frame or context that would make a different performance level more appropriate. It includes performance but also the question as to whether the system in place is appropriate to attain the required performance, such as a thermostat being able to ask the question, why is the temperature switch set at 68 degrees, people are not using the room, perhaps I should turn off the system until the temperature reaches 50 and conserve electricity.

Emotional Intelligence: includes the ability to (a) accurately perceive one's own and others' emotions, (b) exercise mastery over one's own emotions and respond with appropriate (i.e., realistic, undistorted, and adaptive) emotions and behaviors in various life situations, (c) enter into relationships where honest expression of emotions is balanced against courtesy, consideration, and respect, (d) select work that is emotionally rewarding, thereby avoiding procrastination, self-doubt, and low achievement, and (e) balance work, home, and recreational life.

Meme: the basic building blocks of our minds and culture, in the same way that genes are the basic building blocks of biological life.

Meme-space: The total area where your own personal memes are used to interact in space and time.

Marketscape: a term used to describe the full interaction between competitors, suppliers, substitutes, customers, employees and leadership.

Marketspace: a term used to describe the physical and electronic marketplace as one.

Now, near and far vision: Dividing vision up into three components helps to understand that the complexity of our environment is shifting our concern into several concurrent frames, now, near and far. With change and uncertainty occurring at such rapid rates, it may be too much to ask some people to make the intuitive leaps to the far vision when they hardly can see their future right now. Defining vision in terms of now, near and far also allows a person to take a linear approach to what may be the intuitive capability for some and to focus on letting now take care of near and far, keeping in mind what they are painted to be in the future.

Person being coached (pbc): a person who voluntarily enters an interaction towards a result of increasing performance, exploring change and transformation.

Person coaching (pc): a person who engages in an interaction towards performance, change and transformation.

Profound Change: Defined in The DANCE of CHANGE as the change in people's values and behaviors that occur in tandem with "outer" shifts in processes, practices and systems.

Scope of Work: a written document that outlines the challenge, what resources are available, the outcomes desired and support or sign-off on specific actions to be taken.

Single Loop Learning: a term coined by Chris Argyris that refers to a type of learning that can be illustrated as performance. An example given by Argyris is the analogy of a thermostat that automatically turns on when the temperature in the room drops below 98 degrees.

Slack: time not directly accounted for in terms of requirements imposed by either the system or one's self. Referring to slack time in a process where no action is to be taken.

Structure: an entity (such as an organization) made up of individual elements or parts (such as people, resources, aspirations, values, market trends, levels of competence, reward systems, departmental mandates, capital, workload/capacity relationships, and so on) that impact each other by the relationships they form. Taken from *THE PATH OF LEAST RESISTANCE for Managers, by Robert Fritz.*

Structure: an *organization* of thoughts, meaning making or cognitive systems that creates a behavioral result that is unique to that organization.

Structure of Interpretation: includes the commitments, projects, and relationships that make up the world of the observer, as well as the environment in which the observer finds himself. From *COACHING: Evoking Excellence in Others, by James Flaherty*

Structural difference: differences that can be inherent in developmental levels of the current and future realities, the differences in governing variables between Model I status in the organization and Model II in the pbc, or vice-versa or a mismatch in values or principles inherent in the individual and in the organizational role they are in. This also applies to family and community organizations as well.

Appendix B

"*CHANGE-ABILITY*" of ORGANIZATIONS

Why the need to change...adapt

"The ultimate success of any person or organization is directly related to the ability of that entity to anticipate, respond and adapt to the demands of the environment in real time...consistently."

The Fickleness of CHANGE

An initial disturbance in an organism results in a mobilization of energy to restore the balance, and recurrent upsets lead to actions to anticipate the disturbance. This basic principle in an organization is the tendency towards self-preservation of the character of the system. DESIGNING ORGANIZATIONS FOR HIGH PERFORMANCE David Hanna

HOMEOSTASIS

There is a need for balance...yet the bond of what "is" refuses to yield and all the energy of the organization may be directed towards stability...maintenance of the original character and shape--so much so--that it may oppose all the forces against it...to defeat the intended change...even when radical change may be necessary for the survival of the system!

Defining CHANGE-ABILITY

• Change-ability is the **potential** for non-destructive successful change.
• While it is not the "one" defining element of the ability of a company to change, it offers an interpretation of the state of the organization's capability to embrace the elements of change without destroying itself or limiting its capacity for high performance.
• If the Change-ability Index (CI) is above a certain threshold then the likelihood of success of a non-destructive change effort is high.
• Change often occurs in spite of our efforts and to say that change can't

occur because of a low CI score is ludicrous. However, a leader OR COACH may be interested in the ability of an organization to undergo non-destructive change *before* designing a change initiative or coaching program or system.

•There are clear advantages to understanding change readiness before an organization is destabilized through change initiatives. Often the fallout can be deadly to change agents and various constituencies.

Factors of CHANGE-ABILITY

UNDERWRITERS	DECISIVENESS	CULTURE
LEADERS	URGENCY	COMMUNICATION
INTENTION	INEVITABILTY	ORG. DESIGN
OWNERSHIP	CHANGE AGENTS	INNOVATION
METRICS	BEST PRACTICES	INFLUENCE
SYNERGY	CUSTOMER LED	TIME FRAME
SYSTEM VIEW	REWARDS	COMPLACENCY
EXPERIENCE	STRUCTURE	

INSTRUCTIONS

•The following pages describe categories within the change-ability index.

•Each area is rated from "1" being the lowest score and "5" being the highest rating.

•When you score the category think about how widespread your agreement is with the principles described on the page. If you are confident that the desired principles are widespread score the category a "5". If you see deep-seated problems score a "1".

•After you have rated your group or company ask a colleague or an outsider to rate your company also and compare the scores.

_____UNDERWRITERS

The underwriters of change are critical to the success of any change initiative. They sponsor the impetus for change and "pay the bills" for change. The higher the rank of the underwriter, the better the chance your organization can weather the climate of change.

Give yourself a "5" if the underwriter is the CEO or Chairman, as low as "1" if change is sponsored by staff or line employees.

____LEADERS

These are the people who lead the group or organization day-to-day. They set the pace for workflow, provide direction and consultation, as well as design the strategic intention.

Give yourself a "5" if the leaders are highly ranked in the organization and own the change initiative, lower if the leaders are not "well connected" and as low as "1" if the leaders are staff or line employees.

____INTENTION

Are people clear that the future MUST look different than the present and does this opinion comes from the top or is it widespread? Has everyone bought into the group's strategic plan for the future success of the org?

Give yourself a "5" if the entire organization from bottom to top is clear about what their strategic roles are; lower if people are unclear about the strategic intention, "1" if there isn't any strategic intention.

____OWNERSHIP

Is the change effort owned from the top down? Are people convinced of the need for change? Is everyone prepared to do their part to create the change needed with as little of resistance as possible? Is there a strong desire to change and improve performance?

Give yourself a "5" if everyone is motivated to do what it takes, lower if there are only pockets of ownership and "1" if resistance to the change effort is widespread.

_____METRICS

Are measurements widespread in the organization? Is the organization involved in a "quality" management program and are people trained in process metrics? Are their supporting structures such as compensation aligned with the measurement programs?

Give yourself a "5" if metrics are everywhere, lower if metrics are used but not tied to rewards and "1" if you don't know what we're talking about.

_____SYNERGY

Are there other ongoing programs which would support major change, quality, or reengineering and is the company clear on how this "new" change initiative "fits" into the groups strategy and direction?

Give yourself a "5" if the other ongoing programs are a part of strategic intention and can be linked with this change initiative, lower if ongoing programs are isolated and each program is a "fad of the month."

_____SYSTEMS INTEGRITY

Major change requires the redesign of processes and cross-functional teams. If people are turf conscious and are unwilling to cooperate between functions, change is slowed and even prevented.

Give yourself a "5" if you are already aligned into cross-functional teams and work across processes now, lower if there are functional "silos" and power centers established which intend to fight for their perks!

_____EXPERIENCE

Sometimes experience is the best teacher. If your organization has had experience with change efforts before and has successfully found ways to implement change over time, then the chances of this change effort succeeding is high.

Give yourself a "5" if you've already undergone successful change and a 1 if this is your first time!

_____DECISIVENESS

The ability to make effective decisions is crucial to successful change efforts. Does your organizations make decisions efficiently taking into consideration the utility of present decisions with regard to future 2nd, 3rd and 4th orders of consequences?

Give yourself a "5" if decisions are effective and conflict free, lower if decisions are slow and create widespread conflict and resistance.

_____URGENCY

The sense of urgency is the lever that change rests upon. Without a strong pervasive sense of urgency people won't have the inertia to push through the difficult parts of the change process.

Give yourself a "5" if there is a prevailing sense of urgency and people feel the need to change. Score lower if urgency is not widespread or if most people are casual about the need to change very much.

_____INEVITABILITY

Creating a sense that change is inevitable often provides motive force for continuing the change effort when things get really tough. If change is inevitable, then people push through obstacles that keep change from taking root in the culture and improving performance.

Give yourself a "5" if change is thought to be inevitable to most people. Score lower if very few people in the organization see change as necessary.

_____CHANGE AGENTS

Change takes a long time. If change is to create permanent competitive advantage then the change effort must span leadership at all levels. If the company intends for change to be permanent and beneficial then it must provide for the change champions to lead.

Give yourself a "5" if people know they won't get promoted unless they champion the change effort and seek to promote the tenets of the change. If not, lower.

_____BEST PRACTICES

Is benchmarking part of the everyday management scenario? Does your company have an established or ongoing list of "best practices." Are people in the organization aware of competitive practices and seeking to upgrade processes to stay ahead of the game?

Give yourself a "5" if benchmarking is integrated into your decision systems, lower if the company is behind with respect to implementing state-of-the-art processes.

_____CUSTOMER-LED

Is your company inner-directed or outer-directed? Do you know your customers and remember them? Are customers needs at the forefront of process improvement?

Give yourself a "5" if your company is customer focused and led, lower if the company's values place the customer behind company policies and a "1" if process owners don't know who their customer are?

_____REWARDS

What gets rewarded gets done! (Michael LeBoeuf) Are people rewarded for risk and innovation? Are people rewarded for working together on teams? Or are managers rewarded for making budget and keeping things under control?

Give yourself a "5" if team rewards are present and your company rewards innovation and risk-taking, lower if your company rewards continuity and quiet.

_____STRUCTURE

Is the organization flexible and cross-functional or does the organization chart change every week with a lot of turnover? On the other hand, has the organization's hierarchy ever changed or is "that's the way we've always done it" posted on the restroom BB?

You get a "5" if your company is cross-functional and flexible, lower if everyone fights change by just waiting for it to run its course and letting it die on the vine.

_____CULTURE

How do people feel about working here? Do people dread coming to work? Are the work rules rigid and over time people have become rigid and cynical in the way they deal with each other? Is there a lot of team spirit and fun at work. Do people put out extra effort and trust each other?

Score "5" if there is high trust, high effort and fun, a "1" if there is mistrust, low-spirit and minimum effort.

_____COMMUNICATION

A sign of good communication is everyone knows what's going on. It is frequent, goes to all levels, is easily understood, and two-way…in real time!

Score your company "5" if that's the way it is at your place, lower if there is communication, but it seems to be one-way only and top-down and a "1" if nobody reads, listens or cares what anybody else has to say because they're just here to do their job and go home.

_____ORGANIZATION DESIGN

Do you have a flat hierarchy or is there layer after layer of management and many levels between the customer and the top? Are there many employee grade levels and a lot of difference in pay and rank among employees?

Score a "5" if there are 3 or less levels between the customer and the COO, lower if there are many more levels of rank in between with power to block or slow down the change initiative.

_____INNOVATION

How are ideas handled in your company? Is there a lot of red tape to get things done? Are people able to make mistakes and take chances or do you have to "go through channels" to get things changed? Are there multiple sign-offs required and spending limits?

Score a "5" if people help you implement ideas, lower if you're constantly having to fight somebody to get things changed and a "1" if it is faster to do it yourself.

_____INFLUENCE

Are the people in your company open-minded? Do they allow different opinions to be discussed without shooting the messenger? Do they examine the facts and make decisions with respect to merit?

Score a "5" if people can be influenced with the right amount of information, lower if people have their minds made up about things and a "1" if getting rid of them would be easier than trying to change their minds.

_____TIME FRAME

Do you have enough time to complete the required change and meet the transformational objectives? Are you planning to change your organization really fast or do you understand that major change can require 3-10 years or more?

Score a "5" if time frame is not a constraint and as low as a "1" if the time frame is narrow and doesn't account for deep cultural transformation.

_____COMPLACENCY

Last but most important according to John Cotter, celebrated author of LEADING CHANGE, HBR Press, 1996. If people are not worried about change, if they think that someone else will have to change and that they are not required to change-- big problems ahead!

Score a "5" if people are "committed" to changing no matter what! Score a "1" if most people think everything is just fine the way we do it now.

Scoring Table: Fill in Scores & Total

UNDERWRITERS	DECISIVENESS	CULTURE
LEADERS	URGENCY	COMMUNICATION
INTENTION	INEVITABILTY	ORG. DESIGN
OWNERSHIP	CHANGE AGENTS	INNOVATION
METRICS	BEST PRACTICES	INFLUENCE
SYNERGY	CUSTOMER LED	TIME FRAME
SYSTEM VIEW	REWARDS	COMPLACENCY
EXPERIENCE	STRUCTURE	
Total	*Total*	*Total*

_____TOTAL SCORE

Your Change readiness can be viewed in the context of the total score you gave your company from 23-115.

92-115 = high Change--ability potential with minimum damage to existing structure, people and systems.

64-91 = Change-ability moderate--success unlikely unless widespread training and preparation for change is implemented prior to the initiation of the change effort.

<63 = DO NOT PASS GO - Non-destructive change impossible! **FIX THE SYSTEM BEFORE CHANGING!**

Contact for more information: *LEADWISE, LLC*
1-800-823-1251
change-ability@leadwise.com

B-10

Appendix C

About The Balanced Scorecard

[www.bscol.com]

The Balanced Scorecard translates strategy into action - rapidly, measurably, knowledgeably - at all levels of the enterprise. It does this by aligning strategy with organizational structure and resources, leveraging hidden assets and knowledge, connecting people and processes, and by fostering continuous learning and growth.

The Balanced Scorecard provides an enterprise view of an organization's overall performance by integrating financial measures with other key performance indicators around customer satisfaction, internal business processes, and organizational growth, learning, and innovation. The Balanced Scorecard concept was created by Drs. Robert S. Kaplan and David P. Norton in 1992 and has been implemented in hundreds of corporations, organizations, and government agencies worldwide.

It has been the subject of three articles in the Harvard Business Review (HBR), a best-selling business book (now in 18 languages), numerous case studies and public conferences, and has been selected by HBR as one of the "seminal ideas" and most innovative management practices of the past 75 years.

Hundreds of organizations worldwide have implemented Balanced Scorecards to boost performance and achieve results. Gartner Group estimates that by the year 2000, at least

40% of the Fortune 1000 will have implemented a Balanced Scorecard.

The Balanced Scorecard is not simply a static list of measures, but an organizational framework for managing complex programs of change and transformation. Scorecards have been successfully implemented at corporate, business unit, and individual levels, across functional areas such as strategic planning, human resources, quality, and information technology, and in corporations, governments, and organizations of every size and description around the world.

We have learned much from the experiences of early adopters who began using the Balanced Scorecard 3 to 4 years ago, and the results are impressive. While Fortune magazine reports that 9 out of 10 companies fail to execute their strategies, Balanced Scorecard users are not only successfully executing their strategies, but they are doing it fast.

Many of these organizations have achieved dramatic results in only two years, and their executives give much of the credit to the Balanced Scorecard. The Balanced Scorecard Collaborative can show your organization how to achieve similar results.

Visit the Balanced Scorecard Collaborative online [www.bscol.com]

Appendix D

Appreciative Inquiry:
A High Participation Process for
Organization Transformation

Executive Overview

Diana Whitney, Ph.D., John Duncan, Amanda Trosten-Bloom

Appreciative Inquiry begins an adventure. Even in the first steps, one senses and exciting new direction in our language and theories of change – an invitation, as some have declared, to a "positive revolution." Appreciative Inquiry is a powerful process that engages everyone, from 60 to 60,000 people, in an organization in on-going inquiry and dialogue – with customers, with benchmark companies, and with each other – about what's most important and what gives life to the organization when it is at its best.

The inquiry and dialogue lead to redesigning the organization so that high performance is delivered on a daily basis. Through its deliberately positive assumptions about people and organizations, Appreciative Inquiry vitally transforms the ways we approach questions of organizational improvement: strategic planning, culture change, knowledge management, business process improvement, leadership development, union management relations, customer satisfaction, joint ventures and partnerships.

Appreciative Inquiry is being used by organizations like GTE, Smithkline Beecham, Hunter Douglas, Omni Hotel, Red Cross, Veterans Health Affairs, Nutrimental Foods, Front

Range Community College, and British Airways to significantly improve organizational results.

David Cooperrider and Diana Whitney (Appreciative Inquiry, Berrett Koehler, 1999) describe Appreciative Inquiry as "the cooperative search for the best in people, their organizations, and the world around them. It involves systematic discovery of what gives a system "life" when it is most effective and capable in economic, ecological and human terms.

Appreciative Inquiry begins with the art and practice of asking questions that strengthen a system's capacity to heighten its positive potential. In Appreciative Inquiry, intervention gives way to imagination and innovation; instead of negation, criticism and spiraling diagnosis there is discovery, dream, design and delivery. Appreciative Inquiry assumes that every living system has untapped, rich, and inspiring accounts of the positive. When this "positive core" is linked to an organization's change agenda, changes never thought possible are suddenly and democratically mobilized."

In a practical sense, the process improves organizational performance and alignment by:

- One, engaging the full workforce in discovery and dialogue on topics of strategic importance.
- Two, uncovering existing best practices and designing the organization to make these practices an expected routine rather than exceptional performance.
- And three, supporting employees at all levels in an organization to expand the "realm of the possible" and to envision a collectively desired future that can be translated quickly into action and practice.

The process increases employee involvement and morale by putting attention on what employees are already doing well, allowing employees to learn from the customer and each other, rather than looking to managers, supervisors, and consultants to tell them how they should do their job. By engaging people in cross-functional and cross organizational inquiry, silos and "turfism" are overcome, and complex issues requiring cooperation among diverse interests can be openly and resolutely addressed.

Organizations move in the direction of what they study. Appreciative Inquiry reframes the focus of discussion, analysis and the change agenda within an organization. It is a shift from "problem oriented" analysis to positive possibilities and practices. Within an organization the Appreciative Inquiry process begins with the formation of a highly diverse "core team" charged with the tasks of selecting affirmative topics of strategic importance and creating an interview guide. Their challenge is to reframe the typically "deficit based" organizational thinking into a set of affirmative topics.

Discussion of employee turnover becomes inquiry into employee satisfaction and retention. Analyses of root causes of failure become studies of root causes of success. Questions of how to recover lost luggage become questions of how to provide an exceptional arrival experience. Concerns about the cost of rework become excitement about the possibility of zero defects. With this affirmative transformation of the organization's change agenda comes learning, enthusiasm and innovation. High performance grows in the presence of inquiry into what makes an organization its best in economic, environmental and human terms.

Leaders who have taken the risk of embarking on the path of positive change recognize the benefits. Thomas H. White, President of GTE Telephone Operations (Vital Speeches of the Day, vol. LXII, no.15, 1996), put it this way,

"Appreciative Inquiry gets much better results than seeking out and solving problems. That is an interesting concept for me – and I imagine for most of you - because telephone companies are among the world's best problem solvers. We concentrate enormous resources on correcting problem. When used continually over time, this approach leads to a negative culture. Don't get me wrong, I am not advocating mindless happy talk. Appreciative Inquiry is a complex science designed to make things better. We can't ignore problems – we just need to approach them from the other side."

Appreciative Inquiry processes can engage an entire organization in the process of dramatic transformation. As inquiry teams conduct interviews, best practices, highpoint stories and people worthy of recognition are discovered; and successful practices are disseminated throughout the organization.

A work environment alive with success stories, images of positive possibilities, learning and cooperative dialogue emerges. As meetings are conducted to share stories and to design the organization of the future, a new, more democratic organization takes form – an organization co-created through the discovery, dreams and designs of all relevant and interested parties.

Biographies

Diana Whitney, Ph.D., President, Corporation for Positive Change and Founder, The Taos Institute, is an international speaker and consultant whose work focuses on innovative forms of organizing, organization transformation, strategic culture change, and leadership development. Diana is recognized as a leader in the development of Appreciative Inquiry and its applications to large-scale organizational transformation. Her clients include: Smithkline Beecham, Johnson & Johnson,, PECO, The New York Power Authority, GTE, Veterans Health Affairs, Sandia National Laboratories, Intel, British Airways and Hunter Douglas. Her most publications include: Appreciative Inquiry, with David Cooperrider, "Appreciative Inquiry: An Innovative Process for Organization Change" and "The Appreciative Inquiry Summit: Overview and Applications." Email address <whitneydi@aol.com>

John Duncan, President, The Duncan Network, Inc. in Charlotte, NC, is an international consultant who specializes in whole business redesign using Appreciative Inquiry as the philosophical base, helping organizations become self-managing. From his industrial engineering, business management, and organizational psychology background, he has served as lead consultant in over 40 large-scale change projects in the last 20 years. His clients have included BellSouth, Champion International, Coca-Cola, Duke Power, First Union Corporation, Hoechst Celanese, and Johnson & Johnson. Two of John's cases are profiled in *The Self Managing Organization: How Leading Companies Are Transforming the Work of Teams for Real Impact*, by Purser & Cabana, Free Press, 1998. Email address <johnduncan@mindspring.com>

Amanda Trosten-Bloom, Founder and President, Clearview Consultants in Golden, CO, is an organization development consultant whose focus is on co-construction of appreciative organizations. She is among the first consultants to use Appreciative Inquiry for whole-system culture change in business settings. She teaches Appreciative Inquiry as a process for organizational change and facilitates appreciatively based strategic planning, enhancement of customer service, executive coaching, and team building. Along with Diana Whitney, she is co-author of the book chapter, "Appreciative Inquiry: A Path to Positive Change." Email address <clearcons1@aol.com>

You can learn more about Appreciative Inquiry by contacting:
> The Corporation for Positive Change
> PO Box 3257
> Taos, NM 87571
> Voice 505-751-1231
> Fax   505-751-1233

Appendix E

Action Science, A Description

By Tobias C. Brown, MA

Basic Goal

The basic goal of action science is to increase professional and organizational effectiveness by helping individuals and groups to **shift from using Model I to using Model II** in resolving difficult problems.

Problem Types

The action science model focuses primarily on identifying and resolving difficult, complex, real-life problems critical to organizations and society.

Theories of Action

Specific to action science is the **Model I & II theory of action**, a "meta-theory" or "theory about theories" (a hybrid technical and human theory of action).

Data Types

Action science asks whether data, knowledge, or descriptive information is **actionable**. This term is easiest to define by first outlining its opposite, non-actionable data.

Learning Defined

Learning occurs when individuals and groups **detect and correct gaps between descriptive claims and practical outcomes**, intentions and actual results, thoughts and actions, theories and practices (or produce what they claim to know).

Basic Goal of Action Science

Action science is a strategy for designing situations that foster effective stewardship, in any type of organization. As a framework for learning, the approach is designed to help individuals, groups, and organizations to develop a readiness to change to meet the needs of an often-changing environment.

To help individuals in groups to learn how to overcome barriers to organizational change, action science does not simply focus on improving the participants' problem-solving or decision-making skills. It also does not look only at making incremental changes (e.g., identifying opportunities; finding, correcting, reducing, or eliminating threats) in the external environment. Without eschewing these concerns, action science focuses on looking inward, learning new frameworks, establishing new routines.

This website describes action science but to understand and practice action science is, well, not easy. The next step for this web site is to add real-world examples that demonstrate the use of action science.

Problem Types

A critical issue in action science is whether a problem is considered **routine/trivial** VS. **non-routine/difficult**. The difference is not always clear. Nevertheless, action science focuses on identifying and resolving the difficult, complex, real-life problems that are critical to organizations and society. This includes the formidable challenges of leadership, innovation, informed participation, and reducing prejudice. These bewildering problems often emerge and grow when group participants try to formulate and carry out new plans and evaluate their work together.

What are the characteristics of effective groups? Effective groups can resolve difficult problems by taking innovative action relatively soon. As the participants question underlying programs or the credibility of ideas, they maintain high levels of interpersonal openness. They accept that while openness is potentially or actually embarrassing, threatening, or frustrating, openness is necessary to increase trust and individuality in their group. Participants may deny the difficulties inherent in carrying out their challenging plans but group members freely challenge, test, and correct each others claims. Possessing high levels of action science skills, their minimally defensive interpersonal and group relations enable the group members to innovate and respond productively.

Model I & II Theories of Action

The primary distinction in action science is between **theories of action**. Theories of action are the master programs, patterns, designs, sets of rules, or propositions that people use to design and carry out their actions; the governing variables, values, theories, beliefs, concepts, rules, attitudes, routines, policies, practices, norms, or skills that underlie actions.

There are two main types of theories of action. "Technical" theories of action are autonomous or distanced models of expert analysis. They include theories in micro-economic analysis, competitive strategy analysis, activity-based accounting, or rigorous quantitative empirical analysis. "Human" theories of action are theories about interpersonal relationships, effective leadership, administration, group dynamics, or organizational culture.

Action science represents a unique "Model I/Model II" theory of action, a "meta-theory" or "theory about theories," or a hybrid technical and human theory of action. Crafted to help increase professional effectiveness, it aims to help reduce individual and group ineffectiveness caused by defensive interpersonal and organizational relations by removing barriers to change. It helps reduce anti-productive defensive routines in real time, as group members carry out diverse types of technical and human action plans. Reducing ineffectiveness involves shifting from using Model I to using Model II in resolving difficult problems.

Model I Theory-in-Use
Governing Variables -

- Design, manage, and plan unilaterally.
- Own and control the task.
- Unilaterally protect self and others.
- Evaluate others in ways that do not encourage testing the validity of the evaluation.

Action Strategies -

- Define goals and try to achieve them (unilaterally).
- Maximize winning and minimize losing.
- Minimize expressing or generating negative feelings.
- Be rational and minimize emotionality.

Consequences -

- Defensiveness
- Mistrust
- COMPETITION
- Interpersonal manipulation
- Self-service

- Over-protective
- Conformity
- Use of power
- Low freedom of choice
- Low internal commitment
- Low risk taking.
- "Self-sealing, single-loop" learning
- Anti-learning
- Little public testing of notions about why others behave as they do, what they need, etc.
- Decreased effectiveness

Model II Theory-in-Use
Governing Variables -

- Maximize valid information.
- Have free and informed choice for all concerned.
- Have high internal commitment to the choice and constant monitoring of its implementation.

Action Strategies -

- Design situations where participants can originate actions and can experience high personal causation and success.
- Jointly control tasks.
- Make protection of self and others a joint enterprise.
- Craft positions or behaviors into action strategies that openly illustrate how the actors reached their evaluations or attributions, and how they crafted them to encourage inquiry and testing by others.

Consequences -

- Minimally defensive interpersonal relations

- COLLABORATION
- Cooperation
- Trust
- High individuality
- Open confrontation on difficult issues
- High freedom of choice.
- "Double-loop" learning (includes questioning of goals)
- Processes can be disconfirmed
- Public testing of theories and attributions.
- Increased quality of life
- Effective problem solving and decision making, especially for difficult issues
- Increased long-run effectiveness.

Model I

Model I involves single-loop learning processes: any practice that inhibits the participants from experiencing embarrassment or threat and prevents them from identifying, reducing, and correcting the causes of the embarrassment or threat.

Model I is the domain of anti-learning behavior. Model I actors do not encourage testing or validating claims, overprotect participants, and inhibit learning in detecting and correcting non-routine errors. Model I involves single-loop learning processes: any practice that inhibit the participants from experiencing embarrassment or threat and prevent them from identifying, reducing, and correcting the causes of the embarrassment or threat.

Single-loop learning and defensive reasoning processes produce mixed messages. They protect out of thoughtfulness, caring, diplomacy, or concern, as reality demands. However, in caring for and respecting others, criticism gets withheld. By avoiding conflict, the participants consistently fail to deal with difficult issues. As Model I processes do not activate theories-in-use, they reduce the possibility of learning.

Defensive routines produce mixed messages at two levels:

Level I - Denial Routine

- recognize a mixed message, inconsistency, gap, or mismatch between intentions and outcomes
- act like it is not a mixed message or inconsistency, deny that defensive routines exist, bypass embarrassment and threat

Level II - Bypass Routine

- make this bypass action undiscussable (cover-up the bypass)
- make the undiscussable nature of bypasses undiscussable; cover up the cover-up

Example of Mixed-Message

A Mixed-Message, Outsider gets Invited to a Meeting:

> I saw John today and he and Betty have set up a meeting for March. Um. It.. It's just a couple of us and this is the very, very, very first time we're ever going to be talking about the idea of a Web page for the group. You're welcome to come but you need to understand it's just at the very beginning stages and our thought was there would be another meeting where we could have... you know... bigger input with more people. But... the three of us... um... have been talking about this for a while and just

want to get our thoughts together. So. Um...
You're welcome to come but you need to
understand sorta where we are with the process.
Um... Give me a call if you got any questions.

Regarding the meeting, if this is the "very, very, very first time
we're ever going to be talking about the idea of a Web page for
the group," then how is it "the three of us... um... have been
talking about this for a while ..."?

Is the intention here to help me understand the process? If so,
why the mixed-message?

More on Model I

Excluded from this analysis are protective defensive routines
that occur in response to some threatening environmental
situation involving pathological or unjust acts. These
defensive actions can be productive (e.g., if they do not inhibit
learning) as they protect the actors from harm.

Defensive reasoning relies on the idea of deterministic
causality, the claim that "A will cause B." This reasoning
process fails to recognize the richness and uniqueness of
concrete situations. Inevitable gaps, between stored
knowledge and knowledge required to act effectively in new
situations, go unrecognized. Therefore, the need to change the
status quo, the present status of knowledge, gets overlooked.
Not recognizing that any innovation is likely to be inadequate,
the need to monitor the change gets bypassed.

With no monitoring, efforts to reliably repeat innovative
actions are impossible. Specifying the action strategies or
skills required to produce the desired consequences and the
conditions necessary to maintain them is also impossible.
Actions cannot be tested; solving problems cannot contribute

to basic theory, for example, to ideas about how to achieve organizational effectiveness. At the heart of the matter, participants do not integrate theory and practice.

Model I is usually the "theory-in-use" by individuals, groups, intergroups, and organizations, with little variation in how it gets expressed.

Model II

Model II's main characteristic is double-loop learning, a productive reasoning process that involves minimal interpersonal defensiveness. Wide gaps exist between espoused theories and theories-in-use and action science is designed to help participants minimize these gaps.

Model II is the domain of usable knowledge. It has high standards for questioning goals and testing the validity of claims. Model II's main characteristic is double-loop learning, a productive reasoning process that involves minimal interpersonal defensiveness.

Productive reasoning relies on the idea of probabilistic causality, the claim that "A will probably cause B." Probabilistic causality allows for the richness and uniqueness of concrete situations. It recognizes the inherent gap that exists between stored knowledge and the knowledge required to act effectively, the continual need to change the status quo.

Participants who reason productively recognize that any innovation is likely to be inadequate and therefore needs monitoring. They reliably repeat effective actions, making outcomes of initiatives known publicly. They specify the action strategies and skills required to produce the desired consequences and the conditions necessary to maintain them.

Action is testable, so problem-solving contributes to basic theory, theory gets integrated into practice.

Model II is usually espoused but not practiced by individuals, groups, intergroups, and organizations, with a wide variation in how it gets expressed.

The central orientation in action science is therefore that on a nearly universal basis, in practically all cultures and across genders, a wide gap exists between espoused theory (Model II) and theory-in-use (Model I). Action science is designed to help participants minimize these gaps.

Data Types

Also critically important in action science is whether data, knowledge, or information is actionable. This difficult term is defined best by first outlining its opposite, non-actionable data.

What is data? Actionable and non-actionable data both consist of relatively directly observable conversations, or descriptions of actual or proposed problems. The problems involve issues of personal responsibility: where participants evaluate an event or attribute qualities to themselves or others. Observations include statements by the observer that outline their undiscussed thoughts and feelings, or internal monologues related to the descriptions. Action researchers may record these descriptions or conversations on tape as they engage in meetings with participants.

Descriptive Data:

With data that is not actionable, the descriptions of problems, or inferences drawn from observations, are difficult to understand or to accept as valid -- especially by people with contrary views. The premises underlying the observations are not explicit, so testing the validity of the claims using logic or data independent of those who make them, is impossible.

Non-actionable data develops out of pursuing applicable or useful research. It derives from descriptive research, inquiry that focuses on gaining insight or awareness, or on making discoveries. This descriptive research may alternately focus on understanding or developing a solution, proposal, idea, or policy.

By separating descriptive research from action research, useful descriptive data may provide explanations or contribute to developing basic theories. It does not, however, resolve difficult problems. Applicable descriptive data may provide advice but not the actionable knowledge required to overcome and change rigid defensive routines. In describing -- or claiming to resolve a problem -- descriptive data may increase its severity by bypassing the requirement to seek out and overcome its root causes.

The Basic Defensive Reasoning Pattern

Example I

- Recognize a mixed message
- Act like there is no mixed message
- Make this action undiscussable
- Make undiscussables, undiscussable

Example II

- Recognize a mismatch between intentions and outcomes
- Bypass (or deny) the mismatch
- Cover up the bypass

- Cover up the cover-up

Descriptive research does not require participants to specify what actions will produce the desired consequences -- like open confrontation on difficult issues. Missing is an outline of the appropriate behavioral specifications and skills required to produce the conditions necessary to maintain the predicted outcomes.

In action science, descriptive research is necessary but not sufficient for learning. It may induce harm as it remains within the status quo, failing to activate theories-in-use.

Beyond Descriptive Data:

Actionable descriptions, observations, or inferences can be understood, but not necessarily accepted, by individuals holding contrary views. The premises underlying the observations are explicit, so testing the validity of the claims using logic or data independent of those who make them, is possible.

Actionable data develops out of pursuing usable research. This involves combining descriptive research with normative research, inquiry that describes alternate possible frameworks, and prescriptive research, inquiry that informs participants how to get from the present framework to a better framework. Normative and prescriptive research efforts serve action. They help individuals and organizations to better detect and correct errors, create lasting solutions, and develop valid information. They become critical as participants go from describing their insights to formulating and carrying out an innovation -- and evaluating their work together.

Descriptive research in action science is not separate from efforts to resolve practical problems. Descriptions get tested by applying them to efforts to resolve practical problems. Descriptive claims about effective actions prompt changes in how participants craft their actions. Assessing the effectiveness of actions prompts modifications in descriptive claims. Equal concern goes toward advancing descriptive theoretical claims about the underlying basis of actions and to resolving everyday problems, to advancing practice.

The development of actionable knowledge requires that participants specify what strategies will produce desired consequences -- like high internal commitment, trust, and individuality. This fulfills the need to outline appropriate behaviors and skills required to produce the desired results and the contextual conditions necessary to sustain them.

Those who pursue actionable knowledge assume humans have a limited ability to process information. They accept that gaps always exist between stored knowledge and knowledge required to produce effective actions. To develop valid information therefore they engage in cooperation with others to close the gaps. The participants codify and reliably repeat effective actions so their requirements are not merely in their heads but known publicly. They continuously strive to change the status quo and activate theories-in-use.

Learning Defined

In action science, descriptive data is necessary but not sufficient for learning. Learning occurs when participants detect and correct gaps between descriptive claims and practical outcomes (intentions and results, thoughts and actions, theories and practices); produce what they claim to know. Action science calls this "reducing gaps between espoused theories and theories-in-use." Narrowing these gaps involves increasing rigor by testing the inferences participants make in reasoning about problems.

What is reasoning? Reason forms the basis of opinions, beliefs, attitudes, feelings, or actions in that it explains or accounts for the related facts. Participants reason as they advocate a position or reach conclusions about events. Reasoning occurs when attributing causes to actions or when evaluating oneself or others.

Inferences can be rated on a "ladder of inference."

Ladder of Inference

Maximum Inference

Rung 4 - Evaluate an Action -
> "The action was effective (or not effective)."

Rung 3 - Impose Meanings on Actions -
> "The intention the person had in taking the action was to...."

Rung 2 - Impose Meanings on Conversation -
> "The meaning of the conversation is...."

Rung 1 - Experience Some Relatively Directly Observable Data -
> Listen to a recorded conversation, not merely to what he, she, or they recall was said.

Minimum Inference

At high levels of inference someone states an attribution or evaluation like "the action was not effective." A level lower, at Rung Three, meanings are imposed on actions or causes are attributed to them. For example, "In taking the action, his intention was to..." At Rung Two inferences are made about the meanings embedded in a conversation: "When Terry said she was disappointed that the event occurred, she meant the following." At Rung One participants experience some relatively directly observable data, such as a conversation. They may listen to a recorded conversation instead of what someone reports was said in a conversation.

By testing, participants can infer their theory-in-use. They can ask, "Are the attributions we make at high levels of inference (Rungs Four and Three) rigorously connected to some relatively directly observable data (Rung One)? If not, they may infer their theory-in-use does not involve testing the validity of claims against what actually occurs.

Notes

Model II is not the opposite of Model I.

Opposite of Model I Theory-in-Use

Governing Variables -

- Decide unilaterally to not define goals and to not try to achieve them.
- Minimize winning and maximize losing.
- Maximize expressing or generating negative feelings.
- Be irrational and maximize emotionality.

Action Strategies -

- Design, manage, and plan unilaterally.
- Own and control the task.
- Unilaterally harm self and others.
- Evaluate others in ways that do not encourage testing the validity of the evaluation.

Consequences -

- Negativism
- Withdrawal
- Defensiveness
- Mistrust
- COMPETITION
- Interpersonal manipulation
- Self-service
- Over-protective
- Conformity
- Use of power
- Low freedom of choice
- Low internal commitment
- Low risk taking
- "Self-sealing, single-loop" learning
- Anti-learning
- Little public testing of notions about why others behave as they do, what they need, etc.
- Decreased effectiveness.

Last Update: September 15, 1999.

Action Science Network
(actnet@pobox.com)

Author of this summary is Tobias C. Brown, MA Mr. Brown, a student of the work's of Argyris and operates ENHANCED DESIGNS, a web services company in Vermont. He may be contacted at toby@enhanced-designs.com

Appendix F

Personal & Corporate Coaching Distinctions

Summarized from coaching discussions held in 1999

The following material was synthesized by Jan Austin during a coaching design conference call held with coaches from over the US and Canada and is paraphrased by the author and presented for reference only towards the advancement of coaching distinctions.

PERSONAL COACHING

- The individual retains and pays for coaching services
- The individual is in full ownership of the coaching agenda
- Full confidentiality is assured
- Coaching rarely involves obtaining feedback from others
- The client hires and fires the coach at his or her discretion
- Coaching occurs outside of the work environment
- Coaching oriented around the individual values exclusively
- The assumption is that all is well and that the client has the potential to achieve extraordinary results.

CORPORATE COACHING

- The pbc doesn't hire and fire, nor pay for coaching usually
- Contact with those ancillary to the client may be frequent
- Coaching interventions may include individuals and teams
- Coaching typically takes place in the work environment
- The coaching agenda often can impact the individual's job
- Coaching is aimed at improving business results
- The agenda for coaching is often a shared agenda P
- Personal ownership of the coaching agenda is rare
- Coaching often involves obtaining feedback from others
- Coaching considers personal and organizational values
- The assumption by the corporate decision maker (buyer) may be that the individual needs to be "fixed"

*Note the key distinction of *ownership* versus *buy-in* between the paradigms of personal and corporate coaching.

Jan Austin may be reached at thecoach@mindex.com

Appendix G

This is a simple gauge of coaching effectiveness as viewed from the eyes of the person being coached, it is not intended as a predictor or performance evaluation tool.

COACHING SUCCESS ASSESSMENT

Directions: Please circle the appropriate number that best describes how you think and feel about your coaching relationship

The questions are either preceded by "your coach"... or followed by "in our coaching relationship."

1 2 3 4 5   Identifies openings to performance, change & transformation

1 2 3 4 5   Helps create a clear focus of coaching interaction each time it is held.

1 2 3 4 5   Connects my development to an appropriate sense of urgency

1 2 3 4 5   Clear priorities are established during the interaction

1 2 3 4 5   Encourages you to take appropriate action through a planned, systemized process

1 2 3 4 5   Accountability is created around priorities and time lines

1 2 3 4 5   Offers to share experience and knowledge when appropriate

1 2 3 4 5   My coach has no authority, accountability or responsibility for the outcomes I produce

1 2 3 4 5   Takes time to learn about what I do in my job

1 2 3 4 5   I look forward to our meetings and interaction

1 2 3 4 5 The coach is available for prescribed meetings and is accessible

1 2 3 4 5 Time you spend interacting is free from interruption by outside influences

1 2 3 4 5 Information created through the interaction is valuable to your success

1 2 3 4 5 Coaching interaction is valuable to your performance and development

1 2 3 4 5 Insight into the behaviors of others while valuing differences is explored

1 2 3 4 5 Barriers to performance, change and transformation of your personally and the organization are discussed

1 2 3 4 5 The coach always seems to know how to acknowledge my efforts

1 2 3 4 5 The coach tells the truth and encourages me without making me feel bad

1 2 3 4 5 When the coach explains something, the language is clear and concise—I know what is meant all the time.

1 2 3 4 5 The coach continues to encourage my personal development throughout the coaching interaction

1 2 3 4 5 The coach is able to accept constructive criticism without getting defensive

1 2 3 4 5 The coaching interaction is able to identify my blind spots without prejudice or always using negative feedback

1 2 3 4 5 Is fun to be around and likable

1 2 3 4 5 Interaction is focused on creating opportunities

1 2 3 4 5 Makes an effort to understand how I personally feel about my situation

1 2 3 4 5 Has a good grasp of trends and business and their impact on my personal and the organization's development

1 2 3 4 5 Hears what I say and what I don't say about issues we discuss

1 2 3 4 5 Adapts the coaching interaction to my individual differences

1 2 3 4 5   Understands or asks how suggestions and ideas might affect me personally

1 2 3 4 5   Always treats me with respect and dignity

1 2 3 4 5   Is ethical and professional in their interaction with me

1 2 3 4 5   Always avoids talking down or making me feel stupid or inadequate

1 2 3 4 5   Helps me relate my personal goals to organizational goals

1 2 3 4 5   Never makes inappropriate gender or minority based remarks, even in clean fun or jokes

1 2 3 4 5   Helps me create realistic goals and time lines for my development

1 2 3 4 5   Gives me the feeling that they believe in me and are confident that I will succeed

1 2 3 4 5   Demonstrates presence and image of a professional

1 2 3 4 5   Clearly demonstrates skills that guide the interaction and my development

1 2 3 4 5   Is versed in coaching and has my respect

1 2 3 4 5   Always meet commitments regardless of the situation

1 2 3 4 5   Creates an environment of safety and security about sensitive issues

1 2 3 4 5   Establishes and adheres to clear standards regarding our interaction

1 2 3 4 5   Models behavior that I want to develop

1 2 3 4 5   Does not criticize peers, other clients, subordinates during our interactions

1 2 3 4 5   Doesn't use jargon or hard to understand language

1 2 3 4 5   Openly challenges me to stretch myself to develop my potential and realize my dreams without degrading me

1 2 3 4 5   Stands for clear principles and is not afraid to be seen
doing so

1 2 3 4 5   Demonstrates persistence while asking me to move
forward appropriately

1 2 3 4 5   Focuses on success in the interaction rather than on my
failings

1 2 3 4 5   Helps me to constructively view difficult issues

Total Points

___

<100 =   coaching mismatch

100-150 =   average effectiveness

150-200 =   above average effectiveness

>200 =   high performance relationship

Comments that you would like to say about your coach or the
relationship you have with the person coaching you. Please feel
free to relate any positive or negative experiences that you would
like to discuss with the reviewer.

Appendix H

Performance Measurement

How to Measure the Hard Stuff: *Teams and other Hard-To-Measure Work* by Jack Zigon, Zigon Performance Group.

ABSTRACT

Twenty years experience measuring the "hard stuff" have yielded best practices which can save time and improve the quality of performance measures for teams and other hard-to-measure work. This article describes a process for creating performance measures for any kind of work and the learning resulting from implementing these systems. It will conclude with
a case study illustration of the how-to steps and their products.

URL: http://www.zigonperf.com/articles.htm

[Excerpted by the author from: **How to Measure the Hard Stuff**]

Why measure performance?

Most people interested in measuring performance do so for one of these reasons:

You can't manage what you can't measure. Managers, as well as self-managing professionals and teams, can define what's expected, give feedback and provide recognition without performance measures.

You can't improve what you can't measure. It's easy to say, "Let's try this new program" but without data before and after, you can't see if performance is actually improving.

High performance teams and individuals require clear goals. Creating high performance requires a definition so you'll know it when you see it. In addition, all high performers get there because they have a clear picture of where they're going.

Pay for performance requires metrics. If you want to pay based on performance, you need to have some way of knowing when the payout has been earned.

Recent insights into performance measurement

For years, the author separated the techniques of team and individual employee performance measurement because team performance usually required a more complex methodology to handle the more complex performance measurement task. In the last year it has become clear that almost all of these techniques can be used for groups, teams and individuals. A more robust measurement technology is a function of a larger repertoire of techniques and models. The reader is asked to use his/her common sense to apply the model which appears most likely to produce a useful measurement idea.

The approach outlined in this chapter has the following benefits:

Road map for a difficult task. Measurement is hard enough when you know how to do it. Having a clear path allows you to concentrate on creating measures instead of wondering what to do next.

Reduced cycle time. The first generation of this process took a 2-3 days for an individual and months for a team. The latest generation, when coupled with a large collection of measurement ideas, takes anywhere from 3 to 8 hours.

Handles difficult-to-measure work. Not all work can be measured with numbers. This process handles the qualitative, hard to measure jobs as well as the easily quantified.

Multiple ways to align or link. Linkage or alignment with organizational goals is more and more important in today's business environment. This process provides two ways to provide that "line of sight."

Trainable. This process is not rocket science. It can be taught and learned by any workforce with a high school education.

Common problems of team and employee measurement

Measurement is difficult for at least three reasons.
It is not always obvious what results should be measured. Most teams and hard-to-measure individuals will use the obvious measures without asking what results they should be producing and how they will know they've done a good job.

Even if you know what to measure, it is often not clear how the measurement should be done. Not everything can be easily measured with numbers, thus teams and individuals give up when faced with measuring something like "creativity" or "user-friendliness."

Teams are made up of individuals, thus measurement must be done at both the team and individual levels, effectively doubling the size of the measurement task. Developing individual measures that support the team, and don't conflict, is difficult without direction.

Because there are many types of teams and individuals with different measurement challenges, the measurement process presented is not a linear one. You'll need to have a clear understanding of where you want to end up, and then make choices along the way to find the most efficient path to your goal.

For both teams and individuals, we want to end up with a measurement system in which includes:

- A list of the value-added results of the team and team members.
- Performance measures and standards for each of these results.
- A clear picture of the priorities and *relative importance* of the team and individual results.
- A way to track how the team and individuals are performing compared to the performance standards.
-

Based on almost two decades experience measuring "hard-to-measure" work like research and development, design engineering, graphic design, marketing and customer service, and five years of helping teams create measures, the author has refined a third-generation process for measuring performance:

1. *Review the organizational measures.* This step makes sure that the measures "above" and "around" the team and individuals are known and able to be linked to their measures.

2. *Define measurement starting points.* This step offers five alternatives for identifying starting points for measurement. Selecting the best alternatives and using them to identify the team and individual results provides the basis for all further measurement.
3. *Weight the results.* This step allows the relative importance of each result to be discussed and agreed upon

4. *Develop performance measures.* This step identifies the numeric and descriptive yardsticks that will be used to gauge how well the results have been achieved.

5. *Develop performance standards.* This step defines how well the team and individuals have to perform to meet and exceed expectations.

6. *Decide how to track the performance.* This step identifies how the data for each performance standard will be collected and fed back to the team and individuals.

END OF EXCERPT: How to Measure the Hard Stuff

URL: http://www.zigonperf.com/articles.htm

Biography:

Jack Zigon is President, Zigon Performance Group, a PA-based management consulting group specializing in performance measurement and performance management systems for hard-to-measure employees, teams and organizations. His 20+ years of experience has been distilled into time-saving how-to books, searchable online reference libraries, practical workshops and down-to-earth guidance for his clients.

His Measurement Resources website receives thousands of hits per day because of its wealth of free information on performance measurement including links to other sites, hundreds of example performance measures, how-to articles like the one above, an annotated bibliography, performance measurement articles in the news, and even a humor section.

The site can be viewed at www.zigonperf.com/performance.htm

How-to books can be purchased at www.zigonperf.com/store.htm

Contact Jack Zigon:
- email at jack@zigonperf.com
- phone at 610-891-9599.

Appendix I

Questions to ask about Coaching

- Is now the appropriate time to institute coaching?
- What division is ready for a coaching pilot project?
- How does coaching influence the business system?
- Where can coaching be integrated in the organization?
- What does coaching do?
- What is the basis for a scalable coaching program?
- Why use coaching instead of something else?
- Can the same coaching methodology be used everywhere in the organization?
- How can we develop a coaching system in our organization?
- Where is coaching best suited and where doesn't coaching work?
- How will coaching affect our culture?
- What is the best way to integrate a coaching system in an organization?
- How does coaching compare with other methodologies?
- What is and what is not coaching?\
- How does coaching meet complex needs in an organization?
- Will coaching create or influence structural change?
- How will coaching promote the essential business competencies?
- How does coaching contribute to performance, change and transformation?
- What are the overriding goals for coaching in this organization?
  - For Leaders?

- o For Coaches?
- o For Managers?
- o For the Person Being Coached?
- How does coaching fit into the organizational systems?
- Where is the place of leverage for a coaching system?
- What are the ideal characteristics of an effective coach?
- How will we deal with people who discover through coaching they are mismatched in jobs and careers?
- How are we going to leverage the coaching knowledge gained from people coaching?
- How will the assessments be used in coaching?
- Will coaching be tied directly to evaluation?
- What are the key success factors for the coaching system?
- Have we taken the time to develop a strategic architecture for the coaching integration into the organization?
- How will coaching affect leadership? Management?
- Will we grow our own coaches?
- What are the minimum requirements for coaches?
- What are the ratios of pc to pbc?
- How often will we review the coaching effectiveness?

These are just SOME of the questions you should be asking of any coaching program being established in your organization. For more information on supporting your coaching system and developing organizational effectiveness through coaching,

please contact LEADWISE, LLC on the web: www.leadwise.com

or email to coach2strategy@leadwise.com

or call 800.823.1251 to speak to us about executive coaching.

Appendix J

An Essay on an Order of Consciousness

By the author of <u>VIRUS OF THE MIND</u>, Richard Brodie

Level 3

You are reading about something that most people don't even know exists. If you told them, they wouldn't just not believe you—they would have no clue what you were talking about. That's why I wrote this little essay: so that I could show it to someone when they had no idea what I was talking about and, if they were persistent and open-minded, make some progress in their thinking. And meanwhile I could get on with my other projects.

1. In the beginning, there was attraction. Things attract each other because they like to be closer to some things than other things. This is the root of all change in the whole universe.

Sometimes like attracts like and sometimes opposite attracts opposite. When opposites attract, you've got a pair, a couple. That pair is now another unit and you can start the whole process over again. The pair, the new unit, can attract an opposite or a like or just drift along.

When like attracts like, it can end there, like an oxygen molecule made up of two oxygen atoms, or it can continue to attract like, like a Carbon atom. When things continue to attract like, something big gets created.

2. Sometimes a thing will attract just the right stuff to it that the new stuff turns into another copy of the thing. That is self-replication. Self-replication is the most powerful force in the universe. One becomes two, two become four, four become eight, and soon the universe is full of things.

Sometimes a self-replicating thing makes a copy of itself with a mistake in it. The thing with a mistake will either be better, worse, or the same at making copies of itself. If it's better, there will soon be more copies of the new thing than the old thing in the universe.

The only way for new things to get created is by a complex series of mistakes that turn out to be better after all.

3. We are self-replicating things. We are the result of a billion years worth of mistakes that turned out to be better after all.

4. One big mistake that turned out to be better after all was that, of all the animals, we alone can communicate complicated ideas. We can tell stories. We can share recipes. We can make complicated plans. Even dolphins and whales can't do these things, we think.

5. These ideas that we communicate are called _memes_. Memes are a kind of thing. Memes live in our minds.

6. Like all things, memes fit better with some things than others. Some memes naturally fit better in people's minds. Some memes naturally fit better with other memes. When a group of memes fit well together and pull the strings of someone's mouth and vocal cords so that they pass them on to

others, a new, self-replicating thing gets created. The new thing is called a memeplex.

Self-replication is the most powerful force in the universe. One person tells two, two tell four, four tell eight, and pretty soon the whole universe is full of people sharing the memeplex.

Sometimes a self-replicating memeplex makes a mistake in copying itself. The memeplex with a mistake in it will either be better, worse, or the same at making copies of itself. If it's better soon there will be more copies of the new memeplex than the old in the universe.

The only way for a new idea to gain acceptance is by a series of copying mistakes that turn out to be better after all.

7. All our belief systems, religions, and governments are the result of a series of mistakes that turned out to be better at making copies of themselves after all.

8. Every new idea we think of immediately becomes transformed by copying mistakes that change it into something that is better at making copies of itself after all. A key part of the idea may be sacrificed to something better for copying. The only control we have over the spread of our ideas is in making them as resistant to copying mistakes as possible.

9. When we are born, our mind is courted by meme after meme after meme, all the result of thousands of years of practice at getting themselves copied into fresh new minds. This is Level 1. We have our instincts, born of millions of years of the genes our body carries striving to make copies of themselves.

Soon our minds become filled with memes and eventually we may develop a map of life that mostly makes sense. We speak a language that we believe expresses anything we want to say.

We use geometric and physical concepts that we believe explain anything we encounter. We know stories and myths that we believe relate to all of life's trials and tribulations. This is Level 2. We have our roadmap, born of thousands of years of the memes our mind carries striving to make copies of themselves.

10. Each of us has a purpose here. When the memes are quiet, it is possible to feel when we are on purpose and when we are off purpose.

11. Once we realize that there are millions of memes battling inside our mind, there arises the possibility of influencing the outcome of that battle. Until we realize it, there is no possibility.

The battle can be influenced in three ways. First, by noticing the memes. Second, by detaching from them. Third, by obtaining clarity of purpose.

When these three steps are achieved, we can begin to select our memes consciously. We select memes that keep us on purpose. This is Level 3.

12. A purpose is not a goal. A purpose does not feel like guilt, shame, or vengeance. Guilt, shame, and vengeance are emotions used by memes to gain mastery over your life. By choosing memes consciously, we can eliminate the control that memes have over those emotions.

A purpose feels fulfilling, satisfying, joyful, and powerful.

13. A purpose has to do with other people. A purpose is fulfilled by spreading memes. Every time we speak, write, create, or act we are spreading memes. To fulfill our purpose we must be conscious of which memes we are spreading.

Life is largely composed of conversations. Conversations are composed of memes. In Level 1 we are unaware of this. In Level 2 we see the world as a solid, understandable body to be interacted with. In Level 3 we see the world as a canvas to be painted, an instrument to be played, or a block of marble to be sculpted by us for our purpose.

We choose to do this for good or for evil. If we choose good, good is returned to us in unexpected ways. If we choose evil, evil is returned. Either way, it looks like the way we choose is the way of the world.

14. In Level 1, we do not understand the world and consequently fear it. In Level 2, we replace the fear with understanding. The price of understanding is limits. Our approximate models of the universe are never completely accurate, never useful in all situations.

In Level 3, we start with a vision of what we want to create. From there we choose our models. Sometimes a chosen model may seem insane to the other inhabitants of the little patch of space-time we happen to occupy. No matter. Men with a vision of goodwill have often looked insane in times of mistrust and scarcity. But in Level 3, we realize that the universe is not a maze to be navigated; it is a baby to be brought up. When we give it love, clarity, and opportunity, we raise a child to be a joyful, giving, successful adult. This is the opportunity we have to farm our little patch of space-time.

Richard Brodie
June 1999

Richard Brodie is a speaker, thinker and futurist. The creator of Microsoft Word and author of two best-selling books, he writes and speaks on many topics with the broad purpose of inspiring individuals, businesses and societies toward excellence and quality of life.

Mr. Brodie is the author of Virus of the Mind, the first book devoted to memetics, the new science of "memes," the invisible but very real DNA of human society. With formal training in computer science, psychology, and linguistics, Mr. Brodie's background prepared him to be among the first to recognize the importance of this new field, a convergence of evolutionary biology, cognitive science, psychology, and political science.

A key Microsoft employee five years before the software giant went public, Mr. Brodie was chairman Bill Gates's technical assistant and the original author of Microsoft Word, the first computer program to be inducted into the Smithsonian Institution's National Software Collection.

Educated at Harvard, Mr. Brodie is also the author of the well-known "self help book for people who don't need help," Getting Past OK. An accomplished speaker, he is a frequent guest on television and radio shows including Oprah, Donahue, and NBC's Today. His high-profile clients include Andersen Consulting, Knight-Ridder Newspapers, and Microsoft.

Published works:
Virus of the Mind: The New Science of the Meme (Integral Press, 1996)
Getting Past OK: A Straightforward Guide to Having a Fantastic Life (Warner Books, 1993)

World-Wide Web: http://www.brodietech.com/rbrodie
Internet: richard@brodietech.com

Free newsletter! http://www.brodietech.com/rbrodie/meme.htm

FEEDBACK PLEASE!

COLLABORATE WITH US!

We plan to evolve this book with your help. In the spirit of that journey, help us make it better over time and give us your feedback, ideas, questions and challenges!

Email comments to:bk@coach2-the-bottom-line.com, or visit the website and comment there.

If you want, just give us a call at 877.591.1263 and tell the receptionist that you want her to take your comments and pass them on to the author of COACH2.

Please complete the page following this request and FAX TO: 520.752.4613 or mail to: COACH2 Base, P.O. Box 98, Mitchell, NE 69357

For information on speaking, consulting or coaching, please:

Telephone: 877.591.1263
Email: coach2@leadwise.com

Thank you for your interest in the book and in collaboration!

Mike Jay, Author

PS: You must fill out and send or fax us the form on the next page in order for us to activate your COACH-WISE Knowledgebase Subscription, where you can find answers to your coaching challenges. Or visit www.coach-wise.com and complete the registration form online.

Your information will NOT be shared with anyone!

COACH2 REGISTRATION

Bk Version # _____ Place of Purchase_____

(Please include the version number found on the title page!)

What you liked most about the book?

What you liked least about the book?

Here are my specific suggestions for improving this book:

Other Comments:

Please provide us with your registration information:

Date: _____Name: _____

Occupation:_____ Company:_____

Address:_____

City:_____ State:_____ Zip:_____

Phone:____/_____ Email: _____

May we reprint your comments? __YES __No

May we use your name? __YES __No

Login information will be sent via email for www.coach-wise.com